MILITARY PERSUASION
IN WAR AND POLICY

MILITARY PERSUASION IN WAR AND POLICY

The Power of Soft

Stephen J. Cimbala

Westport, Connecticut
London

Library of Congress Cataloging-in-Publication Data

Cimbala, Stephen J.
    Military persuasion in war and policy : the power of soft / Stephen J. Cimbala.
        p.   cm.
    Includes bibliographical references and index.
    ISBN 0–275–97803–6 (alk. paper)
    1. United States—Military policy.   2. National security—United States.   3. World
politics—21st century.   I. Title.
    UA23.C5433   2002
    355'.0335—dc21   2002021571

British Library Cataloguing in Publication Data is available.

Library of Congress Catalog Card Number: 2002021571
ISBN: 0–275–97803–6

First published in 2002

Praeger Publishers, 88 Post Road West, Westport, CT 06881
An imprint of Greenwood Publishing Group, Inc.
www.praeger.com

Printed in the United States of America

The paper used in this book complies with the
Permanent Paper Standard issued by the National
Information Standards Organization (Z39.48–1984).

10   9   8   7   6   5   4   3   2   1

Contents

Acknowledgments

I gratefully acknowledge Dr. James Scouras, Strategy Research Group, for his helpful suggestions on methodology and for making use of his models and data. He is not responsible for any arguments or opinions in this study.

I am grateful to Stephen Blank, Michael Crutcher, William Flavin, and James Holcomb of the U.S. Army War College, Carlisle Barracks, Pennsylvania, for their insights into Russian nuclear arms control and defense policy. I am also very much in debt to Lester Grau, Jacob Kipp, Graham Turbiville, and Timothy Thomas of the Foreign Military Studies Office, U.S. Army Command and General Staff College, Ft. Leavenworth, for their knowledge of Russian security policy and military history. I am especially grateful to David Glantz, editor, *Journal of Slavic Military Studies*, for his suggestions and his encouragement to pursue contemporary issues of Russian military strategy in their historical context.

I owe considerable thanks to Raymond Garthoff and Richard Ned Lebow for sharing their insights into the Cuban missile crisis.

I acknowledge with special gratitude Pavel Baev, PRIO, for his helpful suggestions and critiques of draft studies on Russia's war in Chechnya. I am also grateful to Charles Dick and to Michael Orr, Royal Military Academy, Sandhurst, for their insights on this topic.

I am especially grateful to Robert David Steele, CEO of Open Source Solutions, Inc., for his uncommon insights into the intelligence process and innovative thinking about security issues in general. Paul

Herman of the Directorate of Intelligence, U.S. Central Intelligence Agency, is also thanked for allowing me to present an earlier version of Chapter 3.

Gratitude is willingly extended to Dr. James Sabin of Greenwood Publishing Group for his encouragement to complete this study as well as other works under the Praeger imprint. I gratefully acknowledge John Beck for copy editing that prevented errors of omission and commission.

I acknowledge Penn State Delaware County Campus for administrative support for this project, especially Charele Raport.

None of the persons named here is responsible for any of the arguments or opinions expressed in this study, nor is the university nor any agency of the U.S. government.

This book is dedicated to my wife, Betsy, and to my sons Chris and David, with all my love.

Introduction

On September 11, 2001, the United States experienced an unprecedented attack on its homeland by foreign terrorists. Hijackers crashed two civilian airliners into the World Trade Center in New York City and a third plane into the Pentagon. A fourth seized aircraft crash-landed near Pittsburgh, Pennsylvania, apparently after passengers aware of their fate tried to regain control of the plane for the crew. Other hijackings that day by the same group of plotters may have been thwarted by luck or by local vigilance at airports. An estimated 3,000 American citizens and foreign nationals who were in the World Trade Center or the Pentagon when the planes struck were killed. The carnage and destruction at the World Trade Center site was so extensive and daunting to rescuers that an exact tabulation of victims defied the best efforts of investigators.

The attackers required no elaborate or high-technology weapons; nor did they employ commonly feared tools of mass destruction, such as nuclear, biological, or chemical weapons, to accomplish their aims. They used the simplest of devices: plastic knives and "box cutters" (an odd locution; essentially it means utility knives, used to open boxes in factories and retail stores). Armed with these simple weapons, a daring plan, and much bravado, the terrorists outwitted airline security, circumvented U.S. air defenses, confounded American intelligence, and inflicted a devastating humiliation on the world's "singular global superpower."

The Bush administration soon placed the blame on Osama bin Laden, a Saudi national and former Afghan resistance leader against the Soviet Union in the 1980s. Bin Laden's terrorist network had infiltrated agents in numerous cells throughout the United States. Some of these infiltrators had been in the country for many years. Addresses going as far back as 1992 were identified by FBI investigators. Using ancient arts of subterfuge and deception that go all the way back to the Chinese philosopher of war, Sun Tzu, the perpetrators also employed modern technology for communications, money laundering, and command and control over a decade and across many countries.

U.S. citizens were stunned as the complete dimensions of the plot and of America's unwitting vulnerability began to appear in the press. It turned out that the plotters had identified America's weaknesses in counterterrorism and counterintelligence and exploited those gaping holes in the U.S. security network. Persons on U.S. government terrorist watch lists were permitted to come into the country on tourist, business, or student visas. Once in the country, most were essentially lost sight of. Interagency confusion and turf wars prevented the FBI and the State Department, for example, from sharing pertinent information about suspect terrorists and their associates. Airport security was in the hands of private companies and "rent-a-cops." Although, in theory, the airline captain was the captain of his or her plane in the same way that the ship captain ran his or her ship, in practice the airlines had circumscribed the authority of captains in the interest of customer friendliness. Outrageous and even dangerous passenger behavior had become so commonplace on U.S. airlines that TV magazines featured regular programs entitled "Air Rage."

In addition to the specific features of airline–airport and immigration security that helped to open the door to disaster on September 11, more enduring problems of U.S. intelligence and counterintelligence added to the factors contributing to this unbelievable debacle.

For several decades preceding this incident, the U.S. intelligence community had been stripped of assets and deprived of guidelines that might have prevented this disaster or mitigated its impact. Beginning in the mid-1970s, investigations of the U.S. intelligence community by several committees of Congress and others resulted in punitive legislation and restrictive executive-branch guidelines that inhibited foreign intelligence collection, covert action, and counterintelligence. In addition, a postmodern mind-set came to characterize the operations of U.S. foreign intelligence and domestic counterintelligence. Risk aversion and political correctness were career enhancing. In the Central Intelligence Agency during the 1990s, employees were required to undergo sensitivity training that included sewing "diversity" quilts.

In the aftermath of the end of the Cold War, the demise of the Soviet Union, and the U.S. and allied victory in Operation Desert Storm, an attitude of complacency took root about all things having to do with security and intelligence. U.S. nuclear weapons laboratories allegedly were penetrated by Chinese espionage. Aldrich Ames was unmasked as a traitor for having supplied a decade's worth of gold to his Soviet and Russian spymasters. Ames's information condemned at least twelve Soviet or Russian citizens who had been working as American agents to certain death. Ames's placement in the U.S. intelligence bureaucracy was right out of a John Le Carré novel: At one point he was put in charge of Soviet counterintelligence, responsible for evaluating the bona fides of U.S. Soviet or Russian agents and the credibility of their material. Equally or more embarrassing was the disclosure that Robert Hanssen, a senior and high-ranking FBI agent and Russian counterintelligence expert, also passed secrets to Moscow before and after the Soviet Union dissolved. Hanssen's value to the Russians was priceless: He knew better than anyone the "tradecraft" or the sources and methods used by American spies to obtain information from Russian nationals, including Russian intelligence personnel.

The terrorist hijackers of September 11 exploited the porosity of U.S. foreign intelligence collection and analysis as well as the weaknesses in American counterintelligence. The copious resources expended by the National Security Agency and other collectors on technical intelligence, especially the enormous take from satellite imagery and communications intercepts, was in contrast to the comparatively meager resources devoted to the collection of human intelligence (HUMINT) by the CIA and others. HUMINT is intelligence-community jargon for old-fashioned espionage. The problem was not only one of resources committed, but also a question of sources deemed credible by the evaluators. Beginning with the appointment of Stansfield Turner as director of central intelligence in the Carter administration, the significance of information collected from spies was depreciated and the numbers of experienced persons in the DO (Directorate of Operations or clandestine service) was cut drastically. Turner felt that the future of intelligence collection lay in technical systems and that the value of intelligence gathered by spies was greatly overrated. Although not all future CIA directors were as enthralled with technology as was Admiral Turner, the momentum within the intelligence bureaucracies in favor of reliance on technology as opposed to espionage continued on autopilot until at least the mid-1990s.

Having built down its capacity for human intelligence collection and having grown several generations of analysts and operators who disbelieved in all the traditional arts of deception and espionage, the CIA was further encumbered by "oversight" on the part of Congress that often turned into legalistic micromanagement and post facto recrimination in search of headlines. As the Congress became more and more creative in imposing restraints upon U.S. intelligence sources and methods, U.S. access to reliable and timely sources abroad dried up. For example, in the mid-1990s Congress mandated that the CIA virtually avoid using agents and other sources with histories of human rights violations or criminal backgrounds. This restriction was mainly blowback from the Jennifer Harbury case. Harbury was the common-law wife of a Guatemalan revolutionary who was allegedly killed by a Guatemalan army officer thought to be a CIA asset. Congressman (later Senator) Robert Toricelli publicly charged the CIA with complicity in the death of Harbury's husband, although later evidence failed to prove any CIA connection to the incident.

As additional evidence of the sorry state of human intelligence col-lection, consider the Iran–Contra affair that embarrassed the Reagan administration during its second term. In brief, the president and his advisors wanted to deal arms to Iran in order to secure the release of U.S. diplomats and other American nationals held hostage in Leba-non by Iran-supported terrorists. They also sought to channel aid to the Contra counterrevolutionaries seeking to overturn the left-leaning Sandinista regime in Nicaragua. Congress had forbidden U.S. aid to the Contras for the purpose of overthrowing the government of Nica-ragua. So the president's advisors devised an end run around Con-gress. A National Security Council aide, Colonel Oliver North, put together an off-the-shelf operation to move the arms to Iran and fun-nel the proceeds of arms sales to the Contras. When this off-the-books operation was exposed by news leaks, the administration responded with confusion and uncertainty about who was doing what and why.

Most observers concluded that this was another example of beltway interagency confusion or deliberate deception of Congress by the Reagan administration. But the incident holds more subtle and more enduring lessons. The Reagan administration can certainly be faulted for the bizarre means chosen to assist the Contras and for its inability to explain more clearly to the American public the reasons for doing so. But the very capture of our hostages in Lebanon, including some our most important Middle Eastern intelligence experts, and Ameri-can inability to locate and rescue those persons from captivity spoke volumes about the decline of U.S. espionage since its first two decades after the end of World War II.

The preceding illustrations of U.S. intelligence and security policy failure constitute an appropriate if depressing prelude to the subject of soft power. Soft power is one aspect of knowledge strategy. There are many knowledge-based strategies in business, in education, and in other areas. Our concern in this study is the application of one form of knowledge strategy, called military persuasion, to the problems of avoiding war by means of deterrence or, if necessary and unavoid-able, to the conduct of war itself. A knowledge-strategy approach to war, national security, and intelligence is not called for merely because the United States and much of the world has entered into the "information age" or "third wave" technology. The arts of war and peace making among states, including intelligence analysis and military–strategic planning, have always been about knowledge and information. What the information age has done is to increase the volume of information available to civilian and military users and increase the speed with which this greater volume of information can be transmitted across great distances.

This information revolution means, for national security bureaucrats (including military and intelligence analysts), that the analysis and interpretation of information now proceeds at light speed compared to the pace of a decade ago. The combination of greater volumes of information and demand for faster analysis and interpretation of it strains the processing capacity of U.S. defense, foreign policy, and intelligence institutions that are mostly structured for another era.

U.S. national security and intelligence organizations are structured for the Cold War world and are configured as "second wave" or industrial organizations: strict compartmentation of information; hierarchical authority and command relationships; husbanding of resources and information from other organizations or from other "stovepipes" in one's own organization; and, most important, a mind-set that cannot prioritize tasking or objectives without a simple (if not overly so) definition of the "enemy." Since the end of the Cold War the "enemy" as a focus of U.S. policy planning and strategic thinking has lacked a particular address (the Kremlin) or demonic form (Hitler). The enemy to be deterred is now a set of unacceptable activities instead of a particular government, regime, or person. One reason for strong American public support for the Gulf War of 1991 was that President George Bush was able to personify U.S. geostrategic interests (oil, military access to the Middle East) as containing the evildoer and Iraqi dictator Saddam Hussein.

In the aftermath of the unspeakable attacks on the World Trade Center and Pentagon, the usual calls were heard for reorganization of the government and for creation of a czar for homeland security. Some reorganization may be necessary, but far more important is new strategic thinking for the information age. We need to return to first premises and ask whether our traditional understandings of war and its relationship to policy need rethinking. Our intent is not to disparage any of the great works of political theory or military strategy, but to draw from them in order to construct a new conceptual framework that can be helpful to scholars, strategists, and policy makers. That conceptual framework is defined here as *military persuasion* and is explained in greater detail in the following chapters. In general, military persuasion means the use of the instruments of war and military art in order to influence the mind and will of other state and nonstate actors, and especially as a means of support for one's own political and military strategy.

In Chapters 1 through 3, we outline the idea of military persuasion and provide some pertinent illustrations of the idea. We also relate the concept to some of the present controversies having to do with U.S. security policy, including technology and its place in military strategy. The argument seeks to place psychological strategy, of which military persuasion is one form, in the tradition of past and other contemporary military strategies related to the conduct of war or its avoidance.

In Chapters 4 through 6, we discuss past cases of military persuasion and ask how well policy makers and commanders did. The assumption here is that although they did not realize they were practicing military persuasion in the vocabulary that we are now using, some political and military leaders intuited the successful practice of military persuasion to the advantage of their armed forces or state. Why did some succeed and others fail?

In Chapters 7 through 9, we consider three present and future problems for U.S. policy makers and planners in which the mastery of military persuasion will be important. These cases include the avoidance of interstate war by means of nuclear deterrence and whether that model has any continuing relevancy to the post–Cold War U.S.–Russian security relationship. They also include the role of military persuasion in unconventional conflicts, including peace operations, and the possibly disastrous overlap between nuclear weapons and cyberwar.

The concluding chapter summarizes the major findings from the study and offers formative hypotheses about military persuasion for further research and study, as well as some practical lessons for analysts and policy makers.

PART **I**

THE IDEA OF
MILITARY PERSUASION

1 ———————————

Military Persuasion: The Idea and Some Examples

Military persuasion is the threat or use of armed force in order to obtain desired political or military goals. It is basically a psychological strategy intended to influence the decisions of other parties without necessarily having to destroy their armed forces or societies. When some people hear the language "military persuasion" or "armed coercion" they think of sloppiness in strategy or timidity in the waging of war. Bad strategy can be a result of failed efforts in military persuasion, but nothing inherent in the concept or practice of armed persuasion prevents competence in strategy from being achieved. Because simple destruction is something that people inherently understand and military persuasion is harder to grasp, the nuances of persuasion are sometimes its worst enemies. In an Internet-driven era of sound-bite solutions to complex problems, military persuasion invites detraction and confusion.

Military persuasion is nothing new. War has always been both mental and physical, involving the use of brain power and brute force. Great military theorists from Sun Tzu to Basil Liddell Hart have advocated some aspects of military persuasion. Modern writers in the social science disciplines and in history have discussed other aspects of it. The purpose of this study is to clarify what military persuasion actually is and to explain why militaries and their political masters ought to pay more attention to military persuasion in the future.

The first great military theorist to emphasize the significance of military persuasion was the ancient Chinese philosopher of war, Sun Tzu.

In his classic study, *The Art of War*, dated between 400 and 320 B.C.E., Sun Tzu called attention to the importance of the use of clever strategy and psychology in order to minimize the need for war or the loss of life and destruction attendant to war:

For to win one hundred victories in one hundred battles is not the acme of skill. To subdue the enemy without fighting is the acme of skill.

Thus, what is of supreme importance in war is to attack the enemy's strategy. . . . Next best is to disrupt his alliances. . . . The next best is to attack his army. . . . The worst policy is to attack cities. Attack cities only when there is no alternative.[1]

There is some evidence that contemporary Chinese military planners are taking Sun Tzu's perspective very seriously. Chinese military strategists are now considering various means of offsetting the United States's apparent superiority in computers and information system related to combat. For example, a Chinese concept of information-based deterrence suggests a means by which the weaker side can prevent hostile actions on the part of a stronger side: "If one side can effectively weaken the information capability of the other side, even if its capability in other ways is less, the other side will dare not take any ill-considered action."[2]

Sun Tzu also noted that there are five circumstances or conditions in which victory can be expected: (1) He who knows "when he can fight and when he cannot" will be victorious; (2) He who understands how to use both small and large forces will prevail—there are circumstances in war when "the weak can master the strong" and one must "manipulate such circumstances" to win; (3) the commander whose ranks "are united in purpose" will achieve victory; (4) the one who is prudent and "lies in wait for an enemy who is not" will be victorious; and (5) he whose generals are able and "not interfered with by the sovereign" will win.[3] The al-Qaeda terrorists who struck at the World Trade Center and the Pentagon on September 11, 2001, demonstrated several of these principles in action. They manipulated circumstances so that the militarily weaker side could master the stronger side. They prudently lay in wait for an adversary whose preparedness was imprudent. The terrorists knew when to fight and when not to.

For each of these five principles of war according to Sun Tzu we can identify additional and suitable historical examples subsequent to his writing. Successful application of the first principle, knowing when and when not to fight, is shown in Mao Zedong's campaign against Chinese nationalist forces that led to the seizure of power by the Chinese Communists in 1949.[4] North Vietnamese military strategist Vo Nguyen Giap demonstrated mastery of the second principle, the alternation of small and larger forces, during the Second Indochina War in the

1960s and 1970s.[5] President Bush and General Norman Schwarzkopf conducted a successful coalition war against Iraq using the third principle,
of "ranks united in purpose," in 1991. The defeat inflicted by the Army
of Northern Virginia on the Army of the Potomac at Fredericksburg in
the American Civil War in December 1862 illustrates the fourth principle, of one side that is prudent lying in wait for another side that is
not.[6] The Battle of Midway in 1942 also illustrates the advantage of prudent preparations making possible a successful ambush of a stronger
side by a weaker one. The fifth principle, of generals not unduly interfered with, was not observed by the United States during the Vietnam
War between 1965 and 1973, especially from 1965 to 1969, with disastrous results for policy and strategy.

The who, what, and why of military persuasion have no short answers, but it is worth trying to arrive at some simple answers, or to be
more correct, simplifying answers. Simplification, as opposed to simplicity, is at the heart of theory building. Theory depends upon ab-
straction from the particular to the general; of necessity, this requires
simplification. But simplifying the who, what, and why of military
persuasion demands a point of departure and a focus. The remainder
of this chapter discusses some pertinent past and present examples of
military persuasion. The following chapter elaborates the concept of
military persuasion and discusses related ideas that mark the political
science and military-studies literatures.

THREE EXAMPLES OF MILITARY PERSUASION

The Iranian Hostage Crisis

Consider, as an example, the takeover of the American embassy in
Tehran by Iranian militant "students" on November 4, 1979. More than
fifty U.S. citizens were taken hostage. The Carter administration was
caught by surprise by this coup de main, orchestrated by the newly
empowered Iranian regime that had overthrown the government of
the Shah of Iran. For the remainder of Carter's term in office, the Iranian militants who controlled the embassy manipulated the world and
U.S. media by virtue of their control over the hostages. This psychological strategy of media manipulation was designed to control the
Carter administration by advertising U.S. helplessness and apparent
Iranian reasonableness. The Carter administration tried various diplomatic approaches to obtain the release of the hostages, but to no avail.
Many important diplomatic and intelligence materials were compro-
mised. Carter's 1980 campaign for reelection became imprisoned by
his "Rose Garden" strategy of making the hostage crisis the center of
his concerns. Finally, the U.S. military was ordered to attempt a raid to

rescue the hostages in April 1980, but the raid was aborted in progress by presidential decision as a result of equipment failure, as well as other failures.

The regime in Tehran practiced very successfully various forms of what this study will call military persuasion. First, the Iranian government gave itself official deniability for the hostage crisis by having "militant students" designated as the hostage takers. This provided the regime in Tehran some diplomatic cover and some psychological distance for their illegal acts, although everyone knew that Ayatollah Khomeini, the de facto leader of the Islamic clergy that was now in charge of the country, was making the calls. Second, the Iranians kept negotiating with the United States throughout the crisis while exploiting the Carter administration's obsession with resolving the crisis on some mutually acceptable terms. Khomeini and his advisors understood U.S. society and culture and the mind-set of the Carter administration and exploited that understanding to the fullest. They took advantage of the power of the media in setting Washington agendas by focusing public and government attention on the hostages. Carter's CIA director, Stansfield Turner, recalled that for six months after seizure of the hostages, "75 per cent of my time was taken up with the hostage crisis."[7]

Third, the Iranians were very skillful in managing the perceptions of themselves held by the international community and by the U.S. government and media. They created the impression that "militants" or hard-liners in the government were in conflict with "moderates" who could be reasoned with in order to obtain the release of the hostages. This phony militants–moderates dichotomy kept the Carter diplomacy on a tilt-a-whirl of overtures and marches that left actual control over events to the Iranians.

Fourth, the Iranian regime played out its hand to the greatest extent possible and then folded when it had exhausted its run. The election of President Ronald Reagan was not only a signal that the U.S. public wanted a new foreign policy. It was a specific clue that the American people were fed up with the no-results policy of the Carter administration on the hostage crisis and that the public wanted a prompt resolution. With this assured public backing, President Reagan would almost certainly attempt to resolve the crisis by using a big stick (as he later did by reflagging Kuwaiti tankers in the Persian Gulf when the Iran–Iraq war threatened to disrupt oil shipments there). The U.S. Navy presence in the Indian ocean gave the new president options ranging from coercive diplomacy against Iran to worse. In the words of Kenny Rogers, the Iranians "know when to hold 'em, and know when to fold 'em."

Fifth, the United States was vulnerable to the embassy capture and seizure of American hostages, and to the subsequent diplomatic squeeze employed against the United States by the hostage takers, on account of its few intelligence assets in Iran and the faulty comprehension of Iranian society, culture, and politics by the American intelligence community in the latter 1970s.[8] The U.S. intelligence and policy community believed that the Shah of Iran was invulnerable to domestic overthrow by any source other than his own armed forces and secret police. So long as these pillars of his support remained loyal, the Shah's regime would be secure and the U.S.–friendly tilt of Iranian foreign policy would persist. American intelligence had few if any ties to the forces opposed to the Shah, including some elements of the middle and professional classes. Intelligence estimates overlooked or dismissed the significance of the Islamic clergy and their lay followers, who opposed social and political modernization undertaken by the Shah. When the Shah lost his nerve and abdicated, a temporary power vacuum was filled by a coalition of religious zealots, Revolutionary Guards in support of Khomeini, and a judiciary looking to Islamic law as the touchstone of public policy.

In short, the United States in the year or two prior to the seizure of the American embassy was clueless about the drift of events beneath the facade of the Shah's ruling clique. Thus, it was unable to practice successfully military persuasion once the coup and hostage seizure had taken place. On the other hand, the Iranians practiced military persuasion with a vengeance to confuse and deter any appropriate U.S. response as long as the Carter administration was in office. Only as Ronald Reagan was on the threshold of being sworn in did the Iranian regime release the remaining captives (some had been released earlier as part of Iranian strategy for the manipulation of world media and public opinion) through Algerian intermediaries. The Iranians had used military persuasion with success to confound a superpower and to hold hostage its diplomacy for more than a year. This successful exploitation of military persuasion contributed to President Carter's defeat in 1980; thus, it influenced the outcome of an American presidential election.

Do we exaggerate? There is no more emphatic testimony to Iranian success and American incompetence at military persuasion in 1979 and 1980 than the statement by newly appointed Secretary of State Edmund Muskie in 1980. Muskie was sworn in to replace the departed Cyrus Vance, who had resigned as part of his objection to the planned hostage rescue that eventually failed at Desert One. A reporter asked Muskie what Muskie thought the most important priority was now with regard to U.S. policy and the hostage crisis. He responded thus: "Keep hostage families away from the White House." Muskie was not a man lacking in compassion; during a campaign for the presidential nomination years later he broke into tears in public. He was simply stating his insights with regard to part of the Iranian strategy for manipulating the Carter administration, and he was right.

Nuclear Deterrence

The preceding example might be judged as a biased one. Psychological strategy is at the heart of hostage negotiations because of the high emotional content of the issue: nationalism or patriotism combined with the feeling of victimization. Here is another example, not of a highly dramatic event that takes place within a short time but of an ongoing process that is hardly noticed except in occasional international crises. That process, in the years that we now retroactively define as the Cold War, was referred to as nuclear deterrence.

Nuclear deterrence was an attempt by scholars, policy makers, and military planners to come up with a shared vocabulary and set of concepts to explain the contradictions of war in the nuclear age. Once nuclear weapons and long-range delivery systems were available in large numbers and deployed in survivable basing modes by the United States and the Soviet Union, traditional strategy was stalemated. Traditional strategy was based on competition between the technology base for offenses and for defenses: Experience showed that for every offense (or defense), sooner or later a countervailing defense (or offense) technology would be invented or designed to defeat it.

The nuclear age seemed to repeal this law of inevitable, more-or-less equal competition between offensive and defensive technologies. Nuclear-armed ballistic missile offenses could not be defeated by any defense technologies available during the Cold War. This frustrated missile defense designers on both sides of the East–West divide between 1947 and 1989. Because offenses trumped defenses, deterrence based on second-strike retaliation became mandatory, not optional, for the Cold War American and Soviet "superpowers." The supremacy of offensive technology enforced a shared priority on defensive strategy: deterrence of war by the credible threat of retaliation in lieu of deciding arguments by the actual clash of armies, navies, and air forces.

As Bernard Brodie, one of the earliest and most farsighted of nuclear strategists, first explained in 1946, "Thus far the chief purpose of our military establishment has been to win wars. From now on its chief purpose must be to avert them. It can have almost no other useful purpose."[9] Thus, psychological strategy or military persuasion was to take the place of actual combat because actual combat could no longer be carried out at an acceptable social cost. In addition, the inability of the United States or the Soviets to define a war-winning strategy for any nuclear conflict also tied the hands of their European allies. Conventional war in Europe was simply too risky on account of the tactical nuclear weapons deployed there and the possibility, indeed the near certainty, that escalation from conventional to theater nuclear warfare, and from there to international holocaust, was highly probable. At least, no one could argue that it was improbable and still defend reliance upon the nuclear deterrent.

Nuclear deterrence was a form of military persuasion that continued for most of the Cold War. But the durability of the general concept of nuclear deterrence concealed a number of highly spirited and contentious policy and strategy debates in Washington, in Moscow, and among U.S. allies in NATO. For example, within each military bureaucracy, in Washington and in Moscow, policy makers and military planners were required to sort out important issues that were presented by the possibility of nearly total societal destruction in hours or less. One set of problems was how to manage the operation of nuclear forces in time of peace. This had to be done in order to send the appropriately positive signal of readiness for retaliation if need be, without at the same time sending another signal of provocative intent and preparedness for an immediate first strike. Thus, command and control systems evolved with features that were "fail safe" against accidental or inadvertent nuclear war. And the nuclear ballistic missile submarine (SSBN or "boomer") became the missile platform of choice for the American second-strike force on account of its unmatched survivability combined with its nonprovocative disappearance beneath the sea.

Nuclear crises were the cases in which the dangerous practice of nuclear military persuasion brought the Americans and Soviets close to the flash point. And a variety of types of military persuasion, including but not limited to deterrence, were required once the crisis was in progress to extricate the two sides from mutual disaster. Take the case of the Cuban missile crisis. Soviet Premier Nikita S. Khrushchev decided in 1962 on the bold initiative of placing Soviet missiles in Cuba after having observed the installation of U.S. medium-range missiles in Turkey capable of striking at targets in Russia. He saw his Cuban missile gambit as one of equalizing the nuclear vulnerability of both sides. President John F. Kennedy did not see Khrushchev's missile demarche from the same perspective. Kennedy and his advisors saw the Soviet missile deployments in Cuba as an effort to upset mutual deterrence and as a provocative demonstration of Soviet atomic diplomacy.

During the thirteen days that are now referred to by historians as the Cuban missile crisis of 1962, the American and Soviet leaderships had to engage in crisis bargaining by means of coercive diplomacy and other instruments of military persuasion in order to extricate themselves from prior nuclear brinkmanship carried too far. Chapter 4 of this study goes into more detail about the crisis. It was the beginning of a steep learning curve for both sides. Thereafter, the embrace by U.S. or Soviet leaders of aggressive nuclear bargaining to advantage was more tentative, and their willingness to push matters of political disagreement to the point of military confrontation was less pronounced. Although neither was ready to surrender its primary policy aims of the Cold War, the post–Cuban missile crisis dance between Moscow and Washington was more polite, civilized, and devoid of nuclear braggadocio. Equally important, U.S. and Soviet military operators of nuclear warning and control systems also learned more about how the operations of nuclear forces themselves conveyed psychological messages of threat or reassurance to another state or states.

Image and Information Warfare

Finally, let us consider a third example of military persuasion or, rather, two illustrations of one form of military persuasion. This is the manipulation of thoughts by the presentation of visual images or by restructuring of the information environment.

Images

As an example of the use of visual images, consider Serbia's response to NATO's Operation Allied Force in 1999. The regime of Yugoslav President Slobodan Milosevic was the target of NATO's campaign of military persuasion by means of air attack. One of the targets struck by NATO warplanes was Milosevic's own residence. Serbs played pictures of the destruction of the president's home back across the Internet to Western audiences. Their intent was to reach American and allied NATO populations with the message that NATO was striking at civil as well as military targets. This Serbian spin control was counterspin to NATO's original spin: that the alliance was conducting the most precise air attacks in history and avoiding significant collateral damage. NATO intended this message be sent on account of the surrounding political mission for which NATO air strikes were being carried out: to cause Milosevic and his regime to stop their "ethnic cleansing" campaign against Albanians living in the Serbian province of Kosovo. A military campaign in support of a humanitarian operation needed to justify itself by arguing for the precise character of its targeting. The results with regard to Milosevic's home in Belgrade appear in Figure 1.1.

On the other hand, Figure 1.1 tells about another kind of military persuasion, implicit instead of explicit. The NATO bombing of Milosevic's home was not an accident or a case of "collateral damage." It was deliberate and purposeful. It was intended to send a message to the Yugoslav leader and to his people. The message said, We can destroy

Figure 1.1
Milosevic's Home, Belgrade, Bombed April 22, 1999

Source: Truth in Media, Phoenix, Arizona, April 1999.

not only your objects of military and economic value, but we can attack precisely your person, including your personal estate and family.
This was the same "message" sent by the Reagan administration to
Libyan President Muammar Quaddafi in 1985 by bombing raids that
attacked his "command centers" with the not very disguised intent of
frightening him or killing him. So the picture in Figure 1.1 was intended by the Serbs to send one kind of message: NATO is lying and
NATO is reckless. It also sent another message, unintended by Serbs:
NATO will not allow sanctuary for the Yugoslav leadership as long as
the war continues. Leaders are valid military targets.

Now consider another example of a visual image intended to influence the opinion of American, allied, and other publics during NATO's
war against Yugoslavia. This is a more explicitly ideological image
and one that evokes strong memories, especially for older generations
that remember World War II (Figure 1.2).

The Internet depiction of President Bill Clinton as Hitler is intended
for two different audiences. For Serbs and their allies, including Russians, in conjures up images of fascism (including nazism) and identifies those experiences in people's memories with the current NATO
bombing campaign against Serbia. Milosevic is, by implication, a na-

Figure 1.2
Clinton as Hitler

Source: Truth in Media, Phoenix, Arizona, April 1999.

tionalist leader opposed by a coalition of fascist fellow travelers manifest in NATO's political aims and military capability. It would not be
lost on Serb mind gamers that many Russians, including very influential members of the Russian Parliament, would react favorably to this
image that plays on their visceral identification of the West with nazism
and fanatical anticommunism.

At the same time, the image of Clinton as Hitler is also intended for
audiences in Western Europe as a reminder that war and fascism go
together—especially the waging of an aggressive war and fascist political philosophy. This historical association of fascism or nazism with

military aggression is buried in the subconscious memories of Europeans, especially in Germany and in those countries temporarily occupied by German armed forces during World War II. Playing on this memory of Hitler's aggressive wars, Serbian spinners attempt to induce a connection between present-day NATO and World War II nazism. The picture probably had little, if any, impact in the United States, where Clinton was judged as a left-leaning politician, and nazism was the last charge that would ever be laid at his feet.

This form of visual manipulation of political attitudes is not new in the age of global finance, information, and telecommunications technology. Visual propaganda aimed at modern political audiences has existed since photography was invented. Visual images as part of psychological strategy are even older than that, of course: Drawings by ancient peoples on the walls of caves depicted their gods, warriors, and battles. What is new since the 1990s is the speed with which images can be transmitted, the distances over which they can be sent almost instantaneously, and the volume of visual communications that can travel at these high speeds and long distances. A glut of visual and other communications now encircles the earth like a biosphere—a commosphere? Since there are so many communications stimuli for the individual to cope with once he or she has plugged into the wired world, propagandists on both sides of the NATO–Yugoslav war, and future propagandists as well, will undoubtedly seek to make images more "targeted" to specific audiences much as smart bombs were. One can imagine all kinds of possibilities for visual propaganda using the "morphing" techniques first seen in the film *Forrest Gump* and developed even further since by Hollywood film studios. What is real, and what is not real is now a military persuasion in itself even before a war begins, during it, and afterward.

When the U.S. war against the Taliban regime and al-Qaeda terrorist network began on October 7, 2001, the Pentagon and the remainder of the American government were slow to perceive the requirements for competing in modern, visually driven information warfare. U.S. networks played several videotapes of Osama bin Laden arguing his paranoid philosophy for American and global audiences without screening or editing the content of his messages. President Bush's national security advisors caught on to the damage this might cause and jawboned the networks into a policy of more careful review and selective showing.

But the U.S. side of the media picture remained very slow moving. From October 7 through late December, the U.S. military conducted an innovative and effective campaign in the remotest possible theater of operations (Afghanistan) using a creative combination of high-technology airpower, special operations and other elite forces, Marines, and allied local ground forces. Expert talking heads had warned that Afghanistan had been the "graveyard" of the Soviets, Russians, and Brits; but the United States chose its objectives and campaign tactics to avoid the mistakes made by nineteenth- and twentieth-century would-be conquerors of Afghanistan. Nevertheless, this achievement was hardly exploited for its publicity and persuasive effects because of old Pentagon reflexes about the media. As John Hillen, former Army officer and decorated combat veteran of the Gulf War, noted: "Since Vietnam, where the military's adversarial relationship with the press was cemented, the Pentagon has had a mistrustful and ham-handed way of handling the press and any attention that it cannot control. Some services are better than others, but in general the Pentagon's wartime policy is 'no pictures and no names, please.'"[10]

Hillen is aware that operational security requires concealment of military identities. His complaint is that taking this policy to extremes results in missed opportunities to acquaint the American people with their own military heroes. In twentieth-century wars prior to Vietnam, military heroes like Sergeant York and Audie Murphy were paraded around the country as examples to inspire American youth and patriotism. Nowadays, decorated combat veterans could appear on nationally syndicated talk shows and CNN photo ops or play themselves in movies. This is especially important in the twenty-first century, when the U.S. armed forces are relatively small in size and fewer Americans have any direct experience with military service.[11]

Information Warfare

As John Arquilla and David Ronfeldt have explained it, the Serbian Internet visual propaganda is an example of the use of "netwar."[12] Arquilla and Ronfeldt, among the leading contributors to the study of the impact of the information revolution on military strategy, distinguish between "cyberwar" and "netwar" as variations on the practice we are calling military persuasion. Cyberwar, according to them, is the conducting of a military campaign or plan of operations on cybernetic principles. This essentially means exploiting information technology in order to deny to the enemy a coherent picture of the battle while, at the same time, providing for one's own side the most comprehensive picture of the same engagement. Cyberwar can include tactics as diverse as the physical destruction of command–control centers or air defense radars, on one hand, or the invasion of enemy computer networks with viruses, worms, and other hostile cyberbugs in order to disrupt or confuse those networks and the information they carry.

Netwar, in contrast to cyberwar, is targeted against the polity, society, and culture of the opponent. The object of netwar is to demoralize and confuse. Sometimes this demoralization is even aimed at the opposed combat forces. Tokyo Rose, whose seductive radio voice reached many an American G.I. stationed in the Pacific in World War II, is an example of netwar. Netwar bypasses direct assault on the armed forces of an opponent and goes after its soft underbelly: the social and cultural supports for the war effort.

Wartime propaganda is nothing new as a paradigm of influence: indeed, it is as old as war itself. Arquilla and Ronfeldt recognize, however, that this kind of military persuasion now can call upon new technology: morphed videos transmitted globally in real time; the Internet; faxes; cellular telephones; and other accoutrements of an information age that can leap over the borders of states and the boundaries of armies. Modern Chinese military strategists apparently contemplate a concept of netwar which is based on Chairman Mao's original formulation of "people's war" adapted for modern technology. In modern people's war, according to one concept, no great significance is attributed to the difference between "military" and "civilian" personnel taking part in a conflict. "Anybody who understands computers may become a 'fighter' on the network," according to one PRC military thinker. Adds another: "The development of the Internet opens up new opportunities for the individual to participate directly in an information war."[13] A summary of some of the more important kinds of information warfare appears in Table 1.1.

There are many examples of netwar as a form of military persuasion in modern times. Chechens in 1994–1996 used netwar in order to gain access to international and Russian media to tell their side of the story, much to the embarrassment of the Yeltsin government and the Russian military. Several years later, acting Russian President Vladimir Putin unleashed another Russian offensive into Chechnya. Russian military preparedness and training were better the second time around, but equally important was the improvement in Russian military persuasion aimed at audiences within and outside of Russia. The Russian government successfully depicted the Chechens as invaders of neighboring Dagestan instead of freedom fighters for Chechnya. Russia also assigned blame to Chechen terrorists for several bombings in Moscow in the summer of 1999 that were of suspicious, and essentially unknown, origin. Putin exercised more control over the Russian media coverage of the 1999–2000 war than Yeltsin did during the campaign of 1994–1996. But that was in the old Soviet style. What was more interesting during the latter conflict was the greater ability of Putin, compared to Yeltsin, to soften up the Russian public by demonizing Chechens as bandits, terrorists, and criminals posing a threat to the integrity of Russia itself.

The terrorist attack on the United States on September 11, 2001, was an example of failed netwar. Osama bin Laden and his al-Qaeda network misread American political culture. They assumed that the U.S.

Table 1.1
Varieties of Information Warfare

War Form	Objective	Means	Targets
Cyberwar	Neutralize or destroy military and command system targets	Conduct military operations on information-based principles	Enemy military forces and supporting C4ISR
Net Centric Warfare	Achieve shared awareness, increased speed of command, higher tempo of opera- tions, greater lethality, increased survivability, and a degree of self- synchronization	Increase combat power by networking sensors, decision makers, and shooters	Enemy C4ISR and information and decision networks
Netwar	Influence society and government of the opponent, including public opinion and media	Perceptions management, disinformation, PSYOPs and other means of influ- ence based on information	Enemy society and government, including public opinion, media and armed forces, and security services

Source: Based on *In Athena's Camp: Preparing for Conflict in the Information Age*, ed. John Arquilla and David Ronfeldt (Santa Monica, Calif.: Rand, 1997), Chapter 1; Edward Waltz, *Information Warfare Principles and Operations* (Boston: Artech House, 1998), p. 193.

*C4ISR = Command, Control, Communications, Computers, Intelligence, Surveillance and Reconnaissance

government and the American people would respond to the attacks on the World Trade Center and the Pentagon in the same way that the United States had reacted to earlier attacks on the World Trade Center in 1993 or to al-Qaeda bombings of American embassies overseas. The terrorists anticipated a pro forma firing off of a few cruise missiles against base camps or other notional targets, followed by the usual diplomatic demarches. Instead, the attacks riled the American people who saw them as comparable in magnitude and treachery to the Japa- nese attack on Pearl Harbor on December 7, 1941. President Bush, re- flecting the mood of the entire country, called for a global war against al-Qaeda and other terror networks and the capture or killing of Osama bin Laden; and the United States waged a war that dethroned the Taliban regime in Afghanistan that had shielded al-Qaeda and other terrorists.

The Russian defense ministry and other parts of the Russian government are paying attention to the potential of both cyberwar and netwar. A civilian analyst in the Russian Ministry of Defense, Dr. V. I. Tsymbal, proposed a "broad" and a "narrow" definition of information war (*informatsionnaya voyna*) that correspond to the U.S. distinctions between netwar and cyberwar. According to Tsymbal, information war in the broad sense includes "countermeasures between two states implemented mainly in peacetime" with emphasis not on the armed forces but on "the people's public/social awareness, to state administrative systems, production control systems., scientific control, cultural control, etc."[14] In the narrow sense, according to the same writer, information warfare "has as its goal the achievement of overwhelming superiority over the enemy in the form of efficiency, completeness, and reliability of information upon its receipt, treatment, and use [and is intended] to achieve combat superiority (victory)."[15] Other Russian agencies, including their foreign intelligence and domestic counterintelligence services, are concerned as well with information security and with Russia's possible vulnerability to information attacks. Russia's military is aware of U.S. and allied NATO superiority in advanced technology conventional warfare. Therefore, Russian security experts have studied the importance of "asymmetrical" or "indirect" approaches to offsetting U.S. superiority in this domain, including asymmetrical information strategies such as the use of netwar when the other side is superior in cyberwar.[16]

The preceding examples of military persuasion in very different contexts have set the stage. Let us now explain the concept of military persuasion in more detail in Chapter Two.

NOTES

1. Sun Tzu, *The Art of War*, ed. and trans. Samuel B. Griffith (New York: Oxford University Press, 1963), 77–78.

2. Yu Shifu, Han Xiaoling, and Zhang Qinbin, "On the Outlook of National Security Strategy in the Sunzi (Sun Tzu) and Our National Security Strategy," in *The Fourth International Symposium on Sun Tzu's Art of War*, 82, cited in Kathryn L. Gauthier, "China as Peer Competitor? Trends in Nuclear Weapons, Space and Information Warfare," in *The Dragon Awakes: China's Military Modernization Trends and Implications*, ed. Lawrence Grinter (Maxwell A.F.B., Ala.: USAF Counterproliferation Center, 1999), 28.

3. Sun Tzu, *The Art of War*, 82–83.

4. Bevin Alexander, *How Great Generals Win* (New York: W. W. Norton, 1993), 187–208, is especially good on the period from 1927 to 1935 culminating in the Long March and the arrival of First Army in Yun'an against great odds.

5. Bevin Alexander, *The Future of Warfare* (New York: W. W. Norton, 1995), 160–175.

6. James M. McPherson, *Battle Cry of Freedom: The Civil War Era* (New York: Oxford University Press, 1988), 570–575.

7. Christopher Andrew, *For the President's Eyes Only: Secret Intelligence and the American Presidency from Washington to Bush* (New York: Harper Perennial, 1996), 449.

8. On U.S. intelligence in Iran pertinent to this case, see John Prados, *Presidents' Secret Wars: CIA and Pentagon Covert Operations since World War II* (New York: William Morrow, 1986), 351–353, and Andrew, *For the President's Eyes Only*, 448–455.

9. Bernard Brodie, *War and Politics* (New York: Macmillan, 1973), 377. Brodie's original statement to this effect appeared in his 1946 book, *The Absolute Weapon* (New York: Harcourt, Brace, 1946), 76.

10. John Hillen, "The Real Heroes Aren't On TV," *Wall Street Journal*, December 20, 2001, from Foreign Policy Research Institute <al@fpri.org>

11. Ibid.

12. See John Arquilla and David Ronfeldt, "A New Epoch—and Spectrum— of Conflict," in *In Athena's Camp: Preparing for War in the Information Age*, ed. John Arquilla and David Ronfeldt (Santa Monica, Calif.: RAND, 1997), pp. 1– 22. See also, in the same volume, John Arquilla and David Ronfeldt, "Cyberwar Is Coming," 23–60, and John Arquilla and David Ronfeldt, "The Advent of Netwar," 275–294. I am especially grateful to John Arquilla for encouraging my interest in this topic and for helpful suggestions, although he bears no responsibility for arguments here.

13. Quoted in Gauthier, "China as a Peer Competitor," 30.

14. V. I. Tsymbal, "The Concept of Information Warfare," presentation at a conference in the Academy of State Service of the Russian Federation (Moscow), September 13, 1995, p. 2, cited in Timothy L. Thomas, "Russia's Asymmetrical Approach to Information Warfare," in *Russia's Military Way into the Twenty-first Century*, ed. Stephen J. Cimbala (London: Frank Cass, 2001), 100.

15. Ibid.

16. Thomas, "Russia's Asymmetrical Approach to Information Warfare," esp. pp. 107–116.

2

Military Persuasion and Psychological Strategy

In Chapter 1 I argued that military persuasion is the threat or use of military power for political influence under conditions requiring the intended or unintended "cooperation" of the party being influenced.[1] The object of military persuasion is to induce the party being influenced to want to comply with the demands of the influencer and, having achieved that result, to act in accord with the influencer's demands. The concept of military persuasion, like any concept in social science or military art, stands on the shoulders of those who have already contributed to the study of psychological strategy.

Chapter 1 broadly introduced the idea of military persuasion and provided several pertinent examples. In this chapter I first consider some of the modern intellectual sources and inspirations for the concept of military persuasion. Second, I dissect the "how" of armed persuasion: those drivers of the system that make efforts to use military power in support of psychological strategy, successful or not. Throughout the study I discuss various aspects of military persuasion: "coercive diplomacy," "deterrence," "compellence," or other dimensions. These possible parts of military persuasion must not be confused with the whole. Although each of these has stood alone as the subject of important theoretical and policy studies, I am presenting them here within a more general framework for analysis.

COERCIVE DIPLOMACY, DETERRENCE, AND MILITARY PERSUASION

I draw important inspiration and ideas about military persuasion from one of the most prolific students of deterrence and the psychology of politics: Alexander L. George. George's concept of *coercive diplomacy* is one of the most original contributions to the study of the relationship between force and policy. As George has explained it, coercive diplomacy is a strictly defensive strategy intended to accomplish one of three possible objectives: (1) to persuade an opponent to stop an action already in progress short of its accomplished purpose, (2) to convince the opponent to undo or retract an action already taken or a commitment previously made, or (3) to persuade an opponent to make changes in its government or regime in order to accomplish the defender's political objective.[2]

George excludes from his types of coercive diplomacy *deterrence*. Deterrence aims to persuade a potential or actual opponent not to begin an action that he is thought to be considering but has not yet undertaken.[3] And although its meaning is very similar to his definition of "type A" and "type B" coercive diplomacy, George prefers not to use the term *compellence* because compellence "implies exclusive or heavy reliance on psychological threats, whereas I wish to emphasize the possibility of a more flexible diplomacy that can employ rational persuasion and accommodation as well as coercive threats to encourage the adversary either to comply with the demands or to work out an acceptable compromise."[4]

According to George, coercive diplomacy offers an alternative to military action. If force is used in coercive diplomacy, it takes the form of "an exemplary or symbolic use of limited military action" to help persuade the opponent to back down.[5] By "exemplary," George means "just enough force of an appropriate kind to demonstrate resolution" and "to give credibility to the threat that greater force will be used if necessary."[6] This is possibly a form of "risk" strategy (see later) and it calls for a very fine balancing of military and diplomatic moves. The "coercive" aspect of coercive diplomacy may lie in the force that has not necessarily been explicitly threatened to date, but that the party being coerced recognizes as a possible option for the future. For example, President Harry Truman's use of an airlift to resist a Soviet diplomatic and military squeeze on Berlin in 1948 was an example of nonprovocative compellence or coercive diplomacy supported by the possibility that more dangerous U.S. military measures might be necessary if the blockade were not lifted or interfered with.

The concept of coercive diplomacy as developed by George and the related idea of compellence as developed by Thomas C. Schelling may sound like psychologizing to military traditionalists.[7] But the ideas of George and Schelling are fully in keeping with those of some of the most highly regarded military historians and philosophers of war. For example, the great Prussian philosopher of war, Carl von Clausewitz, in his discussion of the ends and means of military action, explains that destruction of the enemy's combat force is not always the object of military action. But even when it is not, the military potential to bring about such destruction lies in the background of all prewar and wartime calculation:

The combat is the single activity in War; in the combat the destruction of the enemy opposed to us is the means to the end; it is so even when the combat does not actually take place, because in that case there lies at the root of the decision the supposition at all events that this destruction is to be regarded as beyond doubt.[8]

Military persuasion is more inclusive than coercive diplomacy because the latter implies a preference for deescalation of the pace and scope of fighting: military persuasion is open ended whether it is better to escalate, or to deescalate, in order to accomplish policy objectives. Sometimes it is necessary to plan for both. For example, one of the dilemmas of peace enforcement operations is that it is sometimes necessary to escalate with prompt, large troop deployments supported by stiff diplomatic backbone in order to bring about reduced tension and fighting later. Some critics of NATO's air war against Yugoslavia in 1999 faulted NATO's initial assumption that a few days or weeks of bombing would force Yugoslav President Slobodan Milosevic to call a halt to ethnic cleansing in Kosovo. When this assumption was disappointed, NATO faced the unwelcome requirement for escalation to more comprehensive air attacks and, eventually, reluctant preparations for a ground offensive that President Clinton and other allied leaders had initially sought to rule out. As Ivo Daalder and Michael O'Hanlon have noted,

The initial bombing strategy of gradualism can be defended as a reasonable gamble, even if we now know it did not work. But it was wrong to hinge everything on it. At a bare minimum, NATO could have left its future plans ambiguous, and U.S. officials could have consistently underscored that they intended to conduct whatever strikes were needed to achieve their goals. . . . NATO's chosen approach was a dangerous and sloppy way to use force.[9]

Further distinctions among diverse forms of military persuasion are necessary. Coercive diplomacy and compellence must also be distinguished from deterrence. Deterrence occurs before the fact of an undesired action; coercive diplomacy or compellence occur after or during the undesired activity. According to Robert A. Pape, strategies for military coercion can be divided into the following classes: strategies of punishment, of risk, of denial, and of decapitation.[10] Punishment campaigns attempt to raise the cost of continued resistance to one side's demands by inflicting direct or indirect suffering on civilians. Risk strategies, like punishment strategies, target the civilian economy and society in order to coerce the opponent's government. But risk strategies emphasize the capacity for gradually increasing punishment and the expected probability of more to come, instead of the sudden and more comprehensive attacks envisioned in punishment-oriented strategy. Denial strategies, on the other hand, seek to coerce an opponent by demonstrating the ability to defeat the opponent's military strategy in battle and thereby to deny the opponent his political and military objectives at an acceptable cost to the coercer. Finally, decapitation strategies attempt either to kill or to overthrow top leaders in the hope that their successors will be more willing to stop fighting, or to inflict sufficient destruction on the opponent's military command and control systems that effective prosecution of a coordinated war effort becomes impossible.[11]

One of the important issues raised by this taxonomy is to identify the conditions under which one form of military persuasion or another may be employed most successfully. One would anticipate, for example, that denial strategies would be more applicable to conventional warfare than to nuclear crisis management; risk and punishment-oriented strategies, on the other hand, would be more suited to nuclear crisis management than to conventional campaigns.[12] As Bernard Brodie noted with regard to the Cuban missile crisis of October 1962,

From beginning to end, the confrontation that we call the Cuban missile crisis—the most acute crisis of any we have had since World War II—shows a remarkably different quality from any previous one in history. There is an unprecedented candor, direct personal contact, and at the same time mutual respect between the chief actors. Normal diplomatic formalities of language and of circumlocution are disregarded. Both sides at once agree that their quarrel *could* lead to nuclear war, which is impossible to contemplate and which would leave no winner.[13]

The significance of perceptions and of paradoxes of strategy also apply to the choice among Pape's list of strategies and to the entire subject of military persuasion. Those subjects are deferred to the next section, when we dissect the intellectual structure of the concept of military persuasion. Our discussion thus far has established that we are not forced to start from scratch in developing the concept of military persuasion nor in applying it to military affairs. The following list offers a summation of some of the more important ideas and contributing authors noted so far, together with additions that we will note in our third section.[14]

Idea or Concept	Author or Authors
Deterrence	Bernard Brodie, Thomas Schelling, Robert Jervis, others
Coercive Diplomacy	Alexander George, others
Cyberwar and Netwar	John Arquilla, David Ronfeldt
Compellence and Military Coercion	Thomas Schelling, Robert Pape, others
Significance of Perceptions Management, Perspective Taking, Psychological Precision, and Paralytic Warfare	Robert Jervis, Richards Heuer, Steven Metz, Jan Breemer, others
Significance of Paradox and Uncertainty in War and Military Strategy	Modern Interpreters of Clausewitz (Colin Gray, Edward Luttwak, Michael Handel, others)

THE SINEWS OF MILITARY PERSUASION: HOW IT WORKS

Military persuasion, as all strategy and policy, is fundamentally about practice even more than theory. Ideas of war avoidance, war limitation, and war making, together with the policies that they are designed to support, receive their ground truth outside the laboratory or the study. What is valid is what works. Therefore it is prudent now to turn to the actual mechanisms or causal influences that make military persuasion work, or if missing, cause attempts to fail.

The Will of the Opponent

First, military persuasion has as its primary objective the influencing of the opponent's will. This does not exclude military operations intended to destroy the capabilities of the opponent, when and if required. In one sense, all war is about influencing the will of the enemy. But military persuasion seeks to change the other side's own view about the risks and potential costs if it continues on the present, undesired by the first side, path. This change in the opponent's mind-set occurs while the opponent retains some significant capacity to fight back. This influence process takes place through "negotiation" by use of force, threat of force, or both at two levels. Side A attempts to influence Side B's estimate of Side A's intentions and capabilities; Side A also attempts to influence Side B's estimates of its own intentions and capabilities as the fighting continues.

Adolf Hitler's campaign of intimidation against the other heads of state in Europe from 1936 through 1939 is a classic example of military persuasion by influencing leaders' judgments about their own and possible enemy intentions and capabilities. During this time, Hitler and his leading military advisors knew that Germany's military buildup begun in 1933 was far from readiness for a major war. During the diplomatic crisis that was ultimately settled by the Munich agreement of September 1938, the German General Staff feared an Allied intervention on behalf of Czechoslovakia that would expose their actual military weakness. Some generals plotted that in the event of forcible Allied resistance to the capitulation of Czechoslovakia, Hitler should be overthrown. But Hitler read the minds of his opponents, the heads of state and foreign ministries of France and England, better than his generals did. During these years of German military buildup but actual unreadiness for major war in Europe, the German air force (Luftwaffe) staged military demonstrations for visiting foreign dignitaries in order to create the impression that Germany had moved to the head of the class in air power. In addition, the German government released carefully staged film of units marching in formation or preparing for combat in order to exaggerate Germany's actual military strength. These films and demonstrations played into the hands of proappeasement British and French politicians, press mavens, and cultural arbiters. Meanwhile, Germany was depicted by its leadership as only seeking to right the wrongs of the unduly harsh Versailles peace settlement imposed upon it after World War I. The liberation of the Rhineland, the anschluss with Austria, and, finally, the capitulation of Czechoslovakia at Munich with Allied consent—each step was depicted as an incremental concession by the Allies that would finally appease Germany's appetite for a just diplomatic settlement.

Of course, Hitler's clever military persuasion in this regard was almost too much so. He became overconfident of his own skills in manipulation of enemy intentions and inflation of his own capabilities in their minds. Hitler expected that Britain and France would capitulate to his invasion of Poland in September 1939 as they had to his conquest and subjugation of Czechoslovakia. He miscalculated and found himself in a world war that he had not expected to have to fight. Although Germany defeated France in a rapid military campaign in May and June 1940, England would no longer submit to Hitler's strategy of intimidation. Hitler was forced to contemplate a seaborne invasion of the British isles. For a cross-Channel invasion of England to be a viable military option, the German air force had to destroy British land-based air power that could otherwise interdict a force invading from the sea. Thus began the "Battle of Britain" in the summer of 1940: It was both a war of attrition and a military persuasion. The German air force hoped either to exhaust British air defenses by using up pilots and aircraft (a denial strategy) or to inflict a level of destruction and suffering on the British population that would cause further resistance by its government to become unpopular (a punishment strategy). Neither strategy worked.

The attrition strategy failed (although it was a close call) on account of the British talent for improvisation and the successfully conducted military persuasion by England's air defense fighter command. The performance of British Fighter Command in the Battle of Britain is one of the great military persuasions of modern times. Outnumbered by German attackers, the defenders used the combination of new technology (radar) with innovative, flexible, and responsive organization (networking the detection of Luftwaffe bombers with coordination of interceptor response that economized the expenditure of British planes and pilots). The German expectation that the British public, and therefore the government, could be forced to surrender by bombing cities and towns was equally disappointed. If anything, the mass bombardment of London and other urban centers only strengthened the resolve of the British public and government alike to defeat Germany at any cost. In addition, by diverting attack aircraft to punishment strikes against English cities and away from RAF airfields and air-defense command centers, the Luftwaffe mistakenly vitiated the effect of their campaign of attrition against Fighter Command and contributed to Germany's unsuccessful air war against England. Having failed to deliver a knockout blow against Britain's air arm, Hitler was forced to shelve any plans for invading England. England out of Hitler's reach meant eventual defeat for the Germans as the war prolonged and involved the United States and the Soviet Union against Germany.

Interdependence of Ends and Means

Military persuasion also relies upon the mutual interdependence of actors' ends and means, as well as upon the mutual interdependence of their cost and benefit assessments. There is no need for military persuasion if there is no other mind to worry about: when, for example, a stronger state determines to crush a weaker one until the latter is annihilated, regardless of the costs to the stronger state. An imposed Carthaginian peace requires no bargaining and negotiation, and it may even preclude two-way communication. Only the abject surrender or the elimination of the loser is desired. Fortunately, this kind of war is the exceptional conflict among or within states. In most conflicts some interdependence of ends and means and of goals and

strategies exists; thus, bargaining and fighting take place simultaneously. One result of ends and means interdependency in most conflicts is that objectives may have to be revised upward or downward;
more ambitious or less. Many are the heads of state and military planners who embarked on a war that they expected to be short and relatively cheap in blood and treasure, only to be summarily disappointed.

For example, the major combatants in World War I expected a war
that ended by Christmas, and they were correct: It did end by Christmas, but in 1918, not in 1914. The initial expectations of both sides in
the American Civil War when the conflict erupted in 1861 was that it
would be a short war, a matter of months instead of years. And in this
short war, both sides expected to emerge victorious.[15] Only well into
1862 as the casualty figures multiplied did it become clear that a protracted war with unprecedented costs was in progress, and one that
would resist any negotiated settlement short of total military defeat
for the armed forces of the loser.[16] The political and social military persuasion of secession and emancipation hardened against any solution
short of total war as the costs of war mounted and the symbolism of
war's aims became more divisive. The North and South were no longer
mere adversaries: They had become conflicting ways of life and alternate visions of the American future. Military tactics and campaign strategies were adapted to, and in turn caused by, this hardening of positions
and sentiments on both sides.

One of the difficult aspects of interstate rivalry is that states can come
to believe that their commitments are so interdependent that the rene-
gotiation of one commitment will place all others in jeopardy. For example, President John F. Kennedy felt that willingness to negotiate a
peace agreement over Laos without American military invention in
1963 made it all the more necessary to take a firmer stance over the
fate of South Vietnam. The United States could not be seen to have
abandoned allied or friendly neutral governments twice in short succession in the same region. The image of "falling dominoes" is one
that academics and military theorists may deride, but it is a familiar
one to heads of state who fear losing their offices. Even if the dominoes are not really tightly coupled and the loss of one ally does not
entail immediate jeopardy to another, the party out of power can exploit the domino image for gain at the ballot box at the expense of the
government. Dominoes can take on symbolic importance beyond their
military or political value. Both Vietnam for the Kennedy and Johnson
administrations in the 1960s and the Falkland (Malvina) Islands for
the British and Argentine governments in 1982 became talismans of
success or failure in war and foreign policy that cost two regimes (the
Johnson administration and the Argentine junta) their political lives.

Perspective Taking

Related to the ability to rethink one's goals and objectives, a third characteristic of a successfully applied psychological strategy is the ability to engage in "perspective taking." This is the ability and willingness to see into the other side's objectives and motives and to try to appreciate the sources for these objectives and motives. It does not necessarily imply agreement with or sympathy for those motives. For example, a state may take a position in a controversy on account of strong domestic constituencies that have to be appeased, as in the union of Junker and industrialist in Wilhelmine Germany prior to World War I. Or a state may feel that its reputation for resolve is on the line if it fails to stand firm against deterrent or compellent threats posed by an adversary. Reputation was one rationale for U.S. military intervention and later escalation in Vietnam from 1965 through 1968.

The entire Cuban missile crisis resulted in part from a two-way failure in perspective taking. Khrushchev's rocket-rattling diplomacy was based on hubristic boasts about U.S. military weakness relative to that of the Soviet Union on the assumption that this might intimidate the Eisenhower and Kennedy administrations. The effect was the opposite: increased domestic support in the United States for a nuclear and other military buildup. A comparable U.S. failure was to boast publicly in October 1961 about U.S. nuclear strategic superiority, intended as a way to intimidate Khrushchev and deter his nuclear diplomacy. The U.S. action had the opposite effect: The Soviet leader felt suddenly put on the defensive and looked to his Cuban missile gambit as part of his short-term solution.[17] Then, too, Khrushchev may have misread Kennedy's unwillingness to invade Cuba during the Bay of Pigs fiasco and Kennedy's apparent willingness to tolerate the Berlin Wall and Khrushchev's browbeating at Vienna in 1961 as signs of an irresolute or weak president who would be easy to push around.

Perspective taking requires getting to know the opponent better. Consider, for example, the case of U.S. bargaining with imperial Japan in 1945 over the terms for Japanese surrender. The United States obviously held the military cards, but the Japanese could make the process of surrender more or less costly to the Allies. There remained, even after Germany's defeat and Japan's total isolation against history's greatest wartime coalition, a residual capability on the part of Japan to surrender with various degrees of resistance. This continuum of Japanese surrender options ran from maximum resistance, requiring U.S. and Allied invasion of the Japanese home islands, to a surrender by the Japanese government that stood down their armed forces and dissolved their government but retained Emperor Hirohito as a national symbol. The U.S. decision to permit the Japanese to retain their emperor as a unifying national symbol made postwar occupation and the acceptance of military defeat easier for the Japanese to accept.

On the other hand, Japanese perspective taking near the war's end was fatally flawed in ways that only increased the likelihood of the harshest possible surrender terms. Japanese efforts in 1945 to use the Soviet Union as a mediator with its American and British allies in order to arrange favorable terms for peace, as defined by Japan, were not treated seriously by Stalin. He used the pretence of good offices in relaying Japanese overtures in order to ingratiate himself with Washington and London and to set up Japan for the Soviet Union's ultimate entry into the war. Japan's expectation that Stalin would help to conciliate his wartime allies on Japan's behalf was the equivalent of grasping at the straws of imaginary Allied disagreement in order to avoid facing the more fundamental and depressing truth of Japanese defeat.

Manipulation of Symbols and Information: Perceptions Management

A fourth aspect of military persuasion is the importance of mastering the manipulation of symbols and information in support of one's political and military objectives. Reality is often what people think it is. Changing the perception of reality can, under the right conditions, be tantamount to changing "objective" reality that a proverbial person from Mars might see. An example of manipulation of symbols and information is former Soviet leader Mikhail Gorbachev's campaign to reform the communist order from 1985 to 1988. Gorbachev succeeded too well. He effectively stripped the facade of invincibility from the Soviet approach to a planned economy and from the rule of the Communist Party. Gorbachev did not anticipate the side effects: Into the vacuum moved nationalists, democrats, and others with the larger agenda of ending the Soviet Union itself. Another example of an attempt to use the power of symbols was provided in the 1990s by the terrorist organization al-Qaeda and its leader, Osama bin Laden. Al-Qaeda sought to justify its activities by reference to the commands of Islam and to depict its actions against Americans throughout the decade as motivated by religion.

The psychology of symbolism in politics, society, and culture is an important topic in itself; we cannot do justice to it here.[18] But an example from the fields of art and anthropology will bring out one important aspect of symbolization in politics and war. The renowned anthropologist Franz Boas noted, on the basis of his extensive field work on Native American cultures, that in their art two levels of analysis may be distinguished. At the first level, appreciation of a work of art, such as a clay dish or a basket, is based on form alone. At another level, the form is filled with meaning and its "significance creates an enhanced esthetic value, on account of the associative connections of the art product or of the artistic act."[19] Forms that connote deeper meaning can point to differences in social position or social interest. Thus, in the case of the Sioux observed by Boas, men and women used the same ornamental designs to a large extent, but similar designs might have dissimilar meanings for women compared to men. For example, a diamond shape with attached triangular appendages found on a cradle or on a woman's legging is interpreted as a turtle. The turtle is interpreted in this context as a symbol of birth and female maturity. When the same design is found on a male legging, it is assumed to signify or represent a slain enemy.[20]

One example of the manipulation of symbols and information pertinent to strategy is "perceptions management." Perceptions management is sometimes confused with propaganda, but it is more inclusive and frequently more subtle.[21] Perceptions management includes any statements, decisions, and actions taken by one state in order to influence another state's assumptions about the first state's intentions and capabilities. Intelligence, and especially the intelligence discipline called "counterintelligence," is very much about the manipulation of adversary perceptions in a direction favorable to one's own interests. The importance of the counterintelligence function to states lies in the centrality of counterintelligence for perceptions management.[22] For example, the Aldrich Ames case revealed that Soviet capture of a key CIA counterintelligence operative permitted Moscow to control the images and information flowing from the USSR back to Washington.

Steven Metz's very useful concept of "psychological precision" in military strategy provides an example of a construct that includes both perspective taking and perceptions management.[23] Metz notes that the problem of precision has received a great deal of attention from students of technology development related to the "revolution in military affairs." It is equally important for future military planners and policy makers, in his view, to understand the significance of psychological precision: "Psychological precision means shaping a military operation so as to attain the desired attitudes, beliefs and perceptions on the part of both the enemy and other observers, whether noncombatants in the area of operations or global audiences."[24]

According to Metz, overemphasis on technology and an insufficient appreciation for the nuances of other cultures has often impeded U.S. ability to conduct successful military interventions such as low-intensity conflicts or peace operations. One example when U.S. officials used psychological precision to good effect took place in December 2001 during U.S. military operations in Afghanistan against Osama bin

Laden and his al-Qaeda terrorist network. Having acquired a video-tape of bin Laden meeting secretly with fellow conspirators and gloat-ing over the number of American deaths in the attack of September 11, 2001, U.S. officials translated and released the video for worldwide news broadcast. The videotape provided first-person confirmation of bin Laden's culpability for the terrorist attacks on New York city and Washington, D.C. It also showed bin Laden as a psychopath who rev-eled in mass murder. Both effects helped to delegitimate bin Laden and al-Qaeda in the Arab and Islamic worlds.

Related to Metz's concept of psychological precision is Jan S. Breemer's idea of "paralytic warfare." Breemer proposes that while industrial-age warfare was predicated on a way of thought that cen-tered on the notion of destruction, future war may have as its center of gravity the concept of paralysis:

Paralytic warfare is aimed at incapacitating the opponent's war-making sys-tem by causing a complete or partial loss of function involving the power of motion or of sensing in any part of the system. Paralysis-based warfare is *pre-cision* warfare: it relies on a combination of physical and psychological means to incapacitate critical physical and/or sensory sub-systems in order to immo-bilize the opponent's war-making system short of destruction. Whereas im-plicit in the destruction-based model of warfare is a presumption *for* destruction, paralytic warfare is based on a presumption *against* destruction.[25]

Colin S. Gray examines Prussian military theorist Carl von Clausewitz's uncommon insights into the essence of warfare, derived in part from Clausewitz's appreciation that war was a two-way struggle in mind as well as in body.[26] War, according to Clausewitz, involves uncertainty, friction, and other factors that produce a combination of confusion and fear equivalent to a fog. Commanders can never understand the whole of even their own doings in battle, never mind those of the op-position. Those commanders who can master the art of war amid con-fusion, uncertainty, and friction will perform relatively better than those who do not, but even these relatively more astute commanders are not ensured victory. For example, in Operation Desert Storm the United States imposed a great deal of confusion on Iraq by early air strikes against its air defenses, command centers, and communications, thereby establishing visual and electronic domination of the relevant battle space. This early cybertrumping of Iraq's eyes and ears discon-nected the head of Saddam Hussein's war machine from the point of the spear in southern Iraq and Kuwait. On the other hand, U.S. and allied coalition execution of their own war plan did not proceed with-out considerable friction. Examples of friction in the coalition air cam-paign included the inability to locate many of Iraq's mobile SCUD ballistic missile launchers in time to direct air strikes against them before they changed location. Another example of friction in the coalition air war was disagreement over the interpretation and fidelity of Bomb Damage Assessments (BDAs), as between the Pentagon and General Schwarzkopf's command in Riyadh, Saudi Arabia.[27]

One of the most important examples of perceptions management was practiced during the build-up for the Normandy invasion against Hitler's "fortress Europe" in June 1944. Although the size and scale of the invasion was unprecedented, it was necessary to include planning for a strategic deception that would fool the Germans as to exactly where the Allies would attempt to land on the coast of France. Accordingly, one of the most elaborate deception operations in military history, Operation Fortitude, was undertaken to deceive the German high command. The Allies sought to convince German leaders, including those responsible for defense on or near the beaches of Normandy, that the main pincer of the Allied attack would be at Pas de Calais. A multifaceted deception including three major components was set in motion. First, Fortitude North invented activities of a combined British, French, and Russian force assembled in Scotland and primed to attack Norway. Hitler judged that the defense of Norway against Allied attack was vital and had tied down some 380,000 troops there: The Allies sought to keep them there and out of France. Second, Fortitude South, established in the south of England, created a fictitious First United States Army Group (FUSAG) commanded by General George Patton, who was highly regarded by the Germans among American field commanders. Radio transmissions in codes easily broken by the Germans or in the clear were used to simulate communications among nonexistent battalions, brigades, and divisions under Patton's command and preparing to embark for Calais. A third aspect of Fortitude was the "double cross" system. More than 100 German agents attempting to infiltrate Britain by air or sea had been captured since 1939. They were offered the choice of carefully controlled collaboration or execution. Those who chose to live were used to sent seemingly authentic but erroneous messages back to German intelligence, including planted information intended to deceive the Germans as to the planning for Normandy.[28]

Moral Influence

A fifth characteristic of military persuasion is that moral influence is a very important, perhaps the most important, aspect of strategy. The idea is not a new one. Sun Tzu, Chinese philosopher of war and attributed author of the classic study *The Art of War*, said that war should be appraised in terms of five fundamental factors, the first of which is moral influence.[29] Sun Tzu defined moral influence as "that which causes the people to be in harmony with their leaders, so that they will accompany them in life and unto death without fear of mortal peril."[30] This idea has several implications. It implies popular support for war aims and for the methods used to make war. It also implies that the armed forces will not be demoralized by being misused or permitted to be torn apart by political factionalism. And those who find themselves in uniform must feel that, consistent with military discipline and tradition, they are treated with dignity and respect. In each of these aspects of moral influence the successful manipulation of symbols and information, previously discussed, is very important.

Popular support for armies is often thought necessary only in democracies. But history shows that all armed forces and the governments that must provide them rely in the long run on popular support. Military persuasion can only go so far before leaders are strung up and guns and ammunition dry up. Consider the situation in post-communist Russia from 1992 through 1997. The Russian armed forces disintegrated once the Soviet Union dissolved, not only because funds were scarce, but also because the legitimacy of the armed forces was called into question after the Soviet Union fell. The Soviet military had, along with the security services and the party organs, been the major props of the communist state. When the state fell the military drifted into an abyss, unsure of its focus and divided into political factionalism. Although most of the Russian military leadership had no desire to establish military rule in Russia, they became unwilling arbiters of Russia's political fate when they became caught up in internal power struggles in 1991 and 1993.

The disintegration of moral influence in the Russian armed forces became so acute by 1994 that Russia was unable to fight an effective military campaign against rebels in Chechnya.[31] Former Defense Minister Pavel Grachev had boasted in the autumn of 1994 that Russia need send only a few airborne divisions in order to rout Chechen separatists and reestablish Russian control in Grozny, the Chechen capital. Russia's military performance, however, was below even the level set by prewar pessimists. Troops were sent into the fighting with inadequate training, units were poorly coordinated, and leadership at the sharp end of the tactical spear was abysmal. But most important, Russia's intervention had no moral backing. Russia's public opinion largely condemned it, and even officers assigned to the invading troops openly opposed it. Some officers resigned during the campaign, and mothers of troops conscripted and sent to Chechnya appeared in the battle zone to demand the return of their sons and a halt to the war.[32] Had Marshal Georgi Zhukov, chief of the general staff of Soviet forces in World War II and triumphant victor of the Battle of Berlin that ended Hitler's Reich, lived to see Russian military operations in Chechnya from 1994 through 1996, he would have returned his numerous medals in shame.

Moral influence was an important aspect of the defeat of the Taliban militia by American, British, and allied Afghan forces in October and November 2001. The Taliban tyrannized over Afghans by claiming that its eccentric interpretation of Islam justified brutal mistreatment of entire categories of people, especially women and political dissenters. This tyranny had no real basis of popular support among most of the ordinary citizens of Afghanistan, and many of that torn country's tribal leaders also resented the Taliban regime. Once American military operations against that regime began to inflict serious tactical defeats on its leadership and core fighters, the moral influence of the Taliban, based on its claim of political and religious infallibility, melted down. Many of its supposed cadres defected to the Northern or Eastern Alliance opposition forces, and its last power base in Kandahar was eventually besieged and sacked.

As many studies of leadership in and out of the military have noted, leadership is a two-way process: It involves both the leaders and the led, as well as the interactions between the two. It is also highly subjective. Leaders must know the essential facts of their trade, of course: Doctors must know the appropriate treatments for various diseases, and engineers must know what kinds of materials are best suited to bridges as opposed to sidewalks. But beyond the demand for factual mastery of one's trade or profession, the leader must inspire followers with faith, something like Mahatma Gandhi's "soul force" or satyagraha.

What passes for effective soul force varies with the culture, the society, and the situation at hand. Ancient, medieval, and even some postmedieval military leaders were often religious and political leaders as well: Thus, they had a certain supreme apartness or aloofness from the common foot soldier that would seem inappropriate today.[33] On the other hand, in these more hierarchical and less differentiated societies of yesteryear, leaders were expected to lead "from the front" and share the rigors of infantry or cavalry combat with their enlisted personnel. Both the social apartness and the combat togetherness helped to legitimate the commander in the eyes of subordinates.[34] Nowadays it would seem inappropriate, at least in modern Western armies, for generals to lead troops into battle in the fashion of Alexander the Great or Charles XII of Sweden. Still, some modern commanders affect the aura of risk taking when they visit the front lines in order to put on display a feigned kinship between the man at the front and the higher, rearward echelons. Troops usually see through this: Grunts in all modern armies have a patois that expresses characteristic disdain for staff officers attempting to strike an exaggerated pose as one of the trench warriors.

It is therefore of more than trivial interest that the moral force drawn upon by ancient and medieval commanders finds itself manifest in modern times when wars are fought by irregular forces, especially by tribal groups and ethnic or religious warriors.[35] Here the leader and followers may often have a charismatic, as opposed to an institutional or rational–legal, basis for sharing danger. It is also interesting that special-operations forces have this same aura of closeness between commanders and followers: a soul force based on shared and esoteric expertise, to be sure, but also on the small size of special-operations groups compared to larger armies and on a sense of specialized mission that regular forces are not usually equipped to undertake. The distinctive uniforms and insignia worn by special forces worldwide reflect, to their critics, a sense of elitism, but this misses the point. Underlying the specialized training and apartness from regular forces, there is the special forces' *communion*: in dangerous brotherhood tasked to accomplish missions of strategic importance but with small resources, relying on their wits, esprit, and commitment to substitute for numbers.[36] Soul force indeed: Witness the British SAS, who insist upon four-man teams as a number that mixes versatility with horizontal and mutually reinforcing forms of command and control.

The following is a summary of the argument presented in this chapter about the dimensions of military persuasion:

Dimension or Attribute	Commentary
Objective is to influence will of the opponent	The opponent's will includes not only fighting forces or policy makers, but also publics (and see under "moral influence")
Opponents' ends and means are interdependent	Bargaining while fighting or while preparing to fight is regarded as useful, not as a sign of weakness
Perspective taking is a necessary condition for comprehending the strategy of the "other"	Cultural and social barriers to understanding are the largest obstacle here; human intelligence collection is a sine qua non for success
Perceptions management induces the other side to see "reality" as we would prefer	The issue of whose perceptions are to be influenced matters; so, too, does the issue of how much mileage can be expected from the manipulation of perceptions alone (perceptions management is not a silver bullet)

Moral influence is important in motivating troops, sustaining public support, and enabling the government and military leaders to plan coherently and strategize effectively

Sun Tzu was right: In the final analysis, everything else rests on this foundation

NOTES

1. The use of military power for political influence is treated extensively in Thomas C. Schelling, *Arms and Influence* (New Haven, Conn.: Yale University Press, 1966), especially pp. 92–125. See also Stephen J. Cimbala, *Military Persuasion* (University Park, Pa.: Penn State Press, 1994).

2. Alexander L. George, "Coercive Diplomacy: Definition and Characteristics," in *The Limits of Coercive Diplomacy*, 2d ed., ed. Alexander L. George and William E. Simons (Boulder, Colo.: Westview Press, 1994), 7–12. George has a large pertinent literature. See his chapters in Alexander L. George, ed., *Avoiding War: Problems of Crisis Management* (Boulder, Colo.: Westview Press, 1991), especially ch. 3, 4, 11, and 16. Also important on the psychology of international relations is Robert Jervis, *Perception and Misperception in International Politics* (Princeton, N.J.: Princeton University Press, 1976).

3. George, "Coercive Diplomacy: Definition and Characteristics," 9.

4. Ibid. On the concept of compellence, see Schelling, *Arms and Influence*, 70–72. Although George's exclusion of deterrence and compellence from coercive diplomacy has the virtue of emphasizing nonaggressive or nonmilitary approaches to conflict resolution, both terms belong in any viable concept of military persuasion. See, in support of the last point, Robert Jervis, *The Meaning of the Nuclear Revolution: Statecraft and the Prospect of Armageddon* (Ithaca, N.Y.: Cornell University Press, 1989), especially ch. 5 and pp. 237–257.

5. George, "Coercive Diplomacy: Definition and Characteristics," 10.

6. Ibid.

7. Schelling, *Arms and Influence*, 70–72.

8. Carl von Clausewitz, *On War*, trans. J. J. Graham, new rev. ed., vol. 1 (London: Routledge and Kegan Paul, 1966), bk. I, ch. 11, p. 40.

9. Ivo H. Daalder and Michael E. O'Hanlon, *Winning Ugly: NATO's War to Save Kosovo* (Washington, D.C.: Brookings Institution, 2000), 107–108. See also Wesley K. Clark, *Waging Modern War* (New York: Public Affairs, 2001), especially pp. 4–11.

10. Robert A. Pape, Jr., *Bombing to Win: Air Power and Selection in War* (Ithaca, N.Y.: Cornell University Press, 1996), 4.

11. Ibid., 18–19, 58–86. My summary follows the original with the addition of the requirement in denial strategies for being able to deny the opponent its objectives at an acceptable cost.

12. See Schelling, *Arms and Influence*, 26–34 and Bernard Brodie, *War and Politics* (New York: Macmillan, 1973), 375–432.

13. Brodie, *War and Politics*, 426.

14. See third section for pertinent references on perceptions and paradoxes. Other references relevant to this list appear in notes 1 through 17. This list

excludes contributions to the subject from many classical political or military theorists and philosophers prior to World War II (from Thucydides onward) for the sake of economy: there are simply too many to mention. See Martin van Creveld, *The Art of War: War and Military Thought* (London: Cassell, 2000) for an authoritative survey. The text makes specific reference to some very pertinent exceptions.

15. This fallacy in prewar estimation of war's duration and outcome is a historical commonplace. See Geoffrey Blainey, *The Causes of War*, 3d ed. (New York: Free Press, 1988), 35–56.

16. The battle of Shiloh, for example, April 6–7, 1862, was the most costly battle fought in the Western Hemisphere to that date: Killed and wounded on each side exceeded 1,700 and 8,000, and some 2,000 eventually died from wounds. Shiloh was a preview of worse to come. See James M. McPherson, *Ordeal by Fire: The Civil War and Reconstruction* (New York: Alfred A. Knopf, 1982), 225–229.

17. Strobe Talbott, trans. and ed., *Khrushchev Remembers* (Boston: Little, Brown, 1970), 494, in which Khrushchev notes, "In addition to protecting Cuba, our missiles would have equalized what the West likes to call 'the balance of power.'"

18. The significance of symbols in political behavior is addressed in Murray J. Edelman, *The Symbolic Uses of Politics* (Urbana: University of Illinois Press, 1985), 22–43. Also important in this context are studies of the relationship between language and politics. See, for example, Michael J. Shapiro, *Language and Political Understanding: The Politics of Discursive Practices* (New Haven, Conn.: Yale University Press, 1981), 26–27.

19. Franz Boas, *Primitive Art* (New York: Dover, 1955), 88.

20. Ibid., 123.

21. On perception and biases in perception, see Richards J. Heuer, Jr., *Psychology of Intelligence Analysis* (Washington, D.C.: Central Intelligence Agency, 1999), 7–16, 127–146. A still definitive treatment of perceptions in international relations is Robert Jervis, *Perception and Misperception in International Politics* (Princeton, N.J.: Princeton University Press, 1976).

22. Roy Godson, *Dirty Tricks or Trump Cards: U.S. Covert Action and Counterintelligence* (Washington, D.C.: Brassey's, 1995), 184–200.

23. Steven Metz, *Armed Conflict in the 21st Century: The Information Revolution and Post-Modern Warfare* (Carlisle Barracks, Pa.: Strategic Studies Institute, 2000), 78–79.

24. Ibid., 78.

25. Jan S. Breemer, *War as We Knew It: The Real Revolution in Military Affairs—Understanding Paralysis in Military Operations* (Maxwell A.F.B., Ala.: Center for Strategy and Technology, Air War College, 2000), 2.

26. Colin S. Gray, *Modern Strategy* (Oxford: Oxford University Press, 1999), 41, 98–99. See also Michael I. Handel, *Masters of War: Classical Strategic Thought*, 3d ed. (London: Frank Cass, 1991), 81–89, and Edward N. Luttwak, *Strategy: The Logic of War and Peace* (Cambridge, Mass.: Harvard University Press, 1987).

27. Thomas A. Keaney and Eliot A. Cohen, *Revolution in Warfare? Air Power in the Persian Gulf* (Annapolis, Md.: Naval Institute Press, 1995), 72 (on SCUD attacks), 219 (on Bomb Damage Assessment).

28. James Leasor, *Code Name Nimrod* (Boston: Houghton Mifflin, 1981), 26–27.

29. Sun Tzu, *The Art of War*, ed. and trans. Samuel B. Griffith (London: Oxford University Press, 1963), 63.

30. Ibid., 64.

31. Timothy L. Thomas, "The Caucasus Conflict and Russian Security: The Russian Armed Forces Confront Chechnya III. The Battle for Grozny, 1–26 January 1995," *Journal of Slavic Military Studies* 1 (March 1997), 50–108.

32. Various organizations representing soldiers' mothers have engaged in political activism in post-Soviet Russia. Perhaps the best known in the West is the Soldiers' Mothers of St. Petersburg, which documents abusive treatment of recruits and conscripts and other violations of military law and discipline that result in soldiers' deaths, injuries, or resignations from the armed forces.

33. Martin Van Creveld, *The Transformation of War* (New York: Free Press, 1991), 33–62, 95–123. See also Christopher Bellamy, *Knights in White Armour: The New Art of War and Peace* (London: Hutchinson, 1996), ch. 3, 8.

34. John Keegan, *The Mask of Command* (New York: Penguin Books, 1987), 13–91.

35. An exceptional discussion appears in Mary Kaldor, *New and Old Wars: Organized Violence in a Global Era* (Stanford, Calif.: Stanford University Press, 1999), 69–89, passim.

36. The use of special-operations forces in strategic missions receives inadequate attention. An important exception is Colin S. Gray, *Explorations in Strategy* (Westport, Conn.: Greenwood Press, 1996), 163–188. On the special character of low-intensity conflicts and unconventional wars and the pertinent characteristics of special-operations forces, see Sam C. Sarkesian, *Unconventional Conflicts in a New Security Era: Lessons from Malaya and Vietnam* (Westport, Conn.: Greenwood Press, 1993), 188–196.

3

Technology and Deterrence in Military Persuasion

Advanced technology has helped the United States to assume a position of global military preeminence. In addition, U.S. strategic culture shares with American society a tendency toward the worship of technology. Thus, the relationship between the idea of deterrence and technology is of fundamental interest to students of military persuasion. Deterrence, fundamentally a psychological strategy based on insights about human motivation and behavior, was often captured by technology during much of the Cold War and may be in equal danger of being made hostage in the post–Cold War world. Soft power lends itself to subversion by hard coin.

In this chapter we examine the relationship between technology and deterrence in four stages. First, we offer a resume of the idea of deterrence that also provides some assessment of the concept. Second, we examine the problem of asymmetrical warfare and the challenge that various forms of it might present to U.S. planners and policy makers. Third, we discuss the problem of knowledge innovation in technology related to deterrence, using the example of ballistic missile defense. Fourth and last, we consider some aspects of the relationship between "hard" and "soft" power and what that might mean for the future of deterrence.

THE CONCEPT OF DETERRENCE

Deterrence is a novelty among concepts that have acquired familiarity within academic circles. The idea of deterrence grew out of studies by policy analysts and think tanks in the early years of the nuclear age.[1] Although earlier uses of the term "deterrence" to apply to military affairs have been documented, deterrence captured the imagination of U.S. students of nuclear-weapons policy and arms control and became a term of art. Throughout the nuclear age, arguments for and against specific policy proposals or military strategies were couched in terms of their presumed effect on deterrence. A large literature on the subject remains among the artifacts of the Cold War, along with Lenin's tomb and endless studies of the Cuban missile crisis.

For all that, deterrence remains somewhat elusive. Among the references to deterrence that one finds in the literature, one can detect use of the term "deterrence" to mean any one, or all, of the following:

1. deterrence as a *process* of influence by which one party, a threatener or deterrer, affects the estimated costs and benefits attached to actions by another party, the threatened or deterred party.
2. deterrence as a *condition* of having been deterred.
3. deterrence as a *relationship* between two actors that takes place within a relatively short time period and involves at least one explicit threat of military action.
4. deterrence as a *latent feature* of an international system made up of sovereign states and nonstate actors who are reliant upon self-help for survival.
5. deterrence as a one part of a *policy-prescriptive orientation* toward a particular state, especially a potential military adversary; thus, for example, deterrence as a military support for containment policy.

Students of conflict resolution, bargaining, and game theory have also identified various approaches to deterrence in terms of the means of influence by which deterrence is thought to work:

1. deterrence by credible threat to inflict decisive defeat on the adversary's armed forces (deterrence by *denial*).
2. by threat to inflict unacceptable destruction on the society and economic infrastructure of the other side (deterrence by *punishment*).
3. by threat to destroy or paralyze the brain and central nervous system of the other side's war machine (deterrence by *decapitation*).
4. by threat to set in motion a progression of events over which both sides will eventually lose control as a result of Clausewitz's "friction," organizational pathology, misperception, or other forces that will pull the contestants into mutual disaster (deterrence by *uncertainty* or *risk*).[2]

5. *existential* deterrence, or a nuclear-weapons equivalent of cogito, ergo sum: The weapons are there and can inflict unprecedented destruction; therefore, refinements of threat systems and nuanced nuclear diplomacy are superfluous.

Of course, there are subcategories within each of these categories. One of the most obvious is that each of these kinds of deterrent effects can come about rapidly or slowly. In category 1 for example, the conventional armed forces of a state can pose the threat of a campaign of annihilation or of attrition. Reliance on a form of deterrence not suited to conditions can be dangerous. In July and August 1914 a threat system based on fears of rapid conquest failed to deter, and a prolonged war of attrition that destroyed four empires resulted.

Theorists have also recognized that there are relatively more active and passive forms of deterrence. The more active is often referred to as "compellence."[3] Compellence takes place after the fact of an aggression or other undesired action by the other side; deterrence, before the fact. Compellence occurs in at least two forms: to persuade the adversary to stop an activity already in progress, or to persuade the opponent to undo and reverse an action already completed. An example of the first form of compellence was the Berlin airlift in 1948; of the second, U.S. ultimata about the removal of Soviet missiles from Cuba in 1962.

Deterrence is also related to coercive diplomacy. Coercive diplomacy is something like compellence, according to Alexander George.[4] But one can also think of coercive diplomatic demarches that were backed up by military power and took place before the fact of an undesired event. Therefore, in terms of timing, they might be more deterrent than compellent. George emphasizes that coercive diplomacy is a "defensive" not an "offensive" strategy for crisis management and that it needs to be distinguished from pure military coercion. Coercive diplomacy can use the threat of force or even exemplary demonstrations of force, but it is an essentially diplomatic strategy that excludes bludgeoning the opponent into submission. Coercive diplomacy can also resemble an ultimatum, although it need not embody all three components of ultimata: a specific and clear demand, a time limit for compliance, and a credible threat of punishment for noncompliance.[5] This resume of various meanings of deterrence is obviously not exhaustive.[6]

Critics of deterrence theory have charged that it was a rationalization for living with nuclear danger that should have been done away with by means of disarmament or by more aggressive forms of arms control. Others have claimed that deterrence dogmas fortified defense-industry and military demands for greater budgets throughout the Cold War on both sides of the Iron Curtain. Some skeptics have doubted that deterrence is a truly serious intellectual construct, and others have seen the idea as a Trojan horse for psychology or economics applied to military art. The tendency of writing in social science journals to load up on neologisms is off-putting to military officers and, especially, to military historians. Some of both groups blame deterrence theories borrowed from nuclear into conventional warfare for the reversals suffered by U.S. policy and military strategy in Vietnam.

Deterrence, at least the academic versions of it, also suffered from the bandwagon effect that is so important in determining the half life of ideas within the university and among policy elites who still pay attention to professors. During the Cold War, circles of academics who were in regular contact with policy makers and government bureaucrats became very influential in transfusing their ideas into the national dialogue on military strategy and policy. Because most of these academic policy influentials were associated with prestigious universities, their preferred concepts became part of the lingua franca of the national policy debates over nuclear and other military strategy, arms control, deterrence, and defense policies. Some of these academics even served time in the government, and an occasional one, such as Henry Kissinger, acquired substantial power over the making of U.S. foreign policy and grand strategy.

One result of all this conversation about deterrence throughout the Cold War was that a certain elasticity of meaning and laziness of thought took hold. When the Cold War ended and the Soviet Union passed into history, policy makers and scholars began to look over their shoulders and wonder whether any of their Cold War analyses would be left standing amid the rubble of the ruble. Post–Soviet Russia faced an enormously steep learning curve in its attempts to develop a market economy and a functioning democracy. Russia inherited the mantle of the Soviet Union for purposes of nuclear arms control and nuclear-weapons accountability, but the entire context of U.S.–Russian political relations had now changed. So, too, had the military aspects of this relationship. Both Americans and Russians had a hard time accepting this on account of their addiction to Cold War ways of thinking about deterrence and defense.

For example, the United States continued with Russia the strategic nuclear arms reduction talks (START) that had begun under Cold War auspices. The object, admirable in itself, was to reduce the numbers of superfluous warheads and launches on both sides while each side retained a number of survivable warheads and launchers sufficient to guarantee assured retaliation. Notice something peculiar here. The two states were no longer political enemies in principle. Communist ideology had been superseded by post-Soviet kleptocracy. Yet the military dialogue between the two states on strategic nuclear weapons continued very much as if nothing of political importance had changed in 1991. Admittedly, the last sentence is not entirely true. The United States did authorize defense funds for the safety, security, and dismantlement of former Soviet and now Russian nuclear weapons (under the so-called Nunn–Lugar legislation), and other "cooperative engagement" between the two countries took place in security-related matters such as nonproliferation, transparency of warning and assessment, and military-to-military exchanges of personnel. Russian officers were even invited to NORAD to watch with their U.S. counterparts the transition to a new millennium.

But although these attributes of the U.S.–Russian nuclear relationship changed, the essence of that post–Cold War relationship remained locked within a deterrence-oriented model that resembled Cold War redux. A stable balance of nuclear terror between Washington and Moscow was the assumed object of START. Stability was defined as the assured survivability of enough retaliatory power to destroy either society in retaliation for a nuclear surprise attack by the other. Why either America or Russia would launch a nuclear first strike at anyone, including each other, was a subject that received very little exposition or rethinking. In fact, the entire START–deterrence-by-assured-vulnerability model was begging for replacement by a model driven by reassurance and cooperative security. Not only were the United States and Russia no longer adversaries, in the twenty-first century they were fated as security partners, like it or not. The major concern of U.S. twenty-first-century policy makers with regard to Russia ought to be the prevention of Russia's disintegration and the political and military furor that this would let loose in Central Eurasia, the Caucasus, and East Central Europe, inter alia.

The late Herman Kahn, once the eminence grise of defense-policy analysts, argued that deterrence was, at best, a way station, a way of coping with exigencies forced on policy makers until something better came along. Despite this modest beginning, deterrence has outlived most of its creators, proponents, and detractors. Deterrence is very much like that over-the-counter cold medication that we have all learned to depend upon at the first signs of flu symptoms. In lieu of expensive doctor visits or interminable waits for HMO approval, our favorite over-the-counter remedy works fine and does no harm, or so we assume, even if our self-diagnosis is incorrect. Deterrence is perhaps that kind of metasolution where there is insufficient time or knowledge for extensive and detailed diagnosis of the problem. Since the success or failure of deterrence in isolation from other complex social variables is difficult to prove, deterrence may be of sufficiently protean character to outlive another generation of college faculty and policy makers.

ASYMMETRICAL STRATEGIES AND DETERRENCE

The United States demonstrated in the Gulf War of 1991, in Kosovo in 1999, and in Afghanistan in 2001 a growth trend in its capabilities for long-range precision strikes combined with battlefield imaging and management.[7] Aware of this U.S. preeminence in smart warfare, potential opponents will seek offsetting or asymmetrical strategies. Four kinds of asymmetrical strategies have already presented problems for U.S. policy makers in the post–Cold War world or can be expected to. The question is whether any of these strategies is responsive to deterrence as we understand it.

The first is the strategy of unconventional warfare, low-intensity conflict, or small wars, frequently related to the breakdown of states and to disorder based on ethnonationalist, religious, or other primordial values. The deep structure of these problems is enormous, even within cultures where the United States and its European allies have some hands-on experience and sense of affinity. U.S. military interventions in these situations will be controversial for a number of reasons: (1) They will usually take place in parts of the world that are non-Western, offering cultural and social barriers to understanding; (2) Western armed forces may confront irregular forces or unruly mobs who play by no particular rules of war and who are clever at exploiting U.S. interest in the avoidance of collateral damage; and (3) ubiquitous television coverage and other video transparency bring a global network of observers and second guessers into the electronic bleachers. Equally protean and deserving of an essay in itself with regard to the problems it poses for deterrence is the widespread interest in terrorism by self-defined freedom fighters, paramilitaries, hosts both religious and secular, and state-supported entities fighting surrogate wars.[8] The terrorist attacks of September 11, 2001, on the U.S. World Trade Center and Pentagon provide an example of asymmetrical strategy that was horribly effective in its design and execution.

Asymmetrical strategies seek to turn technological strength into political weakness. For example, the United States has become more reliant on long-range precision strikes delivered by air power, even for attacks against suspected terrorist headquarters or facilities, as in Afghanistan and Sudan during Clinton's second term. This has a suspect odor of making policy by the "law of the instrument." Added to the propensity for casualty avoidance that has taken hold of U.S. policy makers since the end of the Gulf War of 1991, the reliance on high technology available and convenient means for situations across the conflict spectrum may have the side effect of self-deterrence. For example, U.S. and allied NATO officials ruled out not only the actual use of a ground war during Operation Allied Force against Yugoslavia in

1999, but also the making of a credible threat to wage a ground campaign using NATO forces. On the other hand, this casualty aversion was not in evidence after the terrorist attacks of 9/11. An aroused American public and a president basking in public support were ready and willing to accept casualties in Afghanistan in order to bring to justice the leaders of the al-Qaeda network and the Taliban regime. The attacks of 9/11 cleared the bar of low-intensity (and other attacks on the American homeland, whether by terrorists or states, are likely to do so as well); but attacks outside of the United States on military bases or civilians may not evoke public wrath and presidential commitment.

A second kind of challenge based on asymmetrical strategy appears at the other end of the spectrum of lethality: the use of weapons of mass destruction (WMD) in order to intimidate and coerce other states or, if necessary, to inflict military defeat or societal devastation on them. The spread of nuclear, biological, and chemical weapons after the Cold War has been much remarked upon in the literature and in policy debates. There is some false comparison among apples, oranges, and tomatoes here. Nuclear weapons inflict the greatest destruction, but they require considerable effort to acquire or fabricate. Chemical weapons are easy to acquire but cumbersome to use in the field and have limited killing capacity. Biological weapons may combine the "advantages" of both nuclear and chemical weapons: easy to acquire and truly massive killing potential.[9] The attributes of various weapons of mass destruction are summarized in Table 3.1. Nonetheless, all qualify as weapons of mass destruction that, in all likelihood, would be threatened or used against cities or military objects of value. In addition to the proliferation of WMD, the spread of ballistic or cruise missiles as the long-range delivery systems of choice for aspiring regional powers poses problems for U.S. and allied military planners.

Weapons of mass destruction combined with ballistic or cruise missiles could enable regional rogues or others opposed to U.S. policy to coerce their neighbors, including some American allies, with the threat of prompt and devastating attacks. WMD and ballistic missiles could also empower regional actors to deter U.S. military intervention in or near their territories by threatening disruptive attacks on U.S. logistics, airfields, ports, communications, or other assets, including expeditionary forces themselves. This is of no small importance given the greater U.S. dependency now, compared to most of the Cold War, on power projection over long distances as opposed to permanent military bases in theater. According to one expert assessment,

From the perspective of a rogue nation facing the formidable conventional military power of the United States and its allies, a LACM (land attack cruise missile), especially if equipped with a BW [biological weapon] agent payload,

Table 3.1
WMD Characteristics

	Killing Potential	Acquisition	Use
Nuclear	Highest	Difficult	Recent testing or simulation—not fired in anger since 1945
Biological	High	Easy	Reported use in several conflicts since WW II, widely tested in laboratories
Chemical	Low	Easy	Documented use in large and small twentieth century wars

is a very politically and militarily cost-effective weapon system. Politically, the mere threat of using a system such as the Biocruise-1000 (a land attack cruise missile with a biological payload and range of 1,000 km) with a payload of 120 kg of anthrax against a major U.S. or allied city could deter the United States from becoming involved in a rogue nation's aggression against a neighbor or bid for regional hegemony.[10]

Weapons of mass destruction may also be used by nonstate actors, including terrorists.[11] The anthrax attacks and hoaxes in the aftermath of the U.S. 9/11 attacks, including use of the U.S. mail to send threatening and toxic letters to members of Congress, reminded Americans that terrorists can make use of WMD to cause mass casualties or to create widespread panic.

The conundrum of "deterring" the spread of weapons of mass destruction and ballistic missile-delivery systems is that deterrence may be the wrong word to describe the problem or the solution. The process of proliferation is driven by both economic and psychological variables that are difficult to put into any calculations of military deterrence. The economic variables relevant to proliferation include the financial incentives of the supplier states to sell weapons and delivery systems in order to earn hard currency. Along with the hard currency may also go a bonus of political influence: Russia, China, and North Korea have all benefited financially and politically from arms transfers to the Middle East and South Asia and elsewhere.

The psychological variables pushing proliferation are related to the prestige value of nuclear weapons among states that are currently nonnuclear. Whereas most states have agreed to extend the Nuclear Non-Proliferation Treaty indefinitely, a significant minority has refused to do so, and some members of that minority (India) are now acknowledged nuclear powers. The United States and its NATO allies are apt to assume, on the basis of their Cold War experience and post–Cold War hopes, that nuclear weapons are at best a necessary evil, to be marginalized as instruments of influence in favor of information-based, advanced conventional forces. This may not be the perception everywhere. In some regions weapons of mass destruction may combine with feelings of nationalistic assertiveness and/or resentment at past treatment by the West.

For example, in Asia some states wishing to flex their military muscles may see nuclear and other weapons of mass destruction as components of a broader military modernization.[12] This broader military modernization may also be designed to change geostrategic space in Asia. India and China, for example, may combine weapons of mass destruction with ballistic missiles and some enhanced C3I (space reconnaissance, modern communications) to extend their military reach well beyond previous confinements. In so doing, they would force the United States, Japan, and Russia to recalculate their estimated costs and risks from military deployments or interventions in the Pacific Basin.

In addition to unconventional warfare and the spread of weapons of mass destruction along with long-range delivery systems, a third kind of asymmetrical warfare is posed by the possible exploitation of the information spectrum for military purposes. The significance of information in warfare is not new, but the widespread dependency of modern militaries on computers, communications, and electronics has opened new possibilities for attack and established new requirements for U.S. national defense.[13] Experts disagree on the significance of cyberwar as an actual military threat, but no one denies that it poses some security problems that will at least spill over into the lap of the Department of Defense (DOD). Attacks on U.S. military computer systems by hackers and other unknowns are now commonplace. Some experts distinguish information attacks pursuant to the conduct of battle from the more diffuse possibilities of attacking the national information infrastructure or other soft targets (see Table 3.2). The United States is ironically both the most advanced state in terms of its ability to exploit the information spectrum for military purposes and the po-

Table 3.2
Varieties of Information-Driven Warfare

War Form	Objective	Means	Targets
Cyberwar	Neutralize or destroy military and command-system targets	Conduct military operations on information-based principles	Enemy military forces and supporting C4ISR
Net Centric Warfare	Achieve shared awareness, increased speed of command, higher tempo of operations, greater lethality, increased survivability, and a degree of self-synchronization	Increase combat power by networking sensors, decision makers, and shooters	Enemy C4ISR and information and decision networks
Netwar	Influence society and government of the opponent, including public opinion and media	Perceptions management, disinformation, PSYOPs and other means of influence based on information	Enemy society and government, including public opinion, media and armed forces/security services

Source: Based on John Arquilla and David Ronfeldt, eds., *In Athena's Camp: Preparing for Conflict in the Information Age* (Santa Monica, Calif.: RAND, 1997), ch. 1; Edward Waltz, *Information Warfare Principles and Operations* (Boston: Artech House, 1998), 193.

tentially most vulnerable state to information warfare on account of its pluralistic society and high military dependency on info-tools.

In addition, the cumulative exposure to cybertools on the part of warriors and policy makers may create a dependency of another sort: a truncated way of thinking about problems. Computers and information systems "think" successfully by narrowing the definition of the problem and by limiting what goes into the algorithms that move the situation from problem to solution. Computers and C3I or C4ISR systems, that is to say, succeed by simplification of a more complex reality. On the other hand, warriors in battle are required to think contextually or "out of the box" because war plans rarely survive initial contact with the enemy, as General von Moltke once said.

The danger that warriors will begin to think like computer programmers or systems managers once given "land warrior" suits and cyber–controls to play with may seem far removed from the actual stuff of deterrence. But consider the relationship between cyberwar and deterrence with regard to early warning of nuclear-missile attack or the possible activation of a missile-defense system for preemptive strike against a presumably attacking offensive missile force. We would not want to trust computers or artificial intelligence systems to make these decisions.

Information warfare as a form of conflict that might tax existing ideas or methods of deterrence is closely related to the use of space for military purpose. Until now the United States has benefited enormously from the militarization of space without the weaponization of it. American military planners now regard space as a place from which various peacetime and, if necessary, wartime activities might be conducted. In addition, space is a potential strategic theater of military operations and a U.S. unified command. Defense Secretary Donald Rumsfeld recently announced a reorganization of U.S. defense management and command and control for space operations. The Department of Defense defines space control as a critical objective for the twenty-first century: Space control means "combat and combat support operations to ensure freedom of action in space for the United States and its allies and, when directed, deny an adversary freedom of action in space."[14] Space-control missions as outlined by the Department of Defense are summarized in Table 3.3.

Space as a strategic theater of military operations lends itself to both symmetrical warfare (as states hostile to the United States acquire their own space defense and attack capabilities) or to asymmetrical warfare (for those who cannot afford or otherwise acquire space-exploiting or space-based weaponry). It would be remarkable if the growth of peacetime U.S. military operations in space were not accompanied by concerns about how or if deterrence will operate in space. One can imagine, at least, that problems of deterrence by denial, punishment, decapitation, uncertainty, or other means could apply to (1) efforts to attack and to defend nonweaponized space assets, including satellites; (2) space-based weapons, or space-based components of weapon systems, and their protection against coercive diplomacy or actual destruction; and (3) cyberwars against components of both ground and space-based weapons or C4ISR systems.

All this potential for deterrence or war in space assumes that we and/or potential adversaries will have more or less reliable knowl-

Table 3.3
U.S. Space-Control Missions

Surveillance	Protection	Prevention	Negation
Precise detection, tracking, and identification of space objects	Detection and reporting of space- system malfunctions	Prevent adversarial use of U.S., allied, or third-party capabilities	Precision negation of adversarial use of space
Ability to characterize objects as threats or nonthreats	Characterization of an attack and location of its source		Strike assessment or BDA against target sets
Detection or assessment when a threat payload performs a maneuver or separates	Withstanding and defense against threats or attacks		
	Restoration of mission capability		

Source: Office of the Secretary of Defense, Assistant Secretary of Defense (Command, Control, Communications, and Intelligence) and Director, Defense Research and Engineering, *Space Technology Guide, FY 2000–01* (Washington, D.C.: 2001), 10-2. Available at: http://www.fas.org/spp/military/stg.htm.

edge about what is going on, and in nearly real time. Our experience with nuclear warning and command and control systems during the Cold War is not necessarily encouraging in this regard. The command and control systems of land- and sea-based nuclear weapons, and of bomber forces for a different reasons, were lumbering and ponderous compared to those that would be required for the use or defense of space-based, speed-of-light, electromagnetic, or kinetic-kill weapons. Eventually some kinds of space-based warning, assessment, and response capabilities would have to be delegated to intelligent systems, the software of which would include decision rules written by persons unknown. Imagine a space-based variant of the Cold War DefCon alerting system: How would it be cued, what would be its minimum threshold of warning, and what would constitute positive identification of threatening phenomenology? Will the policy makers get into the software in order to understand what their real options are? Will the space force live or die based upon the expertise of its underwriting geek force?

U.S. plans to deploy a ballistic missile-defense system are seen by some as the first step in the development of an explicit space-control strategy. A first-generation BMD system using ground-based interceptors will require space-based surveillance and launch detection, communications, navigation, and command and control assets. Denial of these U.S. space assets would be one asymmetrical approach to defeating an American BMD system; destruction of them is another possibility. Conversely, the United States must protect these space assets for its first-generation BMD system even before future missile-defense systems can make use of space-based weapons. Antisatellite weapons have already been tested by various nations, and although satellites in geostationary or higher orbit appear safe for the time being, satellites in low earth orbit (LEO) might be vulnerable to attack by off-the-shelf or near-term ASAT technologies. Will ASATs then necessitate DSATs (defensive satellites) to protect space assets, and where will the DSATs be based, and how will they be controlled?

In conclusion, this section identifies four possibly asymmetrical or deterrence-daunting domains for military activity in defiance of technological supremacy, from the meanest "grunt" environment to the heavens above: unconventional warfare; WMD and missile proliferation, including its possible use by states or nonstate actors; cyberwar; and "star wars" or space weaponization and the reluctance of other states to see the United States dominate the "high ground." Table 3.4 summarizes some of these possibilities.

EVERYTHING OLD IS NEW AGAIN?

Part of the difficulty in relating possible technology futures to military strategy is that covariation in politicomilitary and technical variables cannot be assumed. Political scenarios and technology innovation are often related, but the relationship is mediated by other social and psychological variables. What we need is a better handle on the problem of technology or knowledge innovation.

One possible schematic for understanding knowledge innovation has been proposed by Anthony Oettinger of Harvard University. Oettinger sets up a table that classifies ideal types of knowledge as "cow" (data without context) and "bull" (context without data). He then hypothesizes that each ideal type of knowledge can be relatively static or dynamic in its rate of change. When types of knowledge are classified by rate of assumed change, Table 3.5 results.

Table 3.4
Possibly Asymmetrical Challenges to Deterrence

Type of strategy	Who	Tactics
Low-Intensity Conflict or Unconventional warfare	States or Nonstate Actors	Frustrate U.S. commanders with unorthodox means; exploit U.S. public, media and congressional aversion to casualties and to ambiguous wars
WMD or terrorism	States or Nonstate Actors	Deter U.S. military intervention in regional conflicts by threat of nuclear or biological attacks on U.S. or allied troops, infrastructure
Cyberwar/Netwar	States or Nonstate Actors	Disrupt U.S. military operations or attack parts of the U.S. national information infrastructure by using clandestine attacks on computers, networks, and communications systems
Space war/weaponization	States	Attack ground-based, sea-based, airborne, and space based systems that support U.S. conventional war fighting or nuclear deterrence

These categories of knowledge innovation can be related to the historical development of U.S. debates over ballistic missile defenses. During the Cold War the debate was essentially about "cow": whether antimissile technology could be deployed that was cost effective compared to offenses and reliable against foreseeable offensive countermeasures. The consensus of most U.S. deterrence theorists, arms-control advocates, and military planners during the Cold War was that antimissile technology could not be deployed that was cost effective compared to

Table 3.5
Aspects of Knowledge Innovation

	Cow	Bull
Stasis	Steady-State Cow	Steady-State Bull
Change	Transient Cow	Transient Bull

Source: Anthony Oettinger, "Knowledge Innovations: Celebrating Our Heritage, Designing Our Future" (slide presentation at Harvard University, Program on Information Resources Policy, November 13, 2000). Used by permission.

offenses or capable of defeating offensive countermeasures. Technology dictated that mutual assured destruction or mutual deterrence based on offensive retaliation was the only game in town.

With the end of the Cold War and the demise of the Soviet Union, the thrust of the debate over U.S. missile defenses has now turned away from arguments about technology per se to arguments about the probable shape of the new international order and its implications for U.S. deterrence and defense policies (from "cow" to "bull"). Advocates of American missile defenses in Congress, in the military, and elsewhere in the defense and policy communities now point to the emerging new threats from rogue nations or "states of concern" armed with ballistic missiles and weapons of mass destruction. The Clinton administration signed the Missile Defense Act of 1999 that called for a deployment of National Missile Defense (NMD) of the American homeland as soon as NMD technology became feasible. Clinton's oblique willingness to agree to an eventual deployment of missile defenses against limited attacks (accidental launches or deliberate attacks by rogue states) crossed a Rubicon by putting a liberal Democratic president on the record in favor of defenses under some conditions.

President George W. Bush, in his speech to the National Defense University on May 1, 2001, called for even more ambitious missile defenses than the Clinton plan, along with offensive force reductions. Bush indicated in that speech that the ABM Treaty would have to be drastically amended or abrogated to permit U.S. missile defenses based on a variety of possible technologies, including ground- and sea-based interceptors and airborne lasers.[15] It was therefore unsurprising when President Bush later announced in November 2001 that the United

States was giving official notice of its intention to withdraw from the ABM Treaty.

Following the typology of knowledge innovation, one could imagine disputants in the early twenty-first-century BMD debates arguing for any one of four positions:

1. The situation is a "steady cow–steady bull" condition. There are some test data on theater and national missile defenses that encourage their proponents. But the data also show that there is a long journey ahead for most of these technologies in research and development, and even more time needed for effective weaponization and deployment. Proponents of "steady cow–steady bull" acknowledge that the international system has changed since the end of the Cold War and the collapse of the Soviet Union. But they deny that these changes have invalidated nuclear deterrence based on survivable retaliatory forces. Nuclear deterrence without defenses is still robust from this perspective: Defenses are neither necessary nor useful in order to make deterrence work. Proponents of the "steady cow–steady bull" position also express skepticism about the present and probable future performance of missile-defense technology. In their view, even tests under relatively benign conditions, less stressful than those in the "real world," reveal serious weaknesses in the various components of the U.S.–proposed NMD system and in several candidate theater missile-defenses systems. Finally, adherents of this position judge that the ABM Treaty is worth preserving and that a unilateral U.S. abrogation of the treaty will set off a new nuclear arms race with Russia and China.

2. The situation is a "steady cow–transient bull" condition. The essential data on the effectiveness of defenses relative to offenses have not changed, but the world has. The imminent threat of ballistic missile attack against the U.S. homeland or against forward-deploying American troops and allies requires a fast-track deployment of missile defenses, even imperfectly developed and tested ones. Having even a strawman missile-defense system forces rogue attackers to think twice about the worst-case possibility for them: They will launch against the United States only to have their missiles destroyed in flight; afterward, an angry U.S. president will destroy their society. Proponents of this view also contend that many rogue leaders are beyond deterrence as understood by Western scholars and analysts. Non-Western political leaders and their military advisors may not calculate costs and benefits in the same way that we do. They may have apocalyptic visions of glorious mutual suicide like terrorist truck bombers. Therefore, from this perspective, although deterrence based on offensive retaliation has not been superseded by missile-defense technology, it might be prudent to supplement deterrence based on the threat of retaliatory punishment by deterrence based on the physical capacity to destroy light attacks. But proponents of this position agree with the adherents of position 1, that the ABM Treaty is an important arms-control benchmark and should be amended carefully, preferably with Russian consent and collaboration.

3. The present situation is a "transient cow–steady bull" scenario. Although some data suggest that future missile-defense technologies will be better than their Cold War predecessors, the basic context for the effectiveness of nuclear deterrence has not changed with the end of the Cold War. Proliferation of nuclear weapons and ballistic missiles does make the world arguably more dangerous, but the principal danger from nuclear and missile proliferation is the possibility of attacks by regional rogues against U.S. allies or forward-deployed forces in order to negate the approved Pentagon "two MTW" (major theater wars) strategy. An attack against the American homeland by any state would be an act of national self-destruction because the origin of the attack would be known and the U.S. president would be certain to retaliate. Because of this fact, rogue states seeking to strike at the American homeland with weapons of mass destruction would be more likely to turn to terrorist allies who could smuggle weapons across the U.S. border and attempt a nuclearized version of the New York World Trade Center bombing or the Tokyo subway sarin gas attack.

4. The present condition is one of "transient cow–transient bull." Both technology and the policy context are changing very rapidly. This is good news and bad news for advocates of missile defenses. The good news is that a variety of new approaches to missile defense may come off the drawing boards in the next several decades. This plurality of new technical breakthroughs raises the likelihood that at least one will have the potential to provide a deployable, affordable, and effective offset to (at least) light ballistic missile attacks. In addition, the acceleration of political and social change in the twenty-first century increases the likely appeal of weapons of mass destruction and ballistic or other delivery systems to states who reject the geopolitical status quo, either regionally or globally. The plausible spread of weapons into the hands of highly politicized armed forces in nondemocratic countries also suggests a pessimistic U.S. threat assessment with regard to the likelihood of attacks against U.S. forces or allies.

A world of two-sided transience in data and in context (i.e., in technology as well as in policy) may accelerate beyond the boundaries of the present debate over missile defenses in new and unknown directions. For example, the military uses of space in the twentieth century were for essential missions in support of actual combat: reconnaissance, surveillance, command and control, communications, and navigation. Space has not yet been weaponized. The introduction of weapons based in space, especially if they operate with the speed of lasers, particle beams, or electromagnetic railguns, changes the context for missile attack and antimissile defenses. But the context changes in unpredictable ways. Space-based weapons could not only be used to defend against ballistic missile attacks; they might also be used to attack another state's warning, communications, and navigational satellites. A first strike against the satellite warning and communications of another state would have the potential to render the victim electronically silent and visually blind. The victim state could then be coerced or, if necessary, attacked with impunity.

No scientist can guarantee against the possibility of a breakthrough in technology favorable to antimissile defenses. The question is not only one of technology, but of politics and strategy. Russia's large nuclear force and decrepit C3I system is an Excedrin headache to Russians as well as to potential adversaries and a possible source of crisis meltdown into accidental nuclear war. In order to induce the Russians to buy into below-START levels of strategic retaliatory forces, the United States must not make too convincing a case that it has technology over the horizon that might deter Russia's deterrent. Russia already worries about U.S. cyberwarfare against its strategic vitals, including its nuclear warning and control systems (and Americans should worry that Russian information systems might mistakenly simulate a U.S. cyberattack during a crisis or confuse random errors with attacks).[16]

U.S. missile defenses may impact upon Russian conventional deterrence also. The chain reaction from a nullified Russian nuclear deterrent, given Russia's conventional weakness, also invites bites at Russia's periphery from the Caucasus, from Central Asia, and from its Far Eastern borders. A postnuclear Russia verges on toppling over into a pre-Petrine collection of invasion corridors and internal wars. Reassembling the humpty-dumpty of a disaggregated Russian "near abroad" after key CIS states have fallen into hostile (and anti-Western) hands may demand the combined diplomatic skills of a Holbrooke and a Metternich. Other possible strategy and policy by-products could occur in China and in Europe: Missile defenses of uncertain effectiveness would be a poor trade for a major Chinese ICBM buildup, or for a more assertive European Union unilateral defense.

There is also the policy and strategy paradox of missile and space defenses that, the better they work, the more angst they raise among allies (and others) about shared strategic space. Does the missile shield protect only North America, or does it include Europe, Japan, or even Russia? Interallied controversy about shared control over the missile defense "trigger" could rival in intensity the MLF (multilateral force) debate of the early 1960s. This problem of who protects whom and from what could bedevil theater missile defenses as well. An airborne optical laser cruising at 20,000 feet can be exercised against a variety of missile threats in "out of the area" states not necessarily defined as within the United States or NATO collectively defended aerospace. Is a NATO "theater" missile deterrent a global threat to Indian, Pakistani, or other new or aspiring regional powers?

IDEAS AND MILITARY–TECHNICAL INNOVATION

The preceding example is one of many that could be used to illustrate another point about the relationship between technology innovation and military strategy or policy. Ideas do matter, and the significance of ideas goes beyond creative thinking by imaginative officers or scientists. For new ideas to make a difference in military strategy and in military art, they must find their way into military doctrine as prescriptive norms, and they must be enabled within military organizations as standard operating procedures. Both processes take time, money, and luck. Some ideas are ahead of their time, or at least of the technology of their time. The first prototypes of "flying wing" aircraft were propeller driven and were test flown by Northrop as early as 1947, but the realization of this vision was impractical until the B-2 was deployed in the 1980s. By the time the flying wing became technically feasible, the strategic rationale for the bomber was less obviously justifiable.

Enthusiasts for the Revolution in Military Affairs (RMA) in the U.S. military and policy communities underestimate the complexity of technology innovation as it relates to politics and strategy.[17] They also emphasize the possible payoffs from innovation in C4ISR, precision-strike, and stealth technology that are the most tangible and outcome oriented: targets destroyed, enemy command and control disrupted, and so forth. The impact of the information revolution on military strategy and political decision making in security policy is broader than battle. According to Robert O. Keohane and Joseph S. Nye, Jr., the relative importance of "soft" compared to "hard" power in world politics has changed as one consequence of the information revolution.[18] Hard power is the ability to get others to do what they might otherwise not do by means of coercion: rewards mixed with threats. Soft power is the ability to get others to want the same outcomes that you do. Soft power includes the appeal of a state or nonstate actor's ideas, culture, values, society, and political system.

Other experts have recognized the need to rethink U.S. military strategy and defense organization on account of the requirement to mix hard and soft power. For example, Max G. Manwaring, in his expert appraisal of the "U.S. Plan Colombia" for aid to the imperiled regime in Bogotá, judges that hard power alone cannot save either the political or the military situation in that troubled country (under siege from narcotraffickers, revolutionaries, and paramilitary vigilantes):

Power is not simply "hard" combat fire power directed at a traditional enemy military formation or industrial complex. Power is multi-layered, combining "hard" and "soft" political, psychological, moral, informational, economic, societal, military, police, and civil bureaucratic activities that can be brought to bear appropriately on the causes as well as the perpetrators of violence.[19]

The prescription for combining hard and soft power is also offered as a solution to U.S. national security and intelligence problems. Robert David Steele calls for an integrated national security strategy that would restructure the relationships among government agencies and realign the responsibility for war and peace operations among military commands.[20] Arguing that many of the most important threats to U.S. security are based on social, economic, or other nonmilitary conditions, Steele recommends a transformative strategy that requires four "threat-type" commanders in chief (CINCs) in addition to the existing regional military CINCs. The result of his proposal would be to create ten force components under four new functional CINCs whose responsibilities include everything from public health and civic education to traditional war fighting (the new force structure that would result from his proposals is summarized in Table 3.6).

This schematic is admittedly a radical departure from current practice, but it moves in the right directions: toward multidisciplinary, interdepartmental, and holistic threat assessment as the driver of military organization and of military definitions for the technologies needed for twenty-first-century war and peace making. And it recognizes the need to integrate soft and hard power and to cement that integration into the force and command structure.

With all of its hard power based on nuclear and advanced conventional military technology, the United States could still fall flat in its efforts to combine soft and hard power for conflict avoidance or for the attainment of military victory at an acceptable cost. The 1990s provided little evidence that the collective government memory bank or learning curve has improved since the end of the Cold War. By way of example, much of the U.S. intelligence community is still organized for fighting the Cold War; planning guidance for the George W. Bush Department of Defense emphasized whether the U.S. armed forces could fight in two or one and a half major theater wars until the shock of 9/11 disrupted business as usual; and the rotation of elites and advisors in and out of policy positions in Washington is vivid testimony on behalf of Michels's "iron law of oligarchy." There are visions aplenty in and out of the Pentagon, to be sure, but these visions have a short half life as administrations change, technologies fail or mature, and political priorities shift like tectonic plates. When the chief of staff of the U.S. Army thinks it entirely appropriate to order Ranger-style berets for the entire regular enlisted force and send the contract for beret manufacture to China (a soft power fiasco), scholars and policy analysts can be reassured of a target-rich environment in the twenty-first century.

Table 3.6
A Transformative Force Structure

CINC WAR	CINC SOLIC	CINC PEACE	CINC HOME
Force on Force (Traditional war-fighting missions)	Small Wars (Navy–Marine Corps team, 450-ship Navy, Special Forces, Reserve Foreign Area forces)	State and USIA (1000 new diplomats, 100 new missions, including some to nations that are not states)	Domestic Threat (includes FEMA and NMD as it develops, as well as major remake of National Guard)
	Constabulary (maintains the peace, restores functions of a failed state; heavy on civil affairs, military policy, medical, engineers, and liaison with NGOs and indigenous populations)	Peace Corps (10,000 new volunteers per year, with intent of casting a very wide net of good will, with special emphasis on using American Mujahid in Islamic areas)	Electronic Security (includes cyberwar, security and encryption, etc.; redirects portion of National Guard to give each state an electronic-security battalion and crisis response team)
	Ground Truth (new networks of overt human and covert tactical technical sources of information to obtain ground truth)	Economic Aid (Digital Marshall Plan for the Third World, ten new $100-million water, food, and medicine projects for preventive security)	Citizen Education (a broad program of civic education to support social cohesion and pubic responsibility; restores universal draft)

Source: Robert David Steele, "Threats, Strategy and Force Structure: An Alternative Paradigm for National Security in the 21st Century," in *Revising the Two MTW Force Shaping Paradigm*, ed. Steven Metz (Carlisle Barracks, Pa.: U.S. Army War College, 2001), 159. Parenthetical explanatory remarks are from the original author of this paper. The expanded version of the chapter with extensive footnotes is available at: http://www.oss.net/Papers/white/AlternativeStrategy.rtf.

CONCLUSION

Deterrence is connected to military technology and defense missions in a much more nuanced and problematic way than it was during the Cold War. Deterrence may not disappear as a concept that has passable utility for policy makers or scholars in need of a common vocabulary, but deterrence as a concept will not serve as a universal solvent or justification for intervention or force building as it did during the Cold War. Deterrence will be downsized and "precision guided" very much like the military to which it will be attached: More will have to got from less. Deterrence will no longer be an all-purpose solution in search of compatible problems. The quality of deterrence will matter more than the quantity of it.

NOTES

An earlier version of this chapter was presented to a conference sponsored by the Strategic Assessments Group, Directorate of Intelligence, Central Intelligence Agency. The author is solely responsible for arguments and assertions in this study. I am grateful to conference participants for their comments and for comments on an earlier draft by Robert David Steele, CEO of Open Source Solutions, Inc.

1. The concept of deterrence can be traced prior to the nuclear age as well. See George H. Quester, *Deterrence before Hiroshima: The Airpowers Background of Modern Strategy* (New Brunswick, N.J.: Transaction Books, 1986).

2. Thomas C. Schelling, *Arms and Influence* (New Haven, Conn.: Yale University Press, 1966), 109.

3. Ibid., 69–91.

4. Alexander L. George, "The Development of Doctrine and Strategy," in *The Limits of Coercive Diplomacy: Laos, Cuba, Vietnam,* ed. Alexander L. George, David K. Hall, and William R. Simons (Boston: Little, Brown, 1971), 1–35.

5. Alexander L. George, "Strategies for Crisis Management," in *Avoiding War: Problems of Crisis Management,* ed. Alexander L. George (Boulder, Colo.: Westview Press, 1991), 384–385.

6. On the development of nuclear strategy, see Lawrence Freedman, *The Evolution of Nuclear Strategy* (New York: St. Martin's Press, 1981); Colin S. Gray, *Strategic Studies and Public Policy: The American Experience* (Lexington: University of Kentucky Press, 1982); Robert Jervis, *The Meaning of the Nuclear Revolution: Statecraft and the Prospect of Armageddon* (Ithaca, N.Y.: Cornell University Press, 1989); Richard Ned Lebow and Janice Gross Stein, *When Does Deterrence Succeed and How Do We Know?* (Ottawa, Ontario: Canadian Institute for International Peace and Security, 1990). On the early years of U.S. strategic theorizing, see Marc Trachtenberg, *History and Strategy* (Princeton, N.J.: Princeton University Press, 1991), 3–46. The logic of deterrence and deterrence rationality receives especially insightful treatment in Patrick M. Morgan, *Deterrence: A Conceptual Analysis* (Beverly Hills, Calif.: Sage, 1977); Phil Williams, "Nuclear Deterrence," in *Contemporary Strategy,* vol. 1, *Theories and Concepts,* ed. John

Baylis, Ken Booth, John Garnett, and Phil Williams (New York: Holmes and Meier, 1987), 113–139. The nuclear revolution is put into historical context in Michael Mandelbaum, *The Nuclear Revolution: International Politics before and after Hiroshima* (Cambridge: Cambridge University Press, 1981).

7. Battle imaging and management includes command and control, communications, computers, intelligence, surveillance, and reconnaissance (C4ISR).

8. For pertinent history and concepts of terrorism, see Walter Laqueur, *The New Terrorism: Fanaticism and the Arms of Mass Destruction* (New York: Oxford University Press, 1999), 49–78.

9. Richard K. Betts, "The New Threat of Mass Destruction," *Foreign Affairs* 1 (January–February 1998): 27; Lt. Col. Rex R. Kiziah, *Assessment of the Emerging Biocruise Threat* (Maxwell A.F.B., Ala.: USAF Counterproliferation Center, Air War College, 2000), 11.

10. Kiziah, *Assessment of the Emerging Biocruise Threat*, 49.

11. Walter Laqueur, *The New Terrorism: Fanaticism and the Arms of Mass Destruction* (New York: Oxford University Press, 1999), 49–78.

12. For an expansion, see Paul Bracken, *Fire in the East* (New York: Harper-Collins, 1999), passim.

13. Richard J. Harknett, "Information Warfare and Deterrence," in *The Technological Arsenal*, ed. William C. Martel (Washington, D.C.: Smithsonian Institution Press, 2001), 241–256.

14. Office of the Secretary of Defense, Assistant Secretary of Defense (Command, Control, Communications, and Intelligence) and Director, Defense Research and Engineering, *Space Technology Guide, FY 2000–01* (Washington, D.C.: 2001), 10-1. Available at: http://www.fas.org/spp/military/stg.htm.

15. George W. Bush, "Speech at National Defense University, Washington, D.C., May 1, 2001," *New York Times*, 2 May 2001, A10. See also Steven Lee Myers and James Glanz, "Taking a Look at the Workings of a Missile Shield," *New York Times*, 3 May 2001, A10.

16. *Jane's* reported on May 15, 2001, that Russia had no currently operational photo-reconnaissance satellites. This raises the interesting possibility that, under some improbable but not impossible circumstances, Russia would be reliant upon U.S. optics for reassurance against the possibility of accidental or inadvertent war or deliberate attack.

17. For an assessment of the RMA, see Michael O'Hanlon, *Technological Change and the Future of Warfare* (Washington, D.C.: Brookings Institution, 2000), 7–31. See also Colin S. Gray, *Weapons for Strategic Effect: How Important Is Technology?* (Maxwell A.F.B., Ala.: Center for Strategy and Technology, Air War College, 2001), 20–21.

18. Robert O. Keohane and Joseph S. Nye, Jr., "Power and Interdependence in the Information Age," *Foreign Affairs* 5 (September–October 1998): 81–94.

19. Max G. Manwaring, *U.S. Security Policy in the Western Hemisphere* (Carlisle Barracks, Pa.: U.S. Army War College, Strategic Studies Institute), 18.

20. Robert David Steele, "Threats, Strategy and Force Structure: An Alternative Paradigm for National Security in the 21st Century," in *Revising the Two MTW Force Shaping Paradigm*, ed. Steven Metz (Carlisle Barracks, Pa.: Strategic Studies Institute, U.S. Army War College, 2001), 139–164.

Part II

EXAMPLES FROM THE PAST

4

Military Persuasion in the Cuban Missile Crisis

The Cuban missile crisis brought the world closer to nuclear war than any other Cold War event. Had it been handled like the July crisis of 1914, from which World War I erupted, unspeakable disaster could have resulted for the United States, for the Soviet Union, and for the planet. Fortunately, cooler heads prevailed over the stakes in Cuba in 1962 than in the Balkans in 1914. Of course, part of the reason for this restraint by the crisis leaderships in Washington, D.C., and in Moscow was the fear of the unknown. A two-sided nuclear war had never been fought. But this fear of nuclear escalation does not account entirely for the remarkable restraint practiced by President John F. Kennedy and Premier Nikita S. Khrushchev. After all, it was just as likely that one side might decide to plunge into war below the nuclear threshold before conceding the issues demanded by the other. And, in fact, some advisors to Kennedy and Khrushchev during the thirteen tense days of the crisis recommended exactly that.

The missile crisis was resolved by leaders who used techniques of military persuasion in order to defend their minimum positions while giving ground on their maximum demands. To a remarkable extent, these techniques were improvised by leaders and their advisors for the circumstances, and they were not without danger. Military persuasion was involved because the United States (1) mobilized forces for the invasion of Cuba, (2) put its strategic nuclear forces on their largest ever peacetime alert, and (3) instituted a naval blockade of Cuba that ran a deliberate but calculated risk of a confrontation on the high

seas between American and Soviet naval forces. Additional components of military persuasion were also apparent in both sides' precrisis
and crisis maneuvers. The United States could not extricate itself from
the crisis without engaging in a degree of nuclear military persuasion
that some crisis participants, then and later, felt were unacceptably
dangerous for both sides. Shared nuclear danger was like no other.

COERCIVE DIPLOMACY:
MILITARY PERSUASION IN CUBA

The U.S. naval blockade was one aspect of the Kennedy administration's effort to apply coercive diplomacy, one kind of military persuasion, to the situation in Cuba. According to Alexander L. George,
coercive diplomacy can be used in either of two variants, less demanding and more demanding, in terms of the pressure it places upon the
deterree for compliance.[1] The less demanding is the "try and see" variant; the more demanding is the "ultimatum" approach. The blockade
is an example of the try and see approach. It served to establish
Kennedy's resolve in the eyes of Khrushchev and to position the U.S.
president to exert additional pressure on the Soviet leader if need be.
It lacked, as is typical of the "try and see" option, two components
that the president was later forced to add in order to induce Soviet
compliance. The first of these two additional components was a specific time limit for compliance, and the second was an equally specific
indication of what consequences would follow immediately, absent
compliance. The addition of these components turned the try and see
variant into the harder or ultimatum form of coercive diplomacy.[2]

According to Graham T. Allison, the blockade was not sufficient to
get Khrushchev to agree to withdraw the missiles until it was coupled
with an explicit threat of an air strike or invasion on Tuesday, October
30. Khrushchev's report to the Supreme Soviet after the crisis noted
that "we received information from Cuban comrades and from other
sources on the morning of October 27th *directly stating* that this attack
would be carried out in the next two or three days. We interpreted these
cables as an *extremely alarming warning signal.*"[3] The "other sources"
could have included a warning given to Soviet Ambassador Dobrynin
by Robert Kennedy on October 27, combined with a tacit assurance
that following the resolution of the crisis (but not as an obvious U.S.
concession during the crisis) the U.S. Jupiter missiles would be removed
from Turkey.[4] Raymond Garthoff notes the impressive size of the U.S.
military buildup for possible air strikes and invasion of Cuba, the scale
of which must certainly have been noticed in Moscow. The potential
invasion force mobilized for attacks on Cuba included one Marine and
five U.S. Army divisions (with other Marine and Army reserves if nec-

essary), or more than 100,000 Army and 40,000 Marine combat troops; 579 Air Force and Navy tactical combat aircraft; and 183 Navy ships, including eight aircraft carriers on station. The airborne forces to be dropped on the first day of the invasion (14,500) were comparable in size to the forces dropped during the Normandy invasion.[5]

The experience of U.S. decision making during the Cuban missile crisis suggest that the requirements for prudent crisis management can be in conflict with those of successful coercive diplomacy.[6] Crisis management emphasizes the need for taking escalatory steps in small stages, with allowance for opponents to reconsider their options at each stage. On the other hand, successful coercive diplomacy may dictate a firmer and less flexible position, and on occasion a brutal ultimatum, in order to resolve the crisis on satisfactory terms. George argues that the difference between the try and see and ultimatum versions of coercive diplomacy is not the same as the difference between small and large escalation. Different models of military persuasion are at work.[7] Perhaps so, but the U.S. requirement for an ultimatum and for a knowingly dangerous blockade of Cuba (incidents at sea are notoriously beyond the reach of shore commanders and politicians even under the best communication conditions) pushes the model beyond George's coercive "diplomacy" and into a more ambitious variety of military persuasion. By October 27 the situation (Khrushchev's stalling, the growing impatience of U.S. "hawks" within Kennedy's advisory group, and the continued work on the missiles already in Cuba) called for an ultimatum with a short time fuse.

One difference between the try and see and ultimatum versions of coercive diplomacy is that the try and see approach to coercive diplomacy is open ended with regard to the options that are left to the deterree. Compliance may be structured as much by the creativity of the deterree as by the explicit demands of the deterrer. There is room for the "bargaining space" between the two sides to be adjusted in the direction of the party being coerced. The try and see approach thus allows for the bilateral influence of "perspective taking," which has been shown in some research to be an important influence on the probability of reciprocal concessions in bargaining.[8] Perspective taking is the propensity to adopt the opposite side's perspective in structuring one's own bargaining strategy. Researchers have found that high-perspective takers are less likely to escalate irrelevant demands and more likely to reframe their proposals in positive terms. High-perspective takers are also more likely to have a sense of control over situational factors.[9]

Kennedy and Khrushchev demonstrated some perspective-taking competency after the Cuban missile crisis had broken out, but their performances in perspective taking were less impressive prior to the crisis days of October. Once the crisis got under way, each leader came gradually to see the constraints under which the other was forced to operate. Khrushchev appreciated more completely the domestic policy constraints under which Kennedy labored, as well as U.S. alliance commitments to NATO that limited the array of immediately available policy options. Kennedy, on the other hand, appreciated the difficulty that Khrushchev had got himself into by attempting to conceal the missile deployments and, having been caught in midstream, needing a graceful exit in order to save some face.

If coercive diplomacy is defined to exclude deterrence, it is hard to see how the Cuban missile crisis and its outcome can be explained only as a case of diplomatic military persuasion. Khrushchev was deterred from further escalation by the plausible threat of a prompt U.S. invasion of Cuba and by the possibility of inadvertent escalation growing out of a Cuban confrontation and leading to a U.S.–Soviet war. The need for an ultimatum with a specific time limit for removal of the missiles was a litmus test for the presence of other kinds of military persuasion, in addition to coercive diplomacy. Other aspects of the crisis also make clear the imaginative and impromptu exploitation of events and opportunities by Kennedy and Khrushchev in resolving it. The U.S. ultimatum, for example, was accompanied by a tacit reassurance via Robert Kennedy to Soviet Ambassador Anatoly Dobrynin that the Thor and Jupiter intermediate range ballistic missiles (IRBMs) deployed in Turkey and Italy would eventually be removed. Khrushchev had enough residual military power outside of the immediate Caribbean theater of operations, especially in Europe, to compel caution by the United States in Washington's application of military and political persuasion.

FEARS OF INSECURITY

The U.S.–Soviet relationship throughout the Cold War years was marked by simplification on each side of the political objectives and military doctrine of the other. As only one example, U.S. policy analysts and government officials described Soviet military doctrine from the 1960s through the 1980s, including military doctrine for the use of strategic nuclear weapons, as first-strike oriented and aimed at seeking victory through nuclear war. Deterrence in the Soviet view, as described by much of the U.S. defense community, rested on the ability to fight and win a nuclear war.[10] U.S. analysts who sought to make this case could draw from some statements made by party officials, military–technical literature including important publications in the *Officer's Library Series*, and some evidence of Soviet research and development on future generations of nuclear offensive and defensive weapons. Officials in the Carter and Reagan administrations were especially concerned with Soviet ICBM capabilities for preemptive attack on U.S. missile silos and command centers, and with Soviet ballistic missile defenses already deployed and in development.

Had the same information included a larger component of U.S. perspective taking of the Soviet strategic view, U.S. assessments might not have seemed so ominous. Soviet interest in nuclear offensive and defensive forces could have been interpreted as components of a strategy that emphasized the deterrence of war and the limitation of damage should nuclear war occur. This interpretation might have been supported by the recognition that Soviet interest in first-strike strategies waned as their military planners became less dependent on preemption for survivability of their land-based forces. Then, too, the Soviet force configuration differed from the American: U.S. capabilities spread over three legs of the strategic "triad" placed most survivable U.S. striking power in submarines and bombers. Soviet retaliatory potential as well as first-strike capability resided in the timely launch of their ICBMs, carrying a disproportionate share of their hard-target warheads. The argument that Soviet ICBMs were targeted against U.S. ICBMs and therefore intended as first-strike weapons ignored the equally plausible inference that second-strike counterforce was considered by Soviet military planners, as by U.S. defense officials, as a requirement for credible deterrence.[11]

It was ironic that during the latter 1950s and early 1960s both the U.S. and Soviet governments were marked by fears of strategic insecurity based on misperceptions of actual capabilities and military intentions. Khrushchev's atomic diplomacy of the latter 1950s had sought to exploit U.S. fears that Soviet competency in nuclear rocket weapons greatly exceeded the U.S. ability to develop and deploy those weapons. Khrushchev used extravagant claims of Soviet nuclear superiority to buttress otherwise weak foreign policies and to fend off domestic and foreign critics of his detente policies and military budget cuts.[12] Addressing the Supreme Soviet in January 1960, Khrushchev asserted not for the first time his claim to strategic superiority, argued that world economic trends were moving in favor of socialism, and contended that nuclear war, although certainly devastating for both sides, would result in victory for socialism.[13]

By the fall of 1960 Khrushchev had begun to retreat from some of his more extravagant claims about Soviet nuclear superiority and about the ability of socialism to prevail in nuclear war with comparatively few casualties. His speeches after the fall of 1960 emphasized more and more that the consequences of nuclear war for both sides would be highly destructive. The same thematic focus on the mutually destructive effects of nuclear war appeared in an article in the Communist Party theoretical journal, *Kommunist*, by General Nikolai Talensky in July 1960, and Talensky enlarged his presentation of the same themes in a later article in *Mezhdunarodnaya zhizn' (International Affairs)*.[14] According to Talensky's later article, calculations showed that casualties in a world war would be approximately 500 to 600 million in the main theater of military action (presumably Europe), of an estimated total population of 800 million.[15] One reason for this retreat of Khrushchev and military leaders from previous assertions of nuclear superiority and war-winning capability was the Soviet view that Chinese leaders were far too cavalier about the consequences of nuclear war, challenging the Soviets for leadership of the world communist movement on the basis of ideological claims that disputed Soviet willingness to stand firm in confrontations with the West.

Another reason for a pulling back in Soviet nuclear assertiveness was a recognition by the Soviet leadership that the United States was much more aware by 1960 and thereafter of the actual state of the strategic nuclear balance of power. Eisenhower's last State of the Union address provided an opportunity for the U.S. president to note that "the 'missile gap' shows every sign of being a fiction."[16] Almost immediately after the Kennedy administration took office, press reports appeared that claimed, on the basis of Pentagon studies, that there was actually no "missile gap."[17] Citing new U.S. intelligence estimates, press reports in September 1961 acknowledged that actual Soviet ICBM deployments in 1961 would fall far short of the maximum possible number projected in earlier U.S. estimates. Therefore, the new intelligence estimates, according to press reports, completely eliminated any notion of a missile gap unfavorable to the United States.[18]

Nor was this all. Beginning in October 1961 Kennedy administration officials launched an offensive in public diplomacy to dispel the existence of any missile gap favorable to the Soviet Union. Further, U.S. government officials publicly proclaimed that the United States had now (by autumn 1961) attained strategic nuclear superiority over the Soviet Union. The public-relations offensive began with the speech by Deputy Secretary of Defense Roswell Gilpatric on October 21, 1961, and was followed by similar statements from other high Kennedy administration officials. Gilpatric noted that the United States, even after absorbing a Soviet surprise first strike, would probably retain second-strike forces that were greater than the forces used by the Soviet Union in its attack. "In short," according to Gilpatric, "we have a second-strike capability which is at least as extensive as what the Soviets can deliver by striking first."[19] The actual balance of forces at the time of the Cuban missile crisis (including forces becoming available at the very end of the crisis period, through October 28) appears in Table 4.1.

As Richard Ned Lebow and Janice Gross Stein have noted, the reaction of Khrushchev and his military advisors to this U.S. public diplo-

Table 4.1
Strategic Nuclear Forces, U.S.–Soviet Balance, Cuban Missile Crisis

Weapon	Launchers	Warheads per Launcher	Total Warheads
U.S. ICBMs			
Minuteman 1A	10	1	10
Titan 1	54	1	54
Atlas F	24	1	24
Atlas D	24	1	24
Atlas E	27	1	27
ICBM Totals	139		139
U.S. SLBMs			
Polaris A2	64	1	64
Polaris A1	80	1	80
SLBM Totals	144		144
U.S. Bombers			
B-58	76	2	152
B-47 (y)	338	1	338
B-47 (x)	337	2	674
B-52 (y)	108	3	324
B-52 (x)	447	4	1,788
Bomber Total	1,306		3,276
U.S. Totals	1,589		3,559
Soviet ICBMs			
SS-7	40	1	40
SS-6	4	1	4
IRBM	16	1	16
MRBM	24	1	24
ICBM Totals	84		120
Soviet SLBMs			
SSN5	6	1	6
SSN4	66	1	66
SLBM Totals	72	72	
Soviet Bombers			
Bear-A	75	2	150
MYA-4	58	4	232
Bomber Totals	133		382
Soviet Totals	289		538

Sources: Raymond L. Garthoff, *Reflections on the Cuban Missile Crisis* (Washington, D.C.: Brookings Institution, 1989); Arnold L. Horelick and Myron Rush, *Strategic Power and Soviet Foreign Policy* (Chicago: University of Chicago Press, 1966).

Note: Totals include Soviet MRBM and IRBM scheduled for initial deployment in Cuba but not Soviet MRBM or IRBM deployed in the Soviet Union.

macy was understandably one of concern, even alarm.[20] U.S. intelligence had to have mapped correctly the locations of Soviet ICBMs (SS-6s) in order to determine with such precision that the nuclear strategic balance was so lopsidedly in the U.S. favor. Therefore, Soviet land-based missile forces might be vulnerable to a U.S. first strike. The meaning of U.S. nuclear superiority might not only be the existence of a U.S. relative advantage in nuclear striking power, but also the U.S. ability to jeopardize the survival of the Soviet deterrent. The Soviets were quick to respond to the Gilpatric speech. Two days later, Soviet Defense Minister Malinovskiy, addressing the Twenty-Second Party Congress in Moscow, charged that Gilpatric, with the concurrence of President Kennedy, was "brandishing the might of the United States" and had "threatened us with force."[21] Malinovskiy added that "this threat does not frighten us," but obviously it did.

Soviet leaders gave similar negative appraisals to statements on the subject of nuclear weapons and nuclear war made by U.S. leaders, including President Kennedy, subsequent to the Gilpatric speech. A spring 1962 interview with President Kennedy published in the *Saturday Evening Post* was interpreted in the Soviet press as an attempt to intimidate the Soviet leadership by threatening a U.S. nuclear first strike under some conditions.[22] Taking note of the assertively optimistic trends in U.S. official statements on the nuclear balance of power in July 1962, Khrushchev described the new U.S. appraisals as meaningless. He argued that the real military balance of power could only be determined in the course of a war.[23] This was obvious backing and filling. The general trend in Soviet statements about the strategic balance from mid-1961 was one of the acknowledgment and acceptance of parity as the basis for political relations between the two powers.[24]

Khrushchev's rocket rattling of the immediate post-Sputnik period had set the stage for his own humiliation when the facts were revealed about the true nature of the nuclear strategic balance in 1961. Khrushchev's strategy of nuclear bluff was annoying to the United States and helped to provoke a U.S. response that appeared to the Soviet Union as one based on nuclear bullying. The result of Soviet nuclear bluffing followed by U.S. nuclear bullying was that both sides moved further from a shared understanding of the security dilemma created by their military competition, and especially by their strategic forces.

Perspective taking might have suggested to the Americans in 1962 that the Soviets were less concerned with the "bean count" of United States compared to Soviet nuclear weapons and more concerned with the broader correlation of social and political forces. The role of nuclear weapons and other forces in Soviet military strategy had been to support Soviet policy, including the spread of revolutionary Marxism–

Leninism to states outside of the Soviet bloc (at least until Gorbachev). This could hardly be accomplished by nuclear adventurism against an opponent with superior forces, as Khrushchev was reminded by the Politburo when it decided it no longer required his services. Soviet political strategy is not always compatible with the most risky or assertive military strategy, as their willingness to adhere to the SALT I and SALT II agreements, including the ABM Treaty, attested.

Soviet perspective taking of the American standpoint might have helped to avoid the misjudgment that the United States would accept Soviet missile deployments in Cuba. Although we do not know as much as we would like to know about the Soviet interpretation of U.S. failure at the Bay of Pigs, it seems safe to infer that the episode could not have impressed them favorably with U.S. determination and sagacity. Khrushchev must have wondered why Kennedy authorized the expedition and then failed to rescue the situation when the chips were down. This was a reasonable doubt of Kennedy's resolve on Khrushchev's part: Many Americans doubted it too. Kennedy's reluctance to follow through in the Bay of Pigs might have seemed to Khrushchev a characteristic propensity for hesitation in crises, instead of a singular uncertainty on the part of a new president facing an unexpected debacle. Khrushchev also seems to have erred in assuming that Kennedy perceived only a domestic policy problem with regard to possible Soviet missile deployments in Cuba. Soviet assurances to U.S. officials in September 1962 suggested that no offensive missiles or other objectionable weapons would be deployed in Cuba that might complicate matters for the U.S. president during an election campaign.

President Kennedy and his advisors, in turn, were insufficiently sensitive to the problem of how the Soviets might (wrongfully) interpret U.S. domestic policy debates. Kennedy's reassurances to members of Congress that there were no "offensive" Soviet weapons in Cuba and that he would not accept the deployment of offensive weapons in the future drew a fine and legalistic line between offense and defense. Soviet leaders might well have interpreted this distinction as a loophole that could be exploited to justify the deployment of nuclear weapons in Cuba. After all, whether weapons are defined as offensive or defensive is an issue of purpose as much as an issue of technology. If from the Soviet perspective the purpose of the missile deployments was to contribute to the deterrence of an attack on Cuba or to the defense of Cuba if attacked, then the weapons could from that perspective be described as defensive.

Some U.S. students of the crisis have concluded that only the U.S. ultimatum and threat of an immediate air strike or invasion, conveyed to the Soviet government through Ambassador Dobrynin on October

27 by Robert Kennedy, forced Khrushchev to agree to remove the missiles. An equally plausible argument could be made that the game was up for Khrushchev once the United States obtained unambiguous photographic evidence of the Soviet deployments. From then on Khrushchev's agenda was to save as much political face as possible and to withdraw the missiles while precluding a U.S. attack on Cuba. Obviously, from the standpoint of sheer military power there was little the Soviet Union could do to prevent the United States from using its conventional force superiority to overthrow Castro. On the other hand, the United States was not eager to repeat the Bay of Pigs fiasco, so any U.S. invasion decision would have had to commit major forces against a significant Soviet and Cuban conventional defense.

Khrushchev's missile deployments almost gave the United States a rationale for a difficult and costly military undertaking that Kennedy would have been hard put to justify without the symbolism of Soviet nuclear power deployed in the Caribbean. Khrushchev turned a potentially dissuasive conventional force against all but massive invasion into a lightning rod that would justify exactly that kind of U.S. attack on Cuba.

DETERRENCE AND MILITARY PERSUASION IN CUBA

The significance of deterrence in the Cuban missile crisis and the U.S. ability to exploit deterrence to its advantage are markers for the presence of forms of military persuasion, in addition to coercive diplomacy. The United States was able to use deterrence to its advantage in Cuba once the Soviet missiles had been discovered and the U.S. president was determined to have them removed. Nuclear deterrence entered into the picture only as a backdrop to the successful application of conventional deterrence and a willingness to engage in crisis bargaining based on the appearance of reciprocal concession. The credible threat to destroy Soviet offensive missile emplacements in Cuba by air strike and land invasion, and the corollary threat to remove the Castro regime from power, could be accomplished with conventional forces alone. The burden of geographical war widening or nuclear escalation would be Khrushchev's, not Kennedy's.

The favorable outcome for U.S. crisis management should not obscure the fact that nuclear and conventional deterrence failed prior to the crisis. On the basis of what he must have known about the military balance in nuclear and conventional forces, Khrushchev took an extreme risk in placing Soviet missiles in Cuba. The explanation that he did so in order to adjust an unfavorable strategic balance is consistent with U.S. deterrence theory to a point, but at other points is not.

A strategic nuclear balance of power tilted seventeen to one in favor of the United States should have deterred Khrushchev from his Cuban initiative, according to both orthodox and heterodox schools of nuclear-deterrence strategy. The orthodox school argues that mutual vulnerability and second-strike capability are necessary and sufficient conditions for the preservation of deterrence stability. The heterodox school contends that mutual second-strike capability is not enough for credible deterrence when push comes to shove. The United States, in this second model of credible deterrence, also requires for crisis management a significant relative advantage in nuclear striking power or, in what amounts to the same thing, in capability for damage limitation.[25]

Neither the orthodox nor the heterodox models of deterrence would allow for the kind of challenge Khrushchev made in the face of over-whelming U.S. conventional and nuclear superiority. According to orthodox logic, the United States in 1962 possessed a second-strike capability against the Soviet Union; the Soviet Union did not have a similar capability against the United States. And the heterodox requirements for deterrence were also fulfilled: The United States had significant advantages in nuclear striking power and in the ability to impose a relatively favorable war outcome (if not an absolutely acceptable one). Making reasonable assumptions about the performance parameters of Soviet and U.S. weapons, the following list shows the plausible outcome of any nuclear exchange in the last days of the Cuban missile crisis:

Summary	Numbers
Total Soviet deliverable warheads	41
Total Soviet deliverable EMT	109
Deliverable Soviet reserve warheads	26
Deliverable Soviet reserve EMT	33
Total U.S. deliverable warheads	659
Total U.S. deliverable EMT	655
Deliverable U.S. reserve warheads	591
Deliverable U.S. reserve EMT	587
Ratio of deliverable U.S.–Soviet warheads	16.07
Ratio of deliverable U.S.–Soviet EMT	6.00
Ratio of U.S.–Soviet reserve warheads	22.7
Ratio of U.S.–Soviet reserve EMT	17.78

This list compares U.S. survivors of a Soviet first strike and Soviet survivors of a U.S. first strike. It is not therefore a classical "exchange model," but a statistical comparison derived from an exchange model (information about the exact model used is available from the author).

One can argue that Khrushchev was "irrational" according to the logic of U.S. deterrence theory, but the observation elides the central issue of whether deterrence logic has any explanatory power. Deterrence nomenclature is pervasive in the literature, but demonstrating the explanatory or predictive power of a deterrence model is something else. However, deterrence supported by the credible ability to prevail in battle at an acceptable cost to the threatener is another matter. The United States was in this position in Cuba, unless nuclear weapons were brought into the picture by the Soviet Union in the Caribbean or elsewhere. The United States had established conventional "escalation dominance" in that it could remove the missiles forcibly if it chose without nuclear escalation or geographical war widening. The burden of further escalation was placed upon Khrushchev, but no step that Khrushchev could have taken, subsequent to a U.S. invasion of Cuba, could have saved Soviet missile sites from destruction or, in all likelihood, the Castro regime from military defeat.

Khrushchev attempted to implement his own model of "extended deterrence," but it was more of a political than a military model. The ties between Cuba, as a standard bearer of socialist community buried within the U.S. sphere of influence, and its Soviet benefactor were not those of a military guarantee. Castro sought an explicit Soviet defense guarantee and wanted to go public with the news of Soviet missile deployments in Cuba, but the Soviet leadership demurred on both counts. Cuba was a prize worth keeping in the Soviet camp as long as the risks of doing so fell well short of actual military conflict with the United States. Khrushchev was not prepared to give Castro a blank check in the form of excessive leverage over Soviet decisions for war and peace in the Caribbean.

Evidence for this comes from Soviet behavior before and during the Cuban crisis, and some of the most interesting recent evidence appears in crisis correspondence between Khrushchev and Castro recently published in the December 2, 1990, issue of the Cuban journal *Granma*. In a message to Khrushchev on October 26, 1962 (two days before the crisis was resolved), Castro tells Khrushchev that "aggression is almost imminent within the next 24 or 72 hours" in the form of a U.S. air attack or invasion.[26] Castro then conveys his "personal opinion" that if "the imperialists invade Cuba with the goal of occupying it, the danger that that aggressive policy poses for humanity is so great that following that event *the Soviet Union must never allow the circumstances in which the imperialists could launch the first nuclear strike against it.*"[27] Castro added in this message that if the United States actually invaded Cuba, then "that would be the moment to *eliminate such danger forever* through an act of clear legitimate defense, however harsh and terrible the solution would be, for there is no other."[28]

Khrushchev's response to this request for a Soviet nuclear first strike on the United States following any U.S. invasion of Cuba (sent October 28, the day that the Soviet Union agreed to remove the missiles in return for a U.S. noninvasion of Cuba pledge) was to urge Castro "not to be carried away by sentiment and to show firmness."[29] Khrushchev argued in response to Castro that the Soviet Union had settled the issue in Castro's favor by obtaining a noninvasion pledge from the United States and by preventing war from breaking out. Khrushchev also offered the argument that Pentagon "militarists" were now trying to frustrate the agreement that he and Kennedy had reached. This was why, according to Khrushchev's response to Castro, the "provocative flights" of U.S. reconnaissance planes continued. Khrushchev scolded Castro for shooting down a U.S. reconnaissance plane October 27: "Yesterday you shot down one of these, while earlier you didn't shoot them down when they overflew your territory."[30] The Soviet leader implied that such trigger-happiness would play into the hands of those in U.S. government circles who wanted war: "The aggressors will take advantage of such a step for their own purposes."[31]

The United States, despite its apparent military superiority at the nuclear and conventional levels, was as ready to terminate the crisis without war as the Soviet Union. The U.S. objective was not to sever completely the "extended deterrence" connection between the Soviet Union and Cuba. U.S. crisis-management objectives did emphasize, nonetheless, two aspects of the U.S. view of the Soviet–Cuban connection. The first was that, from Washington's standpoint, the Cuban–Soviet relationship was perceived as one of client and patron, or dependency. This was emphasized in U.S. insistence upon dealing only with Khrushchev on the conditions for removing the Soviet missiles. Second, the United States and the Soviet Union resolved the crisis on terms that called for U.N. inspection and verification of the Soviet missile withdrawal. Fidel Castro objected on both counts. He disliked the willingness of Khrushchev to arrange for crisis termination without having consulted Cuba first, and Castro refused to cooperate in permitting U.N. or other on-site inspection of missile-launcher dismantling and removal. The United States and the Soviet Union worked around this obstacle by arranging for the removal and shipment of the missiles in such a way that the process could be verified by U.S. aircraft surveillance and by other means. Castro objected to the terms on which the crisis was ended on the grounds that they implied a relationship between Havana and Moscow of one-way dependency instead of two-way exchange.

COUNTERARGUMENTS

There are counterarguments to my contention that the results of the Cuban missile crisis of 1962 can be viewed as an escape from inadvertent mutual disaster and, at the same time, an instance of successful but risky military persuasion. I assume that Khrushchev's Cuba gambit was not based on the actual desire for a military showdown with the United States, but on the reasoning that the United States would choose political demarches instead of military threats to get the missiles out. My argument pushes the U.S.–Soviet nuclear-deterrence relationship into the crisis background and ignores the possibility that calculations about nuclear victory or defeat would have mattered to policy makers. The strongest argument in favor of the importance of extended nuclear deterrence in the Cuban missile crisis was the possibility of a trade of U.S. Jupiter missiles in Turkey for Soviet MRBMs in Cuba.

U.S. Jupiter intermediate-range ballistic missiles were deployed in Turkey and Italy during the Eisenhower administration. The decisions for U.S. IRBM deployment in Europe were taken in the aftermath of the Suez crisis of 1956, which shook allied NATO confidence in American guarantees of European security, and in the context of post-Sputnik American concerns about the viability of the U.S. nuclear deterrent.[32] Some arguments used by U.S. proponents of the Thor (in Great Britain) and Jupiter IRBMs were not too dissimilar from those used by the Soviets on behalf of MRBM deployments (and planned IRBM deployments) to Cuba in 1962. U.S. leaders feared after the initial test launches of Soviet ICBMs in 1957 that they needed an interim fix for a perceived status of missile inferiority (although not overall force inferiority, given the size of U.S. bomber forces in the latter 1950s). The Jupiter missiles deployed in Turkey were liquid fueled and used "soft" (above-ground) launchers, which made them vulnerable to first strikes or prompt retaliatory launches.

U.S. leaders saw the Jupiter missile deployments as a concession to the requirements for NATO alliance unity. The host European nation would "own" the missiles and launchers, but the United States would maintain control over warhead dispersal and launch decisions (presumably in consultation with the host state). For the Turkish government, this meant that they had accepted a share of the U.S. nuclear deterrent despite the obvious provocation this would provide for Moscow. The strategic rationale for the Thor and Jupiter deployments was vitiated by technology that made possible sea-based missile deployments and ICBMs based in North America that could cover the same target base in the Soviet Union or in Eastern Europe. The Kennedy administration recognized that the Jupiters in Turkey constituted a technological dinosaur and a potential political provocation. The president had decided in principle to order the removal of the Jupiter missiles from Turkey prior to the development of the 1962 Cuban crisis, but he had not pressed the issue assertively after initial approaches to Turkey were rebuffed by that government.

The Cuban missile crisis thus caught the Kennedy administration with obsolete nuclear missiles deployed in a forward, exposed position, obviously vulnerable to Soviet conventional as well as nuclear attacks. Moreover, Soviet attacks against U.S. missiles in Turkey in response to any U.S. attack on Cuba could draw the entire NATO alliance into a war with Moscow. Kennedy and McNamara, during deliberations of the ExComm, recognized the political irony that obsolete missiles deployed in Turkey were now potential hostages to Soviet horizontal and vertical escalation. In addition, McNamara was especially conscious of the danger of escalation once a U.S. and NATO ally was attacked in the aftermath of fighting in Cuba.

McGeorge Bundy, special assistant to President Kennedy for national security, and James G. Blight transcribed and edited tapes of the October 27, 1962, meetings of the ExComm, and portions of this material appeared in the winter 1987–1988 issue of the journal *International Security*.[33] In these transcripts President Kennedy continually returns to the theme that the Jupiter missiles offered Khrushchev an attractive way out of his predicament that Kennedy might not be able to refuse. Khrushchev's "second" letter of October 27 toughened the terms suggested in his "first" letter of October 26, wherein he agreed to remove Soviet offensive missiles from Cuba in return for a U.S. noninvasion pledge. The October 27 letter (which may have been composed and sent first for reasons still not fully known) insisted upon a trade of U.S. Jupiter missiles in Turkey for Soviet missiles in Cuba. Kennedy was bothered by the apparent symmetry of the trade in the eyes of world, allied NATO, and U.S. opinion.

The president's principal advisors, on the other hand, emphasized the potential damage to NATO solidarity, to U.S.–Turkish relations, and to future credibility of extended deterrence in Europe if the United States made an obvious missile trade under the pressure of the Cuban crisis. As the president kept returning to the apparent plausibility of a missile trade, his advisors sharpened their cautionary notes about the impact on NATO and future deterrence. One example is cited here, from ExComm discussions on how to respond to Khrushchev's two apparently contradictory letters:

Kennedy: How much negotiation have we had with the Turks?

Dean Rusk, Secretary of State: We haven't talked with the Turks. The Turks have talked with us—the Turks have talked with us in—uh—NATO.

Kennedy: Well, have we gone to the Turkish government before this came out this week? I've talked about it now for a week. Have we had any conversation in Turkey, with the Turks?

Rusk: . . . We've not actually talked to the Turks.

George W. Ball, Undersecretary of State: We did it on a basis where if we talked to the Turks, I mean this would be an extremely unsettling business.

Kennedy: Well, *this* is unsettling *now* George, because he's got us in a pretty good spot here, because most people will regard this not as an unreasonable proposal, I'll just tell you that. In fact, in many ways—

Bundy: But *what* most people, Mr. President?

Kennedy: I think you're going to find it very difficult to explain why we are going to take hostile military action in Cuba, against these sites—what we've been thinking about—the thing that he's saying is, "If you'll get yours out of Turkey, we'll get ours out of Cuba." I think we've got a very tough one here.[34]

Kennedy's advisors continue to express hostility to the idea of a missile trade throughout the remainder of this discussion. Rusk comments that "the Cuba thing is a Western Hemisphere problem, an intrusion into the Western Hemisphere." Nitze argues that the president should try to get the missiles out of Cuba "pursuant to the private negotiation" (the terms of the first Khrushchev letter). Bundy cautions that a missile trade, if accepted at this stage of the crisis, means that "our position would come apart very fast." Ball notes that if we talked to the Turks about an immediate missile deal, they would take it up with NATO and "our position would have been undermined." He adds that the United States "persuaded them [the Turks] that this *was* an essential requirement" and now Turkey feels that a matter of prestige is involved. Bundy argues that a missile trade would create the impression of trying to sell out U.S. allies for American interests, adding that "that would be the view in all of NATO."[35]

Despite this consensus of his advisors against the concept of a missile trade, Kennedy held open until the very end of the crisis this option. He approved a back-channel initiative from Dean Rusk to the U.N. secretary general that would have resulted in a "U.N." proposal for a missile trade as the basis for resolving the crisis. The Rusk initiative was developed as an option; the president had not made up his mind at the time whether he would accept a missile trade if Khrushchev refused to deal on the basis of the latter's first letter.[36]

The second counterargument to my assertion that nuclear deterrence remained secondary to conventional deterrence in the Cuban missile crisis is the importance of the perceived role of escalation in bringing the crisis to a conclusion. Pressure to end the crisis in a timely manner came not only from the possibility of a limited war in the Caribbean, but also from the possible expansion of the fighting into general U.S.–Soviet conflict. Absent nuclear weapons, the crisis may have been much more prolonged, and the terms on which it was resolved more ambiguous.

The counterargument that nuclear deterrence in addition to conventional deterrence made a difference in the Cuban missile crisis assumes a connection between nuclear weapons and nuclear deterrence that is not necessarily proved. Whereas conventional deterrence may have operated asymmetrically to support crisis management in favor of U.S. policy objectives, the impact of nuclear weapons on decision making may have been symmetrical. The Soviet and U.S. leaderships might equally have feared loss of control more than either feared a deliberate first strike by the opponent. Notice that this is different from conventional deterrence, in which leaders' hopes and fears are almost directly correlated with expected battlefield outcomes. Leaders planning a conventional war may still guess incorrectly, with disastrous results. Nevertheless, expected battlefield outcomes in conventional war can be projected with more reliability than they can for nuclear war scenarios, however subject to error the former are necessarily going to be. The disconnection between nuclear deterrence and military victory makes the effort to control crisis a military as much as a political objective.

Evidence for this counter-counterargument would be fears on the part of a side with a great deal of nuclear "superiority" in numbers of second-strike weapons that, despite this superiority, loss of control could result in nuclear war with unacceptable outcomes for the superior power. Members of the U.S. ExComm decision-making group, including the president and his leading cabinet officers, do show this perceptual inclination to fear loss of control leading to nuclear escalation despite apparent U.S. strategic nuclear superiority. Secretary of Defense Robert McNamara, estimating the U.S. numerical advantage in strategic nuclear weapons at seventeen to one in October 1962, nevertheless doubted that this relatively advantageous position was meaningfully related to the attainment of U.S. crisis-management objectives without war. In his interview with James G. Blight in May 1987, McNamara explained his reasoning in terms that indicate the irrelevance of relative advantage for a cost–benefit calculus in which unknown risks of absolute destruction are involved:

Look, in my judgment, in fundamental terms, the so-called strategic balance hasn't shifted since 1962. The significant question isn't: How many weapons did we have then and now, relative to the Soviets? The question you should ask is: What did each side have in its arsenal then and now that was, or is, militarily useful? Let me put it another way: What is the likelihood then and now that either side might initiate the use of nuclear weapons and come away with a net gain? The answer to both questions is: Zero! Then and now, for both the United States and the Soviet Union, there are no militarily useful nuclear weapons in their arsenals and thus there is no advantage in using them.[37]

Others on the ExComm did not agree with McNamara's pessimism about the irrelevancy of the nuclear balance of power. C. Douglas Dillon, secretary of the treasury under Presidents Kennedy and Johnson and a member of the ExComm, shared the view of Paul Nitze and other "hawks" that U.S. nuclear superiority was decisive in forcing Khrushchev to back down. Dillon recalled in 1987 that as the crisis wore on he became progressively less worried, in contrast to other ExComm participants who became more nervous about possible war and nuclear escalation. Dillon noted that in the Treasury Department he had not been fully current for the last several years on the details of U.S. force structure. He added,

I was not, when I first heard about it, fully aware of the extent of the nuclear superiority that we had. And, when I became aware of that, then I changed my view entirely and, of course, I agree totally with Nitze and think the McNamara thesis that our nuclear superiority made little or no difference is dead wrong. Our nuclear preponderance was essential. That's what made the Russians back off, plus the fact of our total conventional superiority in the region.[38]

Dillon engages in transference here of the logics of nuclear deterrence and conventional dissuasion, and as the interview continues he advances two supporting points to explain why others, including McNamara, discounted U.S. nuclear superiority. First, the more experienced policy makers on the ExComm were hawkish, according to Dillon, because they had been through crisis-management and decision-making situations before. As he explained, "I think simple inexperience led to an inordinate fear of nuclear damage, the fear of what might happen. McNamara, in particular, felt that way, I guess, although I wasn't so conscious at the time that that was his reason."

One reason for the greater concern on the part of McNamara and other ExComm "doves" about the risks of escalation was undoubtedly the higher sensitivity of the Defense and State Departments to the implications for Europe and NATO of a failure in crisis containment. McNamara illustrates this sensitivity to the European implications of risk assessment when he pushes his ExComm colleagues on October 27 to consider the aftermath of a U.S. air strike and invasion of Cuba. McNamara persists in raising the troubling issue of what U.S. response will be if the Soviets strike at Jupiter missile bases in Turkey.[39] Most other ExComm members do not see the point, so McNamara drives home the danger of nuclear escalation by sketching a plausible scenario. The "minimum" military response by NATO to a Soviet attack on the Jupiter missiles in Turkey, according to McNamara, would involve conventional war in and near Turkey, including strikes by Turkish and U.S. aircraft against Soviet warships and/or naval bases in the Black Sea area. McNamara emphasizes that such exchanges would be "damned dangerous" and the implication of imminent escalation to nuclear war is obvious.[40] He then argues that the United States defuse the Turkish missiles before any invasion of Cuba (presumably making this public), so that the Turkish missiles are removed from their hostage status.

In making this argument about the risks of escalation in an alliance context, McNamara is not necessarily breaking faith with his earlier emphasis on the priority of shared nuclear risk and the irrelevance of putative nuclear superiority. But the acknowledgment of the hostage status of the Jupiters in Turkey and their potentially catalytic role in crisis or wartime escalation is an acknowledgment of the mistake made in deploying those missiles. They were deployed, among other reasons, in order to create deterrence "coupling" between theater forces and strategic nuclear forces. The assumption was that coupling would make extended deterrence more credible than it would otherwise be, by adding additional levels of U.S. force deployments in Europe between conventional war and all-out nuclear war. The same assumption helped to drive U.S. and allied NATO rationales for the decision taken in 1979 to deploy Pershing II and Gloms in Western Europe (begun in 1983, and disbanded as a result of the INF Treaty of December 1987).

As the Jupiter missiles in Turkey in 1962 became nuclear crisis-management hostages and potential catalysts of escalation, so too did the NATO "572" deployments become hostages that slowed the momentum of arms control and detente in Europe during the 1970s. The reason for the irrelevance of Jupiters in 1962, as for the Pershing II and Gloms in the 1980s, had little to do with their technical characteristics (such as the Jupiters' vulnerability and long launch preparation, or the Pershing's range). The political issue is that because nuclear dissuasion cannot be substituted for nuclear deterrence, "intermediate" nuclear weapons do not necessarily support the successful management of crisis and the control of escalation.

Instead, such weapons deployments can contribute to the deterioration of crisis and to the loss of control over escalation. They can do this, as the Jupiters did, by commingling horizontal escalation, or geographical war widening, with vertical escalation, the expansion of conventional into nuclear war. Khrushchev's attack on Jupiter missiles in Turkey would have been a "nuclear" war even if he had only used conventional weapons: Nuclear weapons would be destroyed in the attack, and perhaps fired back at the Soviet Union if its conventional first strike were unsuccessful (the same potential problem faced U.S. air-strike planners once Soviet MRBMs in Cuba were thought to be operational). This "vertical" expansion of the fighting could have been compounded in 1962 by "horizontal" extension of combat to Berlin or Turkey.

It might be contended that the issue of intermediate nuclear weapons deployed in Europe was actually irrelevant to the resolution of the Cuban missile crisis. One could take the strict position that the missiles in Turkey were not a clandestine U.S. deployment but a publicly acknowledged agreement under NATO auspices. The Turkish missiles were a red herring introduced into the Cuban missile crisis by Khrushchev in search of a face-saving exit.

This argument has some validity, but it misses the distinction between precision of policy objective (getting the missiles out of Cuba without introducing irrelevant issues) and the potential for U.S. nuclear weapons deployed abroad to contribute to inadvertent escalation. Kennedy was right to keep the policy focus on the removal of Soviet missiles from Cuba without a publicly acknowledged linkage to subsequent removal of Jupiter missiles from Turkey.[41] On the other hand, transcripts of ExComm deliberations and other evidence suggest that Kennedy also recognized that complications created for his management of the missile crisis by the presence of vulnerable, nuclear-capable missiles deployed so close to Soviet borders. Ironically, the Turkish missiles also served as part of Khrushchev's justification for deploying Soviet MRBMs and IRBMs to Cuba: He would pose to the Americans a threat similar in scope and in geographical proximity to that presented by U.S. IRBMs in Turkey and in other European countries.[42]

The irrelevance of Turkish missiles can be asserted only on the assumption that what mattered in the resolution of the Cuban missile crisis, and perhaps in the instigation of it also, was the strategic nuclear balance of power. Although some members of the ExComm do assert that this balance was of primary importance, other key policy makers, including the U.S. President and secretary of defense, did not assume so direct a connection between nuclear superiority and crisis-management prevalence. Resolution of the Cuban missile crisis in 1962 may suggest that nuclear deterrence is loosely coupled to crisis management, even in a two-sided U.S.–Soviet confrontation, and perhaps even less relevant in multisided crises among nuclear-armed states with less experience in conflict resolution and intracrisis communication.[43]

CONCLUSIONS

Military persuasion was used successfully by the United States to compel the Soviet Union to withdraw its offensive missiles from Cuba in October 1962. This simple statement conceals a great deal. Policy makers "living through" the crisis did not have the same sense of fatalistic success that some later historians or political scientists would. The United States had nuclear and conventional forces superior to those of the Soviets, and the Soviet missile challenge had taken place virtually under the nose of the Monroe Doctrine. The United States was defending a vital interest and the Soviets were not. Granted these asymmetries in capabilities and motivation, it should have been a cakewalk for President Kennedy to reverse Khrushchev's scheme. Nuclear saber rattling, according to deterrence logic favoring Kennedy, would have forestalled any escalation by Moscow in Berlin or Europe. Meanwhile, the United States could have isolated Castro and perhaps finished the Bay of Pigs, ensuring Kennedy's place in history and eventual reelection.

President Kennedy and his advisors did not see the Cuban missile crisis in these terms. Their intent was to achieve the objective of removal of the Soviet missiles from Cuba while controlling the risks attendant to that objective. Toward that end, they chose a form of military persuasion that involved a combination of bargaining and demonstrative military action. The strategy allowed for mutual perspective taking on the part of Kennedy and Khrushchev with regard to each other's motives for settlement and fears of escalation. U.S. military persuasion allowed Khrushchev a face-saving retreat from a course that could only have moved events forward in unpredictable and dangerous ways. The danger was that compellence in the form of a naval blockade against further missile shipments to Cuba would not suffice to cause removal of missiles already deployed there. In the end, threats of escalation with a definite time limit attached were necessary, and fruitful.

NOTES

1. Alexander L. George, "The Cuban Missile Crisis, 1962," in *The Limits of Coercive Diplomacy: Laos, Cuba, Vietnam,* ed. Alexander L. George, David K. Hall, and William E. Simons (Boston: Little, Brown, 1971), 86–143.

2. Coercive diplomacy, according to George, is a defensive strategy that is used to deal with the efforts of an adversary to change the status quo in its favor. The objectives of coercive diplomacy, according to his reformulation of the discussion in 1994, can include persuading an opponent to stop short of its goal, convincing the opponent to undo an action already taken, or persuading the opponent to make changes in its government or regime that will bring about the desired policy change. See Alexander L. George, "Coercive Diplomacy: Definition and Characteristics," in *The Limits of Coercive Diplomacy*, 2d ed., ed. Alexander L. George and William E. Simons (Boulder, Colo.: Westview Press, 1994), 8–9; Alexander L. George, "The Cuban Missile Crisis: Peaceful Resolution Through Coercive Diplomacy," in ibid., 111–132.

3. Khrushchev, quoted in Graham T. Allison, *Essence of Decision: Explaining the Cuban Missile Crisis* (Boston: Little, Brown, 1971), 64–65.

4. See the comments of Dean Rusk on this point in Blight and Welch, *On the Brink*, 174–175.

5. Raymond L. Garthoff, *Reflections on the Cuban Missile Crisis* (Washington, D.C.: Brookings Institution, 1989), 73–74.

6. George, "The Cuban Missile Crisis, 1962," 133.

7. Ibid., 133–134. See also George, "The Cuban Missile Crisis: Peaceful Resolution Through Coercive Diplomacy," 115. As George notes, "The practice of deliberately slowing up and spacing out military actions, which crisis management requires, may be difficult to reconcile with the need to generate the sense of urgency for compliance." George, "The Cuban Missile Crisis, 1962," 134. For further background on this and other crisis-management issues, see Ole R. Holsti, "Crisis Decision Making," in *Behavior, Society and Nuclear War*, vol. 1, ed. Philip E. Tetlock, J. L. Husbands, Robert Jervis, Paul C. Stern, and Charles Tilly (New York: Oxford University Press, 1989), 8–84; Phil Williams, *Crisis Management* (New York: John Wiley and Sons, 1976). Pertinent to the Cuban missile crisis is the discussion in Albert Wohlstetter and Roberta Wohlstetter, "Controlling the Risks in Cuba," in *The Use of Force*, ed. Robert J. Art and Kenneth N. Waltz (Boston: Little, Brown, 1971), 234–273.

8. M. A. Neale and M. H. Bazerman, "The Role of Perspective-Taking in Negotiating under Different Forms of Arbitration," *Industrial and Labor Relations Review* 36 (1983): 378–388, cited in Daniel Druckman and P. Terrence Hopman, "Behavioral Aspects of Negotiations on Mutual Security," in Tetlock, *Behavior, Society and Nuclear War*, 116.

9. Ibid.

10. The various editions of the Pentagon's *Soviet Military Power* during the Reagan years provide ample evidence for my point here. For an overview of this issue, see Robert L. Arnett, "Soviet Attitudes towards Nuclear War: Do They Really Think They Can Win?" *Journal of Strategic Studies* 2 (September 1979): 172–191.

11. For evidence, see President's Commission on Strategic Forces (Scowcroft Commission), *Report* (Washington, D.C.: The White House, 1983).

12. John Lewis Gaddis, *We Now Know: Rethinking Cold War History* (Oxford: Clarendon Press, 1997), 222–223, 235–236, on Khrushchev's strategy for exploiting fictive nuclear superiority.

13. *Pravda*, January 15, 1961.

14. Nikolai Talenskiy, *Kommunist* 7 (1960): 31–41, said that it was necessary to "emphasize that a future war, if the aggressors succeeded in unleashing it, will lead to such an increase in human losses on both sides that its consequences for mankind might be catastrophic." In his *International Affairs* article Talenskiy drew an explicit comparison between the destruction of Soviet cities at the hands of Nazi Germany and the destruction attendant to nuclear rocket war, arguing that the degree of destruction in nuclear war would be "magnified a thousand times" compared to World War II and extended over whole continents. Nikolai Talenskiy, *Mezhdunarodnaya zhizn'* 10 (1960): 33. Both cited in Arnold L. Horelick and Myron Rush, *Strategic Power and Soviet Foreign Policy* (Chicago: University of Chicago Press, 1966), 78–79.

15. Horelick and Rush, *Strategic Power and Soviet Foreign Policy*, 78–79.

16. Ibid., 80.

17. Ibid.

18. Ibid., 83.

19. Ibid., 84.

20. Lebow and Stein, *We All Lost the Cold War* (Princeton, N.J.: Princeton University Press, 1994), ch. 2.

21. Horelick and Rush, *Strategic Power and Soviet Foreign Policy*, 85.

22. Ibid., 86–87. Kennedy had actually said that he would not rule out the possibility of a U.S. first strike under some conditions, which was consistent with previous U.S. policy guidance for nuclear weapons employment in the Eisenhower administration.

23. *Pravda*, July 11, 1962, cited in ibid., 87.

24. Horelick and Rush, *Strategic Power and Soviet Foreign Policy*, 87.

25. I have admittedly collapsed a wide spectrum of opinion into two boxes here. For more complete discussion, see Robert Jervis, *The Meaning of the Nuclear Revolution* (Ithaca, N.Y.: Cornell University Press, 1989); Colin S. Gray, *Nuclear Strategy and National Style* (Lanham, Md.: Hamilton Press, 1986); David W. Tarr, *Nuclear Deterrence and International Security: Alternative Nuclear Regimes* (White Plains, N.Y.: Longman, 1991).

26. "Letter from Castro to Khrushchev, October 26, 1962," *Granma*, December 2, 1990, p. 3. I am grateful to Ned Lebow for first calling this to my attention.

27. Ibid. (italics added).

28. Ibid. (italics added).

29. "Letter from Khrushchev to Castro, October 28, 1962," *Granma*, December 2, 1990, 3.

30. Ibid.

31. Ibid.

32. David N. Schwartz, *NATO's Nuclear Dilemmas* (Washington, D.C.: Brookings Institution, 1983), ch. 4, especially pp. 62–66, 73–74. The Gaither Report had also advocated overseas U.S. IRBM deployments even before Sputnik. Ibid., 65. U.S. Jupiter missiles were formally handed over to the Turks on October 22, the day of President Kennedy's televised address announcing U.S. discovery of the Soviet missiles in Cuba and the decision to impose the quarantine in response. Blight and Welch, *On the Brink*, 172.

33. McGeorge Bundy, transcriber, and James G. Blight, ed., "October 27, 1962: Transcripts of the Meetings of the ExComm," *International Security* 3 (Winter 1987–1988): 30–92.

34. Ibid., 36–37.

35. Ibid., 38–39.

36. Blight and Welch, *On the Brink*, 170–171, 173.

37. Ibid., 187.

38. Ibid., 153.

39. Bundy and Blight, "October 27, 1962," 72ff.

40. Ibid., 75.

41. Numerous arguments to this effect by members of the ExComm appear in ibid.

42. In his memoirs, Khrushchev noted, "In addition to protecting Cuba, our missiles would have equalized what the West likes to call 'the balance of power.' The Americans had surrounded our country with military bases and

threatened us with nuclear weapons, and now they would learn just what it feels like to have enemy missiles pointing at you; we'd be doing nothing more than giving them a little of their own medicine." Strobe Talbott, ed. and trans., *Khrushchev Remembers* (Boston: Little, Brown, 1970), 494. A summary of ExComm deliberations on Khrushchev's possible motives for the deployment appears in Roger Hilsman, *The Cuban Missile Crisis: The Struggle Over Policy* (Westport, Conn.: Praeger, 1996), 79–81.

43. It will be important for U.S. and Soviet scholars to work together in order to establish more confidence in such arguments, admittedly tentative. Some Soviet scholars are now applying modelling and simulation techniques to the analysis of the Cuban missile crisis. See, for example, V. P. Akimov, V. B. Lukov, P. B. Parshin, and V. M. Sergeyev, "Karibskiy krizis: opyt modelirovaniya" [The Caribbean Crisis: Experience of Modelling], *SShA: politika, ekonomika, ideologiya* 5 (1989): 36–49.

5

Military Persuasion and Desert Storm

Military persuasion is a product of cultural and social forces as well as stemming from sources that are strictly political or military. The United States has a less than enviable track record of deterrence and intelligence failure in dealing with non-Western cultures: for example, Pearl Harbor; Chinese military intervention in the Korean War; the Arab–Israeli "October War" of 1973; the Iranian hostage crisis of 1979–1980; and, most dreadfully, the terrorist attacks on the World Trade Center and Pentagon on September 11, 2001. One would suppose, therefore, that conflicts in the Middle East or elsewhere in the Third World involving the United States and a non-Western opponent would be fertile ground for case study in the insufficiently adroit conduct of military persuasion.[1]

So it proved to be in the Persian Gulf, to an extent, in August 1990. Iraq's invasion of Kuwait came as a surprise to U.S. policy makers despite intelligence warnings and previous diplomatic coercion of Kuwait by Iraq. Iraqi leader Saddam Hussein proposed to play at military persuasion while the United States gathered allies and planned for a counteroffensive if necessary to expel Iraq from Kuwait. The United States had to conduct its military planning and its diplomacy with the option to counter Saddam Hussein's version of military persuasion: Sit on Kuwait and threaten to raise the ante if anyone dares to try to expel Iraqi military power from the desert sheikdom. U.S. leaders wanted Iraq out of Kuwait, but they also wanted to avoid a wider war in the Middle East that might turn into an Arab–Israeli war.

Saddam Hussein knew this, and so began some five months of diplomatic military persuasion between the Iraqi dictator and an increasingly determined Bush administration.

Not all aspects of the military persuasion that took place during the run-up to Operation Desert Storm can or should be revisited here. Our main object is to take the harder road: to show how military persuasion extended itself into actual U.S. and allied military planning and into the conduct of military operations. The point is important because the U.S. military went into the Gulf War with an "all or nothing" mindset established in reaction to its reading of the Vietnam experience.[2] Still, we argue that the United States successfully employed military persuasion in the Gulf War. Both political and military constraints on U.S. and allied strategy so dictated. Politically, President Bush and his military advisors recognized that the total destruction of Iraq's armed forces was neither attainable at an acceptable political cost nor desirable from the standpoint of U.S. postwar policy for the region.[3] In military terms, the U.S. air war involved a targeting strategy that rapidly eliminated much of Iraq's command and control and air power, setting the stage for the collapse of its armed forces in and near Kuwait without a protracted ground war.

MAKING THE TOUGH DECISIONS

Another "Korea"?

Iraqi armed forces invaded Kuwait in the early morning on August 2 without provocation and rapidly subdued resisting Kuwaiti defenders within several hours. Within a week Iraq had moved forward into Kuwait some 100,000 troops, armed with modern equipment including surface-to-surface missiles. Iraqi President Saddam Hussein announced that the government of Kuwait had been deposed and that a new regime would be installed more consistent with Hussein's definition of Islamic polity. The Emir of Kuwait and his retinue had fled ahead of Hussein's tanks.

With regard to the invasion of Kuwait in 1990, the United States was in a position somewhat similar to the situation faced by President Harry S. Truman and his advisors in June 1950, when North Korean forces crossed the 38th parallel and crashed into South Korea. Prior to the North Korean attack, various persons, including leading military experts and political figures at the time, were uncertain whether South Korea lay within the U.S. "defense perimeter."[4] Once the attack was actually under way, President Truman and his advisors quickly recognized its strategic importance: The loss of all of Korea to the North Korean regime would be a catastrophic setback for U.S. policy and an immediate strategic threat to America's principal ally in the Far East, Japan. As Robert Jervis has noted with regard to presidential perceptions of U.S. interests in Korea in 1950 and in the Gulf in 1990, "Events and decision makers' instinctive reactions often shape definitions of vital interests, rather than preexisting definitions shaping behavior."[5]

To say that the North Koreans and the Soviets were disappointed by the reaction of Harry Truman to the North Korean attack would be a considerable understatement. The North Korean and Soviet regimes had miscalculated badly. They had forgotten that great powers do not necessarily define all the interests for which they will fight ahead of time in peacetime. War, or the imminent prospect of it, makes calculations different.[6] The North Koreans and the Soviets were disappointed in a way that most students of American foreign policy find quite reassuring. Not all disappointments are of this sort. In 1956, after Egyptian President Gamal Abdel Nasser had nationalized the Suez Canal and the British, French, and Israelis had mounted an invasion to depose Nasser, the United States chose to define its strategic interest quite unexpectedly: with Nasser, and against its NATO and Israeli allies. The attack had to be called off, Nasser emerged from the crisis as a hero, and the advertisement of the limitations to French and British global reach, compared to that of America, was to have long-run effects that are still being felt in the region.

Saddam Hussein calculated, as Kim Il Sung had in 1950, that he could bring about a fait accompli in the form of a complete and total military conquest of Kuwait and the replacement of its regime by an Iraqi puppet. The essential political and military objectives would be accomplished while the United States, its NATO allies, and the other states in the Persian Gulf–Southwest Asia cauldron dithered about what to do. It was a reasonable supposition on the part of the Iraqi ruler. NATO allies of the United States were preoccupied with the winding down of the Cold War in Europe and with the changes going on in the Soviet Union. The Soviet Union, which had for many years built up the Iraqi armed forces through military aid, equipment, and training, would at worst, according to Hussein's reckoning, turn a deaf ear to the entreaties of the Americans or the United Nations.

The common perception that Hussein's reasoning was almost always flawed confuses what is known after the fact about Iraqi military losses with what Saddam could have estimated about the military capabilities and political will of his probable opponents.[7] One could argue that the invasion was a "reasonable" decision given Iraq's economic constraints, Kuwait's heedless twisting of Hussein's tail on oil prices, and confused U.S. signals with regard to American vital interests.[8] It was also the case that Hussein's decisions subsequent to the invasion were not consistently off the mark. His expectation was that the United

States would not be willing to wage war. If it were, it would not have much toleration for high casualties and protracted ground warfare. Therefore, his air forces could even lose and still leave him with an intact army capable of inflicting a political defeat on the United States and its allies by extracting unbearable domestic political costs for them. The chain of reasoning breaks down, as we now know, because the coalition's air campaign proved more destructive and more demoralizing to Iraqi ground forces than Saddam had expected.[9] Nevertheless, air power alone could not cause the departure of Iraqi forces from Kuwait: It required a ground offensive, the beginning of which caused the Iraqi leadership to recognize for the first time that its strategy had totally failed.

Even the United States had, within recent memory, shown more official and unofficial sympathy toward Iraq than Iran during the war those two states fought for most of the 1980s.[10] U.S. public diplomacy during the period of Iraq's military buildup and diplomatic posturing against Kuwait was not, in the event, very deterring.[11] In addition to the much disputed meeting between U.S. Ambassador April Glaspie and Saddam Hussein in late July 1990, higher officials also provided little reassurance that the United States would come to the defense of Kuwait if Kuwait were attacked by Iraq. For example, in Congressional testimony on July 31, 1990, before the House Foreign Affairs Committee, a U.S. Assistant Secretary of State declined to be pinned down on the issue:

Rep. Hamilton: (D. Ind.): What is precisely the nature of our commitment to supporting our friends in the Gulf? I read a statement—I guess an indirect quotation in the press that Secretary Cheney said that the United States' commitment was to come to Kuwaiti—to Kuwait's defense if it is attacked. . . . Perhaps you could clarify?

Mr. Kelly: I'm happy to . . . I'm not familiar with the quotation. . . . We have no defense treaty relationship with any Gulf country. That is clear. We support the security and independence of friendly states in the region. . . .

Rep. Hamilton: If there—if Iraq, for example, charged across the border into Kuwait . . . what would be our position with regard to the use of U.S. forces?

Mr. Kelly: That . . . is a hypothetical or contingency question, the kind of which I can't get into. Suffice it to say we would be extremely concerned, but I cannot get into the realm of "what if" answers.[12]

Undoubtedly, Saddam also believed that the Arab states of the Gulf, Southwest Asia, and North Africa would live up to their well-deserved reputations for finding excuses not to oppose his version of Arab imperialism. An additional factor in Hussein's optimism against any U.S.

military attack was his misperception of the influence of the Vietnam syndrome on the willingness of the United States to employ force under very different circumstances. Hussein's conjecture that any pre-war expectation of high casualties would deter an American military response confused U.S. domestic politics in a conflict of uncertain political purpose with politics in a war of undoubted vital interest.[13]

The Iraqi leadership's reading of U.S. intentions may not have been illogical from Iraq's perspective, but Iraq's fatal vision took mirror imaging too far and combined it with bad history.[14] Most astonishing to the Iraqis was the unequivocal U.S. reaction. President Bush laid down the general thrust of U.S. policy in his address to the nation of August 8. The U.S. president outlined four policy objectives that must be met in order to resolve the crisis on terms judged satisfactory to American interests. First, the United States insisted upon the "immediate, unconditional and complete withdrawal" of all Iraqi forces from Kuwait.[15] Second, the legitimate government of Kuwait had to be restored. Third, the stability and security of the Persian Gulf were defined explicitly by the president, as by more than one of his predecessors, as vital U.S. interests. Fourth, President Bush indicated that he would be concerned about the lives of American citizens living abroad, including those in Kuwait and Iraq.[16]

President Bush ordered an immediate embargo of all trade with Iraq and with allied cooperation froze all Iraqi and Kuwaiti financial assets in the United States and elsewhere. U.S. diplomacy sought to isolate Iraq as an aggressor state and to mobilize international opinion against it. Toward that end, U.S. leaders succeeded on August 6 in getting the U.N. Security Council to approve for the first time in twenty-three years mandatory sanctions under Chapter VII of the U.N. Charter. This gave international blessing to the U.S. effort to ostracize Iraq from other military, economic, and political support. Further to the discomfiture of Iraq, the Soviet Union under Gorbachev did not even make sympathetic noises in the direction of Baghdad. Instead, Gorbachev sided with Bush and with the United Nations in declaring the Iraqi aggression illegal, and in calling for a restoration of the status quo ante. This was the first post–Cold War crisis in which the superpowers acted in diplomatic concert, and it gave to the Americans virtual carte blanche for a military response of the most unambiguous sort.

The response was not long in coming. Bush immediately authorized the deployment of elements of the 82nd Airborne Division to Saudi Arabia; much more would follow. By the middle of September 1990, the United States had some 150,000 troops in the region, including air force and naval personnel. This expectation was realized along with the commitment of forces and support from a total of twenty-six countries, including forces from Egypt, Morocco, and Syria. Many more

U.S. forces were to follow in October and November, with increasing controversy over the political objectives motivating the deployments.

An Ounce of Prevention

The United States had first poured this sizable contingency force into the Gulf and its environs as an exercise in deterrence. The particular form of deterrence chosen was what Alexander George has termed coercive diplomacy: the combined use of arms and diplomacy in order to induce an opponent to behave in a preferred way, while remaining short of actual war.[17] The objective was not to get into a large and direct shooting war between the United States and Iraq, but to discourage further Iraqi aggression, primarily the threat of attack on Saudi Arabia. Because it partakes of military persuasion rather than war, coercive diplomacy is intellectually demanding on the resources of military planners and policy makers alike.

It is customary for analysts to define the problem of preventing Iraq's attack on Kuwait as one of deterrence and the subsequent mission of getting Iraq to withdraw from Kuwait as compellence. Deterrence aims at prevention, and compellence at the undoing of an action already taken or in progress.[18] One can overstate the difference between deterrence and compellence, implying that deterrence is always passive and compellence always active. This is far from the case. It is sometimes impossible to make a deterrent threat credible by words or military preparedness without an actual demonstration in battle. At this point, defense and deterrence may be commingled. One can respond to an attack with forcible defense per se, which is simply designed to defeat the attack and to destroy the attacking forces and eliminate their combat power. Or one can use defense as a way of making a statement relative to intrawar deterrence: Defense, once in progress, makes more apparent the willingness of the defender to pay actual costs in lives lost and resources expended in battle. What was previously a hypothetical possibility, that the defender would resist, is now a certainty.[19]

The idea of intrawar deterrence is not as self-contradictory as it might sound. The purpose of fighting can be twofold: to force the attacker to use up combat power and to send a message that there is a potentially higher risk in the continuation of combat for the attacker compared to the defender. The United Nations sought to send both messages during the Korean War. The North Koreans were put on notice that conventional defenses of the United States, South Koreans, and other allies would deny to North Korea an inexpensive victory or, once the fighting had stabilized in 1951, any victory at all. North Korea was also led to believe, as was China, that continued fighting might expand in ways that were not simple extensions of the ground and tactical air warfare previously fought to a standstill. The Eisenhower administration warned the Chinese and the North Koreans through intermediaries that the United States would not necessarily confine future fighting to the Korean peninsula unless more progress was made toward the conclusion of an armistice in 1953. The deterrent threat against additional North Korean or Chinese escalation was posed in part by the availability of American and other forces that were prepared to continue fighting, and in part by the possible expansion of the war into other theaters of operations and by the U.S. potential use of tactical nuclear weapons.[20]

President Bush and his advisors assumed that the ability to exclude Iraq from meaningful allied support was a necessary condition for the establishment of escalation dominance in the crisis. The United States moved rapidly and successfully on the diplomatic front to obtain military and other support from NATO allies, and troop commitments were obtained from Egypt, Syria, and Morocco for deployments in support of U.S. forces in Saudi Arabia. The Soviet Union was also engaged in support of the U.S. aim to reverse the results of the attack on Kuwait. The U.N. Security Council supported the embargo of trade with Iraq in goods other than foodstuffs and medicine. As the diplomatic noose closed in on Saddam as a result of effective U.S. international politicking and a globally shared dependency on oil, Iraq's options became more limited. Divested of support for its war effort by its former Soviet ally, Iraq in desperation turned to its former enemy, Iran. During September 1990 Saddam Hussein offered attractive terms to Iran for terminating their conflict, including the repatriation of Iranian prisoners of war. Further diplomatic isolation of Iraq was brought about by its own incompetence: Sacking of the French embassy in Kuwait resulted in a French decision in September to dispatch an additional 4,000 troops to the region.[21] France had previously declined to join in the active naval quarantine against Iraq on the grounds that doing so would make it a cobelligerent.

The diplomatic aspects of crisis management were supported by an extensive military buildup that would rise to some 430,000 U.S. forces in the Persian Gulf region by the end of January 1991. Having inserted the trip-wire force to establish U.S. commitment, the Bush administration then built it into a formidable air, ground, and sea-based force supported by allied deployments that were more than ceremonial. The commitment of other Arab forces to the defense of Saudi Arabia testified to the isolation Hussein's diplomacy had imposed on him. The difference between the U.S. ability to mobilize international support for its position and Iraq's inability to do so created military alternatives for the Americans and limited the military options available to Iraq. As the U.S. and allied military buildup proceeded, the window of opportunity for a blitzkrieg against Saudi Arabia of the kind Saddam had imposed on Kuwait rapidly closed.

Therefore, the United States had succeeded by mid-September 1990 in employing a variant of coercive diplomacy that prevented Iraq from accomplishing further aggressive aims in the region. This variant of coercive diplomacy is termed by Alexander George the "try and see" variation.[22] This is the more passive of the two basic forms of coercive diplomacy; the other form is an ultimatum with a time limit for compliance attached to it. The difference between the two variations can be illustrated by reference to the Cuban missile crisis of 1962. The try and see variation was the blockade imposed against further shipments of missiles into Cuba; the blockade could preclude additional shipments of medium- or intermediate-range ballistic missiles, but it could not by itself cause the Soviet Union to remove the missiles. Only the additional pressure of an ultimatum that the missiles had to be removed within twenty-four hours, with the warning that if the Soviets could not do so the United States would, finally forced Khrushchev's hand on October 28.[23]

After having deployed a blocking and deterring force into Saudi Arabia and the Gulf region, the United States was in a position analogous to that of President Kennedy after having imposed the quarantine against Soviet missile shipments into Cuba in October 1962. The United States had established a line Saddam could not cross without raising the risks of escalation, as Khrushchev could not have repeatedly violated the quarantine without risking at least conventional war between the superpowers. The analogy is one of approach to decision making, and of the character of the relationship between force and policy. Obviously the United States was in a superior military position relative to that of its antagonist, in 1962 as in 1990. The United States could have won a conventional war in the Caribbean in 1962; the Soviet Union would have been left with the option of nuclear escalation or conventional war in Europe with a very high probability of nuclear escalation. In similar fashion, the U.S. position of force superiority relative to that of Iraq was obviously a very important factor in calculations being made in Baghdad and in Washington. An all-out war in the Gulf would be costly, but the eventual expulsion of Iraq from Kuwait and the destruction of Hussein's regime seemed to be highly probable, if not inevitable, outcomes.

From Passive to Active Military Persuasion

The deterrent objectives of the U.S. deployments seemed easier to accomplish than the compellent ones, however. It did not suffice, according to U.S. policy, merely to deter Iraq from attack on Saudi Arabia.

U.S. political objectives, as previously noted, included the withdrawal of Iraqi forces from Kuwait and the restoration of the emirate government in power prior to the invasion. This compellent mission was more complicated than the deterrent one, in both political and military terms. Politically, the allies and U.N. support that the United States had signed onto the deterrent mission now complicated the planning for any use of military force for the purpose of compellence. The Soviet Union was not eager to go beyond its commitment to the slow squeeze on Iraq by blockade and embargo. Tightening of the blockade by the interdiction of air traffic to and from Iraq was proposed by nine European states for consideration by the U.N. Security Council on September 18. This in itself, a further refinement of the try and see variant of coercive diplomacy, would be complicated to administer, and posed the risk of inadvertently strafing or forcing down a civilian jetliner.

Compellence required the Iraqi leadership to reverse a course of action previously undertaken, as opposed to the simpler task of deterring further aggression perhaps being contemplated. An unprovoked attack on Iraq launched by U.S. forces without U.N. approval would not have broad international, allied NATO, or Gulf Cooperation Council support. The United States needed a compellent option that supported the diplomacy of slow squeeze and wasted away at the Iraqi military position. Instead, during September Iraq moved further toward the termination of its war with Iran, transferring its forces from that front into Kuwait. U.S. planners who had anticipated in August an Iraqi force in Kuwait of some 250,000 troops faced the prospect that by the end of December 1990 there might be as many as 600,000 Iraqi forces deployed in forward defensive positions or in operational reserves of high readiness stationed behind the covering forces. However inferior in professional competency to the crack U.S. divisions being deployed in Saudi Arabia when fighting on the offensive, the Iraqi forces in Kuwait presented a significant defensive capability against any ground invasion.

On November 8, 1990, President Bush announced a virtual doubling of the U.S. military deployments to the Gulf. This was taken by many in Congress and in the news media as a shift from a defensive to an offensive strategy. Leaders in Congress, although it had gone into recess following the election two days earlier, indicated their concern and demanded to know whether the Bush administration had abandoned the blockade for a course of action leading to war. The official Bush explanation was that the addition of some 200,000 combat forces to the estimated 230,000 U.S. forces already deployed in the Persian Gulf area did not constitute a transition from a defensive to an offensive military strategy. Instead, it amounted to a tightening of the screw, an increase in compellent pressure by a demonstrative show of force that might or might not be used. As explained by a U.S. "senior official" in early November 1990, "What we are trying to do is tell Saddam Hussein, 'Look, we are serious.'"[24] The administration was not yet prepared to issue an ultimatum demanding Hussein's withdrawal, although the ground was being prepared for that next step as the compellent pressure on Iraq was being tightened. U.S. Secretary of State James Baker sought and received the approval of the Soviet leadership for a conditional use of force if other options were to no avail. And U.S. officials worked with other U.N. delegations throughout November on candidate resolutions authorizing the use of force against Iraq; American diplomats worked against the deadline of the expiration of U.S. chairmanship of the U.N. Security Council on December 1.

The "senior official" cited earlier also noted, in contrast to some other Bush administration policy makers, that the new U.S. military deployments were not related to any assumed failure of economic sanctions. The official told reporters that it was too soon (early November) to draw any conclusion about how well sanctions might ultimately work.[25] The new deployments were designed to support the sanctions by conveying to Saddam a sense that his time for compliance was not unlimited: They represented an ultimatum of a sort, although with no specific time line for compliance.[26] This relatively passive form of compellence failed to move Iraq. In response, Saddam Hussein mobilized another 150,000 to 200,000 forces for deployment into or near Kuwait, raising his expected total to over 600,000 by January 1991. It therefore became clear to U.S officials that a stricter form of coercive diplomacy would be necessary, one of the more active forms of compellence.

In the last week of November 1990 the United States worked at a hectic pace to establish a consensus among the permanent members of the U.N. Security Council in favor of dropping the last shoe. On November 29 the Security Council voted twelve to two (one abstention) to authorize the use of force against Iraq if Iraq did not withdraw from Kuwait by January 15. During the forty-seven-day period between passage of the resolution authorizing members to use "all necessary means" to enforce U.N. resolutions on Kuwait, the Security Council announced a "pause of good will" and a concentration on diplomatic approaches to resolve the crisis.[27] This made little immediate impression on Iraq, which vowed defiance immediately prior to the expected Security Council resolution authorizing force if necessary.

U.S. officials indicated that they sought the time limit not as a guarantee that American and allied forces would take the offensive after that date, but as an open door through which subsequent attacks could be launched at any time. Although this seemed to give the United States the upper hand in the competition in coercive bargaining, the ultimatum variant of military persuasion was not without risk. An ultimatum gave Iraqi planners an outside date to use as a guideline for military preparedness. Possible first-strike moves by Iraq in the interim between the authorization of force after a deadline and the arrival of the deadline were not precluded. Iraq also had the option of coercive "reprisal" attacks in response to the U.N.–imposed deadline, attacks short of all-out war but stressing of the coalition supporting U.S. and U.N. objectives.

One obvious question to which the answer was not known at the time of the passage of the U.N. resolution authorizing force against Iraq was how the U.S. Congress would figure into the equation of U.S. compellence. A Congress strongly in support of the president would add to the credibility of compellent threats, but forcing Congress to stand up and be counted on this issue risked defeat for the administration, lacking a congressional majority. Both houses of Congress eventually voted to authorize U.S. use of force against Iraq in January, and, armed with these resolutions together with that of the United Nations, Bush was legally and politically protected against charges of "Presidential war."[28] In the weeks ahead this would prove to be a considerable asset for him with regard to the support of the international community, Congress, and the U.S. public.

By virtually doubling the size of the force deployed in the Persian Gulf immediately after the fall elections, Bush had circumvented a congressional and public debate over the shift from deterrence to compellence as the mission of U.S. forces. A force of roughly 200,000 could be maintained in Saudi Arabia almost indefinitely without significant strain on U.S. resources and patience: A force of 400,000 or more (ultimately more than 500,000 U.S. forces) was too large for such an extended, constabulary mission. Pressures would surely build within the armed forces and within the administration for a resolution of the crisis by war or by Iraq's voluntary withdrawal from Kuwait. While Bush administration officials publicly scorned the idea of "saving face" for Saddam and viewed his aggression against Kuwait as criminal and inadmissible, they understood that the avoidance of war would require some kind of bargaining over minor aspects of the crisis, if not major stakes. The other option was to fight, and the Bush military persuasion could threaten to fight with more credibility following the U.N. resolution of late November authorizing force if necessary.

However, once the guns speak, military persuasion is not silent. The United States would still be fighting for political objectives and holding together a diverse multinational coalition, including Arab states of heterogeneous ideological persuasion and regime character. The "economy of violence" Machiavelli recommended would call for a rapid and decisive campaign against Iraqi forces in Kuwait, but it was less clear how much further the United States and its allies ought to go. Military forces find targets of opportunity hard to resist, and plenty of hints emitted from high places in Washington to suggest to Saddam Hussein that his regime's days, and perhaps his own, were numbered should war begin.

TARGETING FOR MILITARY PERSUASION

The uppermost question in the minds of U.S. and allied planners with regard to planning for the outbreak of war should compellence fail was the decision whether Saddam Hussein should be permitted to survive in power. Wartime operations might give the coalition the opportunity to depose him, but not necessarily at an acceptable cost in battlefield casualties and allied disunity. Hussein's strategy for the conduct of war could be assumed to include a postwar world in which he maintained effective control over Iraq's armed forces and security services, allowing for his later return to the Middle East and Persian Gulf stage of prime-time players. If Bush objectives for going to war against Iraq included dethronement of Saddam and the breaking of his political and military power over Iraq, then U.S. and allied military operations fell short of the commitment necessary to attain those objectives.

Variations of the Instant Thunder air war plan, first developed in the Pentagon and modified in Riyadh, called for a variety of strikes against military and other targets and posited ambitious battle-damage objectives. The eighty-four targets are enumerated by target class in Table 5.1, together with expectations for target destruction conveyed in early Distant Thunder briefings.

The U.S. Joint Chiefs of Staff (JCS) had concluded that only the massive use of air power against a wide variety of targets could force Iraq out of Kuwait and bring the war to an acceptable conclusion.[29] Air Force planners interviewed academics, journalists, "ex-military types," and Iraqi defectors to determine "What is unique about Iraqi culture that they put a very high value on? What is it that psychologically would make an impact on the population and regime of Iraq?" Israeli sources allegedly advised that the best way to hurt Saddam Hussein was to target his family, his personal guard, and his mistress.[30] The expectation that the air war alone could either loosen Hussein's grip on Kuwait or cause the destruction and capitulation of Iraq's forces in the Kuwaiti Theater of Operations (KTO) was to be disappointed, despite one of history's most one-sided bombing campaigns over a period of thirty-nine days preceding the outbreak of a 100-hour ground war.

Planners frequently approach the problem of targeting as a question of the destruction of so many physical things: bridges, air defenses, depots, and so forth. This is a legitimate concern, but from the point of view of the relationship between force and policy not the most impor-

Table 5.1
Instant Thunder Air War Plan: Early Target Categories and Damage Expectancies

Category of Target	Number of Targets	Objectives
strategic air defense	10	destroyed
strategic chemical	8	long-term setback
national leadership	5	incapacitated
telecommunications	19	disrupt ordegrade
electricity	10	destroy 60 percent in Baghdad, 35 percent of the country
oil (internal consumption)	6	destruction of 70 percent
railroads	3	disrupt or degrade
airfields	7	disrupt or degrade
ports	1	disrupt
military production and storage depots*	15	disrupt ordegrade

Source: Adapted from Michael R. Gordon and General Bernard E. Trainor, *The Generals' War: The Inside Story of the Conflict in the Gulf* (Boston: Little, Brown, 1995), 86, 89.

*Presumably this includes known nuclear, biological, and chemical weapons production and storage facilities (NBC targets).

tant issue. Targeting can also be treated as the effort to disrupt or destroy the coherence of an enemy organization. The command system of an opponent is its "brain," without which the body is susceptible to paralysis or disintegration. Targeting the command and control system of an opponent, including the opponent's leadership, is thought by some analysts to be an economical approach to victory, compared to a prolonged war of attrition. The countercommand approach commends itself especially when political power and enemy leadership are concentrated in one or a few hands. Undoubtedly this was one reason why the headquarters of dictator Muammar Quaddafi were specifically targeted during the U.S. raids against Libya in 1986.

However, targeting for military persuasion, as opposed to targeting for destruction, is more complicated than the killing of one individual or the elimination of a few persons in a leadership group. Targeting for military persuasion is an influence process directed at a reactive military organization.[31] Military organizations react and adapt to changed conditions according to repertoires of procedures and professional expectations. The U.S. and Allied bombing offensives against Germany in World War II proved to be less effective than the most optimistic proponents of strategic air power had assumed on account of the ability of German civil and military organization to adjust previously established routines and priorities. As another example, the air-delivered knockout blows against the British Isles anticipated by prewar planners and futurists did not materialize, and those that did failed to coerce Britain into surrender in 1940.[32] In the latter case, misjudgment about Luftwaffe targeting priorities shifted the thrust of their attacks away from potentially crippling strikes against British airdromes to terror raids against cities. The age of information warfare equips commanders with more numerous and more diverse media of observation, communication, and assessment. This may increase or decrease their vulnerabilities, as C. Kenneth Allard has argued with unusual emphasis:

The command structure is the one part of a military organization that, more than any other, must function as a weapon of war. It must either be a lethal, predatory weapon, capable of preying upon and killing other command structures—or else it runs the risk of becoming a bizarre, expensive techno-gaggle more likely to generate friction than to reduce it.[33]

The relationship between the coercive and attritive uses of air power is therefore one of subtlety and reciprocity. The persuasive face of air power is linked to its decisive use in either of two ways against command and control or other targets sets. First, devastating attacks against a small but highly important target set may be indicated, especially if striking or destroying that target set might bring the entire system to a halt or render it confused and paralyzed. Second, prompt and massive strikes against a variety of military and economic assets must convince the enemy that further destruction is both possible and potentially ruinous to him. As Eliot A. Cohen has noted, "To use air power in penny packets is to disregard the importance of a menacing and even mysterious military reputation."[34] The two-faced potential of air power for military persuasion and for attrition may require a willingness on the part of policy makers for immediate and dramatic escalation now in order to quicken the decision in the enemy's capital to avoid further punishment and denial later.

The history of command and control systems shows that there is no one right way to organize a defense establishment or a fighting force. It follows that there is no all-purpose magician's trick that will destroy the cohesion of one.[35] Military persuasion cannot be based on optimistic assumptions about toppling the opponent's command system. In some cases the "system" will consist of one dominant leader and his or her immediate coterie of retainers. Destruction of this group of persons might change short-term war aims, but there is little historical evidence that the change would be for the better. Hawks are as likely as doves to emerge from the rubble when the top leadership group is eliminated by internal coup or external attack.[36] As Fred Charles Ikle noted in his definitive study of conflict termination, it is arguable whether those who favor continuation of fighting or those who are prepared to surrender an unfavorable position are truly "patriots" or "traitors." It frequently happens that a "peace of betrayal" can only be brought about by a military hero from an earlier era.[37]

The original Instant Thunder plan was modified considerably by Air Force planners in the "Black Hole" planning cell under the direction of Lieutenant General Charles Horner and Brigadier General "Buster" Glosson. The resulting plan retained from Instant Thunder the concept of working from the "inside out" in order to destroy or incapacitate highly valued target classes, but it rested on no single theory or approach to command and control disruption, and it called for attrition of Iraq capabilities in order to impair the Iraqi war machine and as a means of causing Iraq to rethink its continued occupation of Kuwait.

MILITARY PERSUASION IN BATTLE

On January 16, 1991, the United States and its allies launched a massive air campaign against Iraq. The objective of the campaign was to induce Iraqi compliance with the demands of President Bush and the United Nations for a prompt withdrawal of his forces from Kuwait. The U.S. and allied air campaign was unprecedented in its scope. More than 2,000 U.S. and other coalition aircraft flew as many as 3,000 sorties per day. The setting for the application of air power was ideal. Bombing targets were not obscured by jungle, woods, or other natural interference and camouflage. Iraq's air force was no match for the combined air power of the allies. As former U.S. Air Force Chief of Staff General Michael Dugan noted, "If there ever was a scenario where air power could be effective, this was it."[38]

From an operational standpoint, the U.S. air campaign against Iraq had a number of overlapping phases. The first phase involved attacks against Iraqi command and control targets; against nuclear, chemical, and biological warfare manufacturing facilities; and against other components of the Iraqi military infrastructure. In preparation for this, the suppression of Iraqi air defenses was emphasized in order to clear the skyways for the operation of coalition aircraft throughout Iraqi battle space. In the next phase an interdiction campaign was designed to isolate Saddam Hussein's crack Republican Guard and other forces from reinforcement and resupply of forward-deployed elements in the KTO. In the final phase air support would be provided to the ground forces of the coalition as they moved against the Iraqi forces remaining in Kuwait.[39]

The Iraqi air force, including its air defenses, was caught by surprise on January 16. This might seem monumentally absurd, since President Bush had received U.N. authorization to use force against Iraq as of January 16. The expectation that the United States would attack eventually did not transfer into an accurate prediction by Iraqi intelligence about the specific timing of the attack. In a classical case of "signals to noise" confusion, the flurry of last-minute diplomatic exchanges and proposals in search of a peaceful resolution to the Gulf crisis by various world leaders probably obscured from Iraq the resolution and immediate preparation for war of the U.S. and allied air forces. The initial attacks on January 16 were devastating, clobbering Iraqi air defenses and command and control targets with such effectiveness that the Iraqi air force was essentially out of the picture of air-superiority combat.

These initial successes in the strategic air war left the missions of interdiction and close air support for the ground phase of the war to be accomplished. The interdiction campaign against a "target-rich" environment included Iraq's entire military infrastructure, not omitting its stationary defensive forces in Kuwait and its mobile armored and mechanized forces in Kuwait and in Iraq. The objectives of the interdiction campaign were to weaken further the command and control of the Iraqi armed forces so that they would be forced to fight in disaggregated globules, to reduce the combat power of Hussein's crack Republican Guard forces so that they could not intervene decisively to rescue other Iraqi forces later cut off and destroyed in Kuwait, and to continue the destruction of other military and defense-related targets in order to increase the price that Iraq would have to pay to keep fighting.

The third point is most pertinent to the discussion here. The U.S. and allied air campaign was designed not only to destroy a complex of targets in Iraq for the purpose of denying those capabilities to Saddam Hussein, but also to punish the Iraqi leadership by influencing their expectation of further damage to come. The air campaign was as much a competition in military persuasion as it was a war of destruction. The hope in some compartments of the U.S. and allied governments was that the bombing campaign by itself might induce the Iraqis to withdraw from Kuwait without the necessity for a major ground offensive. It was also the case that a mainly coercive air campaign could not avoid inflicting significant numbers of enemy casualties and causing some unplanned collateral damage. As Eliot A. Cohen noted in his assessment of the U.S. and allied air war against Iraq, there is no getting round the point that force "works" by causing destruction or death or by presenting the enemy with the fear of destruction and death.[40] And making fear believable in the enemy's mind requires that you actually have both the capability and the will to carry out the necessary punishment and denial missions.

A distinction must be made between the operational–tactical and the strategic level of warfare, relative to the political objectives of President Bush and U.S. allies, in order to assess the limits of the coercive air war in the Gulf.[41] Even under the most optimistic assumptions about the effectiveness of air power, ground operations would be necessary in order to "mop up" those Iraqi forces remaining in Kuwait, unless Iraq chose to withdraw them voluntarily. Air power can neither hold ground nor forcibly disarm soldiers in their defensive redoubts. These limitations of air power are acknowledged, but incidental to the argument whether air power could accomplish the strategic objectives of the United States in Iraq by itself. The theory that it could rested on assumptions about the coercive effectiveness of air power in both punishment and denial roles.

Western strategists generally accept that the punishment capabilities of nuclear weapons are more meaningful for deterrence than their denial capabilities. Most U.S. strategists also generally assume that, for conventional forces, the reverse is true: Conventional denial capabilities are more important than conventional deterrence based on the threat of retaliatory punishment. Thus, it would be argued by many strategists that a coercive air campaign with conventional forces should be counterforce rather than countervalue. Its objective should be to destroy the instruments of military power of the opponent in order to induce the opponent to see the futility of further fighting.[42] In addition to avoiding gratuitous attacks on civilians, a counterforce-oriented campaign reduces the competency of the enemy force, thereby influencing the decision calculus of the enemy leadership against continued fighting.

Although these arguments are widely held in the U.S. defense community, they must be qualified in several ways. In conventional war the decision calculus of an opponent may not be amenable to influence based on subjective estimates of future losses until the point at which the back is broken of the opponent's entire war machine. Instead of gradually shifting his will to fight from the "yes" into the "no" column, air and other attacks may meet with stiff resistance until a "catastrophic fold" appears in the opponent's ability to fight back. Sudden collapse of an opponent's fighting power may shift his decision calculus overnight from extreme optimism to extreme pessimism. Hitler insisted that wonder weapons, including newer versions of V-2 rockets, would come to his rescue even as his leading generals saw their forces collapse on the Eastern and Western fronts. During the last months and weeks of war Hitler issued orders affecting imaginary or mostly destroyed forces. Only the virtual collapse of the city of Berlin on his head finally persuaded the Führer that all was lost.

A second qualification is that air power, especially in the massive doses administered by the allied coalition against Iraq in January and February 1991, is not a surgical instrument. The precision of bombing has improved dramatically since World War II, and even since Vietnam. Nonetheless, the colocation of civil and military installations and inevitable bombing errors ensure that massive numbers of sorties against "military" targets will also include significant amounts of "collateral damage." There is no such thing as a purely counterforce air war, except on a very small and therefore insignificant scale. This argument, if correct, implies that not only the denial aspects of counterforce campaigns but also the inadvertent punishment that inevitably accompanies them are important in inducing the opponent to "cooperate" by negotiating for war termination.

Third, military persuasion against an enemy government that is losing a military campaign is more likely to be successful if that government is divided into various factions. The "outs" can exploit the losses already sustained by the armed forces and by the civilian population to bring policy judgments to bear against the prior decisions of the "ins." If, on the other hand, the enemy leadership is united in its pursuit of war aims, or if dissenters lack powerful and influential voices compared to those in favor of continued war, the potential for military persuasion is diminished.[43] One of the factors that limited the effectiveness of U.S. air power in Vietnam was the lack of any "peace party" within the political leadership of North Vietnam. Although they emphasized tactical flexibility in their use of diplomacy and fighting tempo, North Vietnam's strategic compass never deviated from the objective of taking over South Vietnam. In similar fashion, Saddam Hussein brooked no opposition to his decisions, reducing the opportunity for any dissident faction to organize in favor of early war termination. In cases such as these the influence of air power may be as dependent upon the expectations of an undivided enemy leadership about future punishment, including their own survival, as it is dependent upon the diminished future competency of their armed forces. Conventional deterrence, unlike nuclear deterrence, depends upon punishment and denial capabilities based in the same military forces.

The U.S. air war against Iraq is but one case among many that demonstrates that the coercive and destructive aspects of the use of force cannot easily be separated in battle. Policy makers may adopt a try and see variant of military punishment just as they have adopted try and see variations of crisis diplomacy.[44] The Bush administration in the first stages of the crisis clearly preferred to induce Saddam Hussein to withdraw his forces from Kuwait voluntarily, just as President Kennedy preferred to induce Khrushchev to withdraw his missiles from Cuba voluntarily. Kennedy avoided actual war, and Bush did not, although the military balance in both cases favored the United States. Nevertheless, the initial phase of the U.S. war against Iraq was not just a campaign designed to bring about the destruction of Iraqi military capabilities. President Bush indicated repeatedly that the destruction would stop if Iraq withdrew from Kuwait and that the destruction would continue if Iraq did not withdraw. Given the U.S. declaratory objective of compelling Iraqi withdrawal from Kuwait and nothing more, the coalition air war against Iraq fit the paradigm of coercive bargaining.[45] The *Gulf War Air Power Survey* (GWAPS) summary of objectives and accomplishments in the air war against Iraq supports the preceding argument for the interdependency of coercive and attritional air warfare (Table 5.2).

Subsequent to the Gulf War of 1991, some expert analysis was deliberately cautious in attributing to air power the keys to strategic victory against Iraq. The authoritative *Gulf War Air Power Survey* noted that precision attacks against Iraqi leadership and command, control, and communications "clearly fell short of fulfilling the ambitious hope entertained by at least some airmen that bombing leadership and C3 targets might put enough pressure on the regime to bring about its overthrow."[46] The same study noted that "bombing alone therefore, failed to achieve the objective of eliminating the existing Iraqi nuclear weapons program" and that attacks on oil refineries and storage in Iraq "bore no significant results."[47] Coalition targeting of Iraqi nuclear assets fell short of expectations because prewar intelligence about Iraq's nuclear program was misleading. Figure 5.1 summarizes the locations of nuclear-weapons-program targets as revealed by post–Desert Storm U.N. inspectors.

Air Vice Marshal Tony Mason's centennial assessment of air power noted that "after 100 years there is still no incontrovertible evidence that strategic bombardment has been decisive in breaking the determina-

Table 5.2
Summary of Air Campaign against Selected Target Sets: Desert Storm

Target Sets	Intended Objectives or Effects	Actual Results
IADS (SAD) and Airfields	Early air superiority • suppress medium- and high-altitude air defenses throughout Iraq • contain or destroy Iraqi Air Force	IADS blinded and suppressed, or in some cases intimidated • low-altitude AAA, infrared surface to air missiles remained Iraqi Air Force bottled up on bases • possible two air-to-surface Iraqi sorties 375 of 594 HABs destroyed or damaged • Iraqi AF flees to Iran beginning January 25
Naval	Attain sea control • Permit naval operations in northern Persian Gulf	All Iraqi naval combatants neutralized or sunk • other vessels sunk Silkworm missiles remain active throughout war
Leadership and Telecommunications/C3	Disrupt government, destroy key government control facilities Isolate Iraqi leadership from forces in KTO and weaken leadership control over people	Some disruption, to uncertain degree • Saddam remains in power • no decapitation of politico-military high command Telecommunications reduced substantially • links to KTO are never completely cut • international communications cut
Electricity and Oil	Shut down national grid • minimize long-term damage to civilian economy Cut flow of fuel and lubricants to Iraqi forces • avoid lasting damage to oil production	Rapid shutdown of grid • electric grid down 55 percent by January 17, 88 percent by February 9 • lights out in Baghdad Some unintended damage to generators Refining capacity down 93 percent by day 34

Table 5.2 (*continued*)

Target Sets	Intended Objectives of Effects	Actual results
		Destruction of about 20 percent of the fuel and lubricants at refineries and major depots
		• 43 day war precluded long-term effects
NBC and SCUDs	Destroy chemical and biological weapons	Some chemical weapons destroyed
	• prevent use against coalition	• most survived
	• destroy production capability	• chemical use by Iraq deterred
	Destroy nuclear program	• no biological weapons found by UN
	Prevent or suppress use	Nuclear program "inconvenienced"
	• Destroy production and infrastructure	• most program elements survive
	• Keep Israel out of war	Firings somewhat suppressed, not salvos
		• SCUD operations pressured
		• aircraft destroy few (if any) MELs/TELs
Railroads and Bridges	Cut supply lines to KTO	All important bridges destroyed
	• prevent retreat of Iraqi forces	• many workarounds by Iraqis
		Short duration of war limits effects
Republican Guard and Other Ground Forces in KTO	Destroy the RG	RG immobilized
	Reduce combat effectiveness 50 percent (armor and artillery) by G-day (start of ground war)	—attrition by G-day is less than 50 percent
		—some RG units and 800 tanks escape
		Front-line forces are destroyed in place or waiting to surrender
		—attrition by G-day is greater than 50 percent
		—morale destroyed by air bombardment

Table 5.2 (*continued*)

Source: Thomas A. Keaney and Eliot A. Cohen, *Gulf War Air Power Survey* (Washington, D.C.: U.S. Government Printing Office, 1993), republished as Thomas A. Keaney and Eliot A. Cohen, *Revolution in Warfare? Air Power in the Persian Gulf* (Annapolis, Md.: Naval Institute Press, 1995), 102–103. Adapted by author.

IADS, Integrated Air Defense System; SAD, Strategic Air Defense; AAA, Antiaircraft Artillery; HABs, Hardened Air Bases; KTO, Kuwaiti Theater of Operations; MELs/TELs, mobile SCUDs; RG, Republican Guard; SAM, Surface-to-Air Missiles; IR, Infrared; Military support, breaching targets, and KTO SAMs are included within other categories.

tion of any opponent to carry on fighting."[48] The cautious appraisal of air power's centrality to victory in the Gulf or previously would no doubt be contested by air enthusiasts in and out of uniform. My concern is not to resolve that debate, but to call the reader's intention to the yardstick by which critics are evaluating the performance of air power in Desert Storm or elsewhere. The GWAPS notes that air power did not create enough pressure to induce regime overthrow; Mason suggests that strategic bombardment is not incontestably able to break wills.

Both statements are noteworthy for what they assume about the object of air power in the Gulf War: not only to destroy target sets in order to forcibly prevent Iraqi action, but also to induce Iraqi compliance with behavior desired by the coalition. The goalposts are rooted firmly in evaluative criteria related to military persuasion: Air power is judged for its effectiveness as a persuader, albeit a persuader by means of destruction. Indeed, one of the valuable lessons of Desert Storm is that the psychological use of air power against military and war-supporting infrastructure targets may be more dissuasive than the comprehensive attack on populations or other target sets envisioned by air power's founding fathers.[49] "Contextual" in this case does not, on the other hand, imply "limited" in the sense that operational and tactical decisions are muddled by policy ad-hocracy.[50]

One argument for the goodness of fit between the U.S. and allied air war against Iraq and a psychology-of-influence model was that the choice of continued suffering was left up to Saddam Hussein. Bush would have been under great pressure from the U.S. Congress and from members of the allied coalition, especially Arab members, if Saddam Hussein had taken up the challenge of conciliation and begun to remove his troops from Kuwait in January or early February 1991, even at a slow pace. Saddam would not play this diplomatic card until later, after coalition air attacks had caused significant if not decisive losses to his ground forces deployed in Kuwait and Iraq. Only the imminent expectation of total military defeat for his forces in Kuwait would change his deci-

Figure 5.1
The Nuclear Program as a Target System

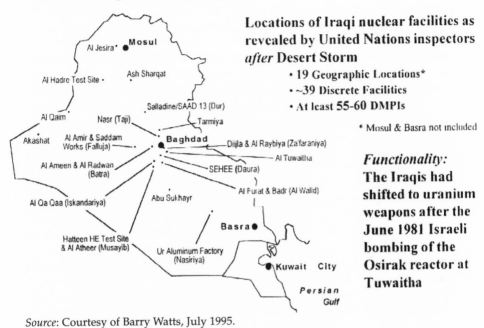

Locations of Iraqi nuclear facilities as revealed by United Nations inspectors *after* Desert Storm
• 19 Geographic Locations*
• ~39 Discrete Facilities
• At least 55-60 DMPIs

* Mosul & Basra not included

Functionality:
The Iraqis had shifted to uranium weapons after the June 1981 Israeli bombing of the Osirak reactor at Tuwaitha

Source: Courtesy of Barry Watts, July 1995.

sion calculus for or against continued war. This defeat might also be accompanied by the destruction of the remainder of his offensive military power, as he surely realized by the middle of February, and perhaps by his own political disestablishment.[51]

Hussein's "strategic" objectives once crisis management faded into combat were apparently threefold. First, he sought to create a war of attrition, including an extended phase of ground fighting, which would make the war unpopular with the U.S. public, Congress, and media. Extended ground fighting with high casualties would also alienate allied members from the U.S. coalition.[52] Hussein's second objective was to expand the war geographically (horizontal escalation) by bringing in Israel. This would also, in his view, divide some Arab members of the coalition from the United States. A third Iraqi objective became clear only in February, as Saddam entertained visits from Soviet officials offering to mediate the conflict. This objective was to hold the United States to its declaratory objective only, of expelling Iraqi forces from Kuwait, and to deter or otherwise prevent the expansion of U.S. and allied war aims to the destruction of all of Iraq's military power and the removal of Saddam as a player in the postwar world.

The problem for Iraq was that each of these objectives required that elements of military persuasion, of bargaining while fighting, had to be amalgamated with elements of traditional war fighting in order to succeed. But Iraq was unable to impose any unacceptable costs on the United States and its coalition partners. As the coalition proceeded to destroy Hussein's air and ground forces, his bargaining leverage for the postwar world diminished progressively. When the effectiveness of his armed forces reached the point of "catastrophic" failure, his future influence rested solely on his potential to prolong an already lost military campaign. Having missed the opportunity to negotiate for war termination while military persuasion was still open to Iraq, Saddam Hussein ensured that the final terms of armistice would be that much more unfavorable for his country.

CONCLUSION

The United States played military persuasion against Iraq in 1990 and 1991 at several levels. Iraq's coercive diplomacy against Kuwait assumed that the United States could be surprised by Iraq's invasion in August 1990. Iraq also assumed that the United States and its allies, having been surprised at least temporarily, would acquiesce in a fait accompli. The Bush administration responded with military persuasion in its tool kit at several levels. First, Bush mobilized an allied coalition that included major Arab powers, thus isolating Saddam Hussein from diplomatic support and denying his asserted symbolism as the embodiment of Islamic brotherhood and/or Arab nationalism. Second, the Bush administration backtracked the international coalition in support of containment against Iraq into U.S. domestic policy support: A favorable U.N. resolution to expel Iraq became a wedge that pried a slender but favorable majority from the U.S. Congress for the same mission.

In addition, and even more interesting, was the use of military persuasion by the United States and its allies in preparing for war and during the conduct of battle. Iraq's brain as much as its brawn was the target of selective yet brutal attacks. Crippling the brain and central nervous system of Iraq's military and intelligence set the stage for further destruction of its ground forces, logistics, and command and control by air power. Reeling in confusion, Iraq's ground forces began stumbling backward once the ground war commenced (but only then, an important point about coercion based on air war only in a major coalition war). Military persuasion also influenced the timing of Iraq's decision to quit Kuwait and agree to peace terms: It still had some limited bargaining power that was rapidly being wasted. Some of that residual bargaining power in the hands of Iraq was the result of inadvertent military persuasion: media coverage of the carnage over the "highway of death" as retreating Iraqi ground forces were pounded by unanswered U.S. air strikes.

The case of Desert Storm also gives some encouragement to more expansive thinking about the concept of military persuasion than hitherto. The concept of military persuasion owes a great deal to modern pioneers in thinking about the relationship between force and diplomacy or bargaining, especially to Alexander George and Thomas Schelling, whose works are frequently cited here.[53] But military persuasion is more than the psychology of bargaining or negotiating for advantage supported by the existence, threat, or use of force. Military persuasion is also about the symbolic uses of politics, including symbolic interactions among friendly and hostile actors.

One must enter this level of analysis to answer the otherwise unanswerable: Why did Saddam Hussein persevere in the face of long odds and a military losing hand? Part of the answer can be found in the staged symbolism, or role play within a play, that Hussein contrived for himself. He was Nebuchadnezzar in the process of recreating the Babylonian empire against enemies numerous and culturally disbarred from civilization. In turn, the United States was caught in its own post–Cold War role playing. President Bush was Franklin Roosevelt all over again, creating a "new world order" in the aftermath of a major military victory. And the U.S. military was also playing out a symbolic catharsis. It was paying itself back for having been denied its entitlement to victory in Vietnam. Finally, by putting the command centers in Baghdad in the bull's-eye, the U.S. leadership was making it personal with Saddam Hussein for having deceived President Bush and for having played bad faith with American policy after having received U.S. intelligence and other aid during Iraq's protracted war against Iran in the 1980s. Saddam Hussein learned nothing about George Bush from the experience of Manuel Noriega. Bush had no patience with leaders of regimes who turned against U.S. policy after having benefited from prior American support.

NOTES

I am grateful to Professor Don M. Snider, U.S. Military Academy, West Point, and to Dr. Paul K. Davis, RAND, for important insights pertinent to this study. Neither bears any responsibility for information or arguments made by the author.

1. It may be prudent for future policy makers to model more than one personality type for adversary leaders. See Paul K. Davis and John Arquilla, *Deterring or Coercing Opponents in Crisis: Lessons from the War with Saddam Hussein* (Santa Monica, Calif.: RAND, 1991), 14. Deterrence as practiced during the Cold War may not be very meaningful for post–Cold War rogue states

or terrorists, especially for those acquiring weapons of mass destruction. See Keith B. Payne, *Deterrence in the Second Nuclear Age* (Lexington: University Press of Kentucky, 1996), 56–58.

2. Powell's role in revising U.S. national military strategy during the Bush administration is described in Stephen J. Cimbala, "The Role of Military Advice: Civil–Military Relations and Bush Security Strategy," in *U.S. Civil–Military Relations: In Crisis or Transition?* ed. Don M. Snider and Miranda A. Carlton-Carew (Washington, D.C.: Center for Strategic and International Studies, 1995), 88–112.

3. According to one analysis of U.S. Gulf War aims, "Many of those who loudly applauded the Bush administration's inexorable march toward a military confrontation with Saddam Hussein later roundly condemned the White House for what they regarded as a premature cease-fire, and for Bush's failure to support post-cease-fire Kurdish and Shia uprisings against Baghdad and to use force again to compel Saddam's compliance with cease-fire terms." Jeffrey Record, *Hollow Victory: A Contrary View of the Gulf War* (Washington, D.C.: Brassey's, 1992), 52.

4. U.S. Secretary of State Dean Acheson is said to have raised doubts about the importance of Korea in a speech given in January 1950, in which he defined a number of U.S. vital interests in Asia, not mentioning Korea specifically. This was not, however, a formulation that excluded the possibility of a U.S. response to North Korean aggression, as North Korean Premier Kim Il Sung and Soviet General Secretary Joseph Stalin soon learned.

5. Robert Jervis, "What Do We Want to Deter and How Do We Deter It?" in *Turning Point: The Gulf War and U.S. Military Strategy*, ed. L. Benjamin Ederington and Michael J. Mazarr (Boulder, Colo.: Westview Press, 1994), 118.

6. Geoffrey Blainey, *The Causes of War*, 3d ed. (New York: Free Press, 1988), 146–156.

7. I am grateful to Paul Davis for emphasizing this point in a critique of an earlier draft of this chapter.

8. On Saddam's motives, see Richard Herrmann, "Coercive Diplomacy and the Crisis over Kuwait," in *The Limits of Coercive Diplomacy*, 2d ed., ed. Alexander L. George and William E. Simons (Boulder, Colo.: Westview Press, 1994), 234–235.

9. Michael R. Gordon and General Bernard R. Trainor, *The Generals' War: The Inside Story of the Conflict in the Gulf* (Boston: Little, Brown, 1995), 331.

10. Bruce W. Jentleson, *With Friends Like These: Reagan, Bush, and Saddam, 1982–1990* (New York: W. W. Norton, 1994).

11. Bernard E. Trainor, "War by Miscalculation," in *After the Storm: Lessons from the Gulf War*, ed. Joseph S. Nye, Jr. and Roger K. Smith (New York: Madison Books/Aspen Institute, 1992), 198, notes that the U.S. track record for deterrence over the preceding four decades was successful against the main threat of Soviet aggression but less successful against lesser threats, as a number of regional and local wars attest.

12. Testimony of John Kelly, Assistant Secretary of State, July 31, 1990, to U.S. Congress, House Foreign Affairs Committee, cited in Davis and Arquilla, *Deterring or Coercing Opponents in Crisis*, 67–68.

13. John Keegan, "The Ground War," in Ederington and Mazarr, *Turning Point*, 77.

14. The difference between "mirror imaging" and "perspective taking" should be noted here. Mirror imaging is a decision pathology in which the opponent's motives are assumed to be analogous to one's own. Perspective taking implies the awareness of the opponent's motives in his or her own terms, regardless whether they correspond to one's own assumptions and motives. Mirror imaging leads to closure and bias; perspective taking to openness and objectivity.

15. The White House, Office of the Press Secretary, *Address by the President to the Nation*, August 8, 1990.

16. Ibid.

17. Alexander L. George, "The Development of Doctrine and Strategy," in *The Limits of Coercive Diplomacy*, ed. Alexander L. George, David K. Hall, and William E. Simons (Boston: Little, Brown, 1971), 1–35.

18. Thomas C. Schelling, *Arms and Influence* (New Haven, Conn.: Yale University Press, 1966), 69–73.

19. Ibid., 78.

20. Richard K. Betts, *Nuclear Blackmail and Nuclear Balance* (Washington, D.C.: Brookings Institution, 1987), 31–47.

21. *Time*, September 24, 1990, pp. 31–35. This raised the total French forces committed to the immediate theater of operations to 7,800.

22. George, "The Development of Doctrine and Strategy."

23. This has become a somewhat contentious point among historians of the Cuban missile crisis, as to whether Robert Kennedy did or did not issue an ultimatum through Soviet ambassador Anatoly Dobrynin on October 27. In his report to the Supreme Soviet on the Cuban crisis, Soviet Premier Nikita S. Khrushchev noted, "We received information from Cuban comrades and from other sources on the morning of October 27th *directly stating* that this attack [a U.S. air strike and/or invasion of Cuba] would be carried out in the next two or three days. We interpreted these cables as an *extremely alarming warning signal*." Quoted in Graham T. Allison, *Essence of Decision: Explaining the Cuban Missile Crisis* (Boston: Little, Brown, 1971), 64–65.

24. Dan Balz and R. Jeffrey Smith, "Bush Ordered Escalation to Show Resolve, Aide Says," *Philadelphia Inquirer*, November 11, 1990, p. 16-A.

25. By Christmas, however, Vice President Dan Quayle was stating in public that sanctions had failed to dislodge Saddam from Kuwait. It now seems apparent that President Bush had determined to expel Iraq from Kuwait by means of force, if necessary, by mid-November at the latest. According to Jeffrey Record, in the fall of 1990 it was an open secret in Washington that "the Bush administration's worst nightmare was a voluntary Iraqi withdrawal from most or all of Kuwait, which would have effectively eliminated war as an administration option." Record, *Hollow Victory*, 40.

26. Ibid.

27. *New York Times*, November 30, 1990, p. A1.

28. However, the vote was very close, supporting the point made earlier that Saddam's apparent hardheadedness in not being compelled to withdraw from Kuwait voluntarily was not as irrational or unreasonable as some now depict it to have been. See Davis and Arquilla, *Deterring or Coercing Opponents in Crisis*, 54. The Senate vote to authorize force, for example, was fifty-two to forty-seven in favor.

29. Rick Atkinson, "Hussein, Baghdad Would Be Air Force's Top Targets," *Philadelphia Inquirer*, September 17, 1990, p. 10-A.

30. Ibid.

31. Paul Bracken, *The Command and Control of Nuclear Forces* (New Haven, Conn.: Yale University Press, 1983), 92–93.

32. See George H. Quester, *Deterrence before Hiroshima: The Airpower Background to Modern Strategy* (New York: John Wiley and Sons, 1966).

33. C. Kenneth Allard, "The Future of Command and Control: Toward a Paradigm of Information Warfare," in Ederington and Mazarr, *Turning Point*, 188. This passage has the virtue of benign overstatement, but of a nevertheless valid point. Command systems are not literally weapons of destruction, but a bad command system can be the medium for self-destruction through ossified command channels, poor situation awareness, confused intelligence assessment, and so on.

34. Eliot A. Cohen, "The Mystique of U.S. Airpower," in Ederington and Mazarr, *Turning Point*, 63.

35. A generalization aptly documented in Martin Van Creveld, *Command in War* (Cambridge: Harvard University Press, 1985).

36. Fred Charles Ikle, *Every War Must End* (New York: Columbia University Press, 1971), ch. 4, pp. 59–83.

37. Ibid., 66.

38. Michael Dugan, "The Air War," *U.S. News and World Report*, February 11, 1991, p. 26.

39. Gordon and Trainor, *The Generals' War*, 212; Dugan, "The Air War." Dugan's description of the phased air campaign notes that the phases are overlapping and not altogether sequential.

40. Cohen, "The Mystique of U.S. Airpower," 61.

41. For comparison, see the analysis of U.S. air power in Robert A. Pape, Jr., "Coercive Air Power in the Vietnam War," *International Security* 2 (Fall 1990): 103–146.

42. An argument to this effect appears in ibid.

43. Ikle, *Every War Must End*, ch. 4, pp. 60–83.

44. George, "The Development of Doctrine and Strategy."

45. The argument holds even if the actual Bush objectives were more ambitious, including the dethronement of Saddam Hussein. The large numbers of tactical sorties and the uncontested control of airspace over Iraq by the coalition can be read to suggest a massive, indiscriminate air war of attrition for the purpose of destroying Iraq's military capability. However, the United States, perhaps mistakenly, did not seek to disestablish the Iraqi regime by direct application of military force (hoping for Saddam's internal overthrow does not constitute a politicomilitary objective), nor was the destruction of Iraq's defensive capabilities intended. A smaller, user-friendly Iraq was the political postwar objective, not a power vacuum in the Middle East that Iran would exploit. The expectation that Saddam would be overthrown by his own praetorian guard overestimated his vulnerability to domestic pressure, but that U.S. and allied intelligence misestimate does not carry any weight in the argument as to whether the United States waged a limited or unlimited air and ground war.

46. Thomas A. Keaney and Eliot A. Cohen, *Gulf War Air Power Survey* (Washington, D.C.: U.S. Government Printing Office, 1993), 21, cited in Tony Mason, *Air Power: A Centennial Appraisal* (London: Brassey's, 1994), 301.

47. Keaney and Cohen, *Gulf War Air Power Survey*, 25, 21, cited in Mason, *Air Power: A Centennial Appraisal*, 301.

48. Mason, *Air Power; A Centennial Appraisal*, 272.

49. Robert A. Pape, Jr., "Military Persuasion and Military Strategy: Why Denial Works and Punishment Doesn't," *Journal of Strategic Studies* 4 (1992): 423–475.

50. This charge has been laid against the U.S. bombing campaign in Vietnam from 1965 to 1968 by military critics. See Mark Clodfelter, *The Limits of Air Power: The American Bombing of North Vietnam* (New York: Free Press, 1989), 77–88.

51. U.S. Secretary of State James A. Baker III outlined postwar U.S. objectives for the Gulf and Middle East regions in testimony before the U.S. Congress, House Foreign Affairs Committee on February 6, 1991. His statement hinted at a continued U.S. military presence in the region, and included among five major goals the economic reconstruction of Iraq. Baker was noncommittal on insisting that Saddam Hussein resign as a precondition for U.S. postwar aid. *New York Times*, February 7, 1991, p. A-17.

52. This objective was not as impractical is it now seems. According to one expert assessment, low U.S. and allied casualties in Desert Storm were the result of a fortuitous synergism between new technology and the imbalance in skills between Iraq and its opponents. In the absence of either Iraqi mistakes or new technology effective at proving ground levels, U.S. and friendly casualties "would likely have reached or exceeded prewar expectations." See Stephen Biddle, "Victory Misunderstood: What the Gulf War Tells Us about the Future of Conflict," *International Security* 2 (Fall 1996): 140.

53. I mean no exclusion of other important contributors to this genre, as notes throughout the text make clear.

6

Intelligence and Military Persuasion: The 1983 "War Scare"

Intelligence is about the collection of information, the analysis of that information, and the distribution of that information to customers or clients. This brief description is admittedly misleading. Intelligence, in the sense of foreign intelligence organs that serve a government or state, is not only a collection of boxes on an organization chart. Nor is intelligence reduced to the product collected, analyzed, and distributed by intelligence agencies and others, however interesting and intriguing it may be. Intelligence is, like Billy Joel's description of New York, a "state of mind." Intelligence is not only a competition between military threat assessors and case officers on two or more sides: It is also, and preeminently, a window on the soul of a country and society.

History permits us to open a window on the intelligence of a great power, the former Soviet Union, during a tense time in the Cold War. It was early in Ronald Reagan's first term, and the president's harsh anti-Soviet rhetoric coincided with a leadership-succession crisis in Moscow and a Soviet economy that even its leadership agreed was failing miserably. Had U.S. intelligence been able to see into the high circles of Soviet Communist Party leadership and intelligence services as well in 1983 as they later could do with the advantage of post-Soviet archives, the results would have surprised and stunned some American political leaders in 1983. Some very pessimistic intelligence estimates were provided to the top leaders in Moscow in 1983, based on what the Soviets saw as a pattern of U.S. hostility and attempted intimidation dating back at least to 1979. U.S. officials were unaware of this Soviet pessimism at the time, including some estimates of U.S. intent so dark as to anticipate an American nuclear surprise attack.

Were Soviet leaders really fearful of warlike American intentions in 1983, or is this "war scare" hypothesis a mere contrivance by historians? This study reviews some of the available evidence in support of the war scare thesis. In order to evaluate the war scare arguments, it is necessary but insufficient to consider the historical or anecdotal evidence. One must also ask what difference it would have made given the fact of mutual deterrence that existed between the two nuclear superpowers for the decades of the Cold War. Accordingly, we also consider quantitative evidence on nuclear force structure and operations pertinent to the political atmosphere between Washington and Moscow in 1983. Together the anecdotal and quantitative evidence shed light on why a crisis might have turned to war in 1983 despite the apparent irrationality of any such conflict by any policy standard.

OPERATION RYAN

In May 1981 Soviet KGB Chairman and future Communist Party Chairman Yuri Andropov addressed a KGB conference in Moscow. He told his startled listeners that the new American administration of President Ronald Reagan was actively preparing for nuclear war. The possibility of a nuclear first strike by the United States was a real one. Andropov announced that for the first time ever the KGB and GRU (main intelligence directorate of the Soviet armed forces general staff) were ordered to work together in a global intelligence operation named *Raketno-Yadernoye Napadeniye* (Nuclear Missile Attack).[1] During the next three years or so the Soviet intelligence services were tasked to collect a variety of indicators, including political, military, and economic information, suggestive of any U.S. and NATO intent to launch a nuclear first strike. RYAN was, according to some sources, the largest intelligence operation conducted in time of peace in Soviet history.[2] Collection of indicators continued well into 1984 and was contributory to partial Soviet leadership paranoia that outran even the normal suspicions of intelligence professionals in Moscow Center.

In an attachment to a Center directive to KGB residents in NATO capitals in February 1983 it was stated that the threat of an immediate nuclear attack has acquired "an especial degree of urgency."[3] KGB agents were tasked to detect and assess signs of preparation for RYAN in political, military, economic, and other sectors. The attachment noted that the United States maintained a large portion of its strategic retaliatory forces in a state of operational readiness. Soviet intelligence estimated that all American ICBMs, 70 percent of U.S. "naval nuclear facilities," and 30 percent of the American strategic bomber force were alerted and capable of rapid response. Thus, according to the instructions in the attachment it was imperative to detect U.S. or NATO decisions or preparations for war as far ahead of D-day as possible. The authors go into considerable detail summarizing U.S. and NATO systems for military alert, including the aspects related to nuclear weapons.[4] Information about the U.S. Single Integrated Operational Plan (SIOP) for nuclear war and about NATO's general defense and nuclear support plans was specifically emphasized in the tasking from Center to the various residencies. Uncovering of the process leading to a decision for war by the United States and its NATO allies, and of the related measures by those countries to prepare for war, was imperative: It would enable Soviet leaders "to increase the so-called period of anticipation essential for the Soviet Union to take retaliatory measures."[5]

What had brought the Soviet Union to this brink of pessimism and near fatalism about U.S. intentions and, in the case of Andropov, nearly apocalyptic doomsaying? A series of events treated in isolation by political actors at the time apparently combined, in unexpected and potentially dysfunctional ways, to produce a mentality among some members of the Soviet high command that shifted policy expectations in Moscow tectonically from 1979 through 1984. If so, the sequence of events and their impact on Soviet decision makers fulfill the law of unanticipated consequences that often appears in social and political decision making. This "law" is well known to social scientists and everyday practitioners of the arts of politics. It says that some of the effects of any decision or action will be unexpected and unpredicted, and that some of these unexpected and unpredicted effects may be contrary to the policy intent of the original decision makers. This problem of unanticipated consequences certainly applies to the possibility of a U.S.–Soviet crisis slide in 1983, since the last thing that either intended was an actual outbreak of war.

THE INF DECISION

In December 1979 NATO took a decision to modernize its intermediate nuclear missile force (INF) by deploying 572 new cruise and ballistic missiles in five European countries beginning in November 1983. This "dual track" decision also called for negotiations with the Soviet Union with the objective of limiting or eliminating its SS-20 intermediate-range mobile ballistic missiles, first deployed in 1977. The Soviets were strongly opposed to the NATO INF modernization: The connection between the Soviets' SS-20 deployments and NATO's theater nuclear force modernization was one of challenge and response from NATO's perspective, but not in the Soviet view.[6] Moscow mounted an aggressive active-measures campaign through a variety of European peace movements and in other ways in order to stop the scheduled NATO deployments. The Soviet campaign failed to divide the Western alliance or to dissuade it from beginning its deployments on the original timetable. U.S. ground-launched cruise missiles (GLCMs) first arrived in England in mid-November, and on November 23 Pershing II intermediate-range ballistic missiles were first deployed in West Germany.[7]

The Soviet military establishment was most concerned about the Pershings. Pershing IIs deployed in West Germany could be launched across trajectories that Soviet early warning installations were poorly equipped to detect in good time. In addition, a Soviet intelligence appreciation in February 1983 estimated that the Pershings could strike at long-range targets in the Soviet Union within four to six minutes. This compared very unfavorably with the twenty minutes or so that Moscow assumed it would have to detect and react to missiles fired from the continental United States.[8]

The Pershings reestablished for NATO a credible threat of escalation dominance below the threshold of general (global) nuclear war. Moscow could not initiate the use of theater nuclear weapons in Europe with any confidence that it could establish local or regional military superiority while American and Soviet strategic nuclear forces remained uninvolved and their respective homelands spared.

NATO and Soviet assessments of one another were complicated by the dual-purpose character of each side's modernized theater missiles. The missiles served to enhance deterrence, but they would also increase nuclear war-fighting capabilities if deterrence failed. The missile deployments were a competition in political intimidation as much as they were an enhancement of deployed and usable military power. The competition in political intimidation was also an issue of alliance unity and management for the United States. NATO's steadfastness or weakening in the face of Soviet threats and blandishments would signal diminished U.S. influence within the Western alliance and a collapse of alliance unity on nuclear force modernization. Moscow's defeat once NATO INF deployments began was an affirmation of NATO solidarity and renewed U.S. leadership competency in alliance nuclear affairs. These political effects meant more to beleaguered Soviet military planners and political leaders than NATO's commitment to deploy additional firepower in Europe.

STAR WARS

On March 23, 1983, President Ronald Reagan surprised many of his own advisors as well as American listeners with his proposal for the Strategic Defense Initiative (SDI), rapidly dubbed "Star Wars" by media pundits and critics. Reagan also surprised allied NATO and Soviet audiences. The president shared with the U.S. public his vision of a peace shield that would protect the U.S. homeland from nuclear attack, even a large-scale attack of the kind that the Soviets could mount in the early 1980s. The reaction in Moscow was predictably negative, but unpredictably hysterical.

The Soviet leadership might have denounced the U.S. initiative as a potential abrogation of the ABM Treaty and a complication of the U.S.–Soviet relationship of mutual deterrence, while at the same time pointing out that no feasible near-term technology could accomplish what the president demanded. Instead, the Kremlin reacted with public diplomacy filled with venomous denunciations of the Reagan administration and privately concluded that SDI was part of a U.S. plan to develop an effective nuclear war-fighting strategy. Even if SDI were not a feasible technology within the present century, making sure that the United States could not deploy enough missile defense to neutralize Moscow's deterrent might cost a strapped Soviet economy more than it could bear. As Robert M. Gates has noted,

SDI was a Soviet nightmare come to life. America's industrial base, coupled with American technology, wealth, and managerial skill, all mobilized to build a wholly new and different military capability that might negate the Soviet offensive buildup of a quarter century. A radical new departure by the United States that would require an expensive Soviet response at a time of deep economic crisis.[9]

SDI therefore presented to the Soviet leadership a two-sided threat of military obsolescence and economic stress. As in the case of INF, a Soviet propaganda campaign against SDI (in part by drawing upon well-informed U.S. critics who pointed to the gap between aspirations and available technology) failed to deter the Reagan administration from persisting in its research and development program on missile defense. This attempted great leap forward in defensive technology, combined with a U.S. strategic nuclear offensive force modernization and increased defense spending that began under President Carter and continued under Reagan, faced the Kremlin leadership with depressing possibilities far into Moscow nights. The Soviet economy would not permit matching of U.S. offensive and defensive force innovation and modernization. A future time of troubles might confront Soviet leaders by the end of the decade, faced with upgraded U.S. theater and intercontinental missile systems and early SDI technology for antimissile defenses. Even a first-generation SDI system might, according to Moscow pessimists, introduce enough uncertainty into the estimated effects of a Soviet second or retaliatory strike to weaken con-

fidence in mutual deterrence and in strategic stability. A group of Soviet scientists issued a statement in May 1983 opposing the U.S. antimissile system in language that also reflected the views of top Soviet
political and military leaders:

In reality, an attempt to create a so-called "defensive weapon" against the
nuclear strategic weapons of the other side, which the U.S. president has announced, would inevitably result in the emergence of another element strength-
ening the American "first strike" potential. . . . Such a "defensive weapon"
would leave no hope for a country subjected to massive surprise attack since
it (the weapon) is obviously not capable of protecting the vast majority of the
population. Antimissile weapons are best suited for use by the attacking side
to seek to lessen the power of the retaliatory strike.[10]

KAL 007

Another contributory factor to exacerbating U.S.–Soviet tensions in
1983 was the shootdown of Korean Air Lines flight 007 by Soviet air
defenses on September 1, 1983. U.S. intelligence monitored and re-
corded the transmissions between the pilot of the Soviet fighter–interceptor that shot down the plane and his ground controllers. American
policy makers, including President Reagan and Secretary of State
George Shultz, referred to the contents of these intercepts as proof that
the Soviet Union had deliberately and knowingly destroyed the civilian airliner in cold blood. U.N. Ambassador Jeane Kirkpatrick, playing selected excerpts from the pilot's transmissions for the benefit of
U.N. and American media audiences, claimed that the Soviets "decided to shoot down a civilian airliner, shot it down, murdering the
269 people on board, and then lied about it."[11] However, some U.S. Air
Force assessments of communications intelligence and other data available shortly after the shootdown disputed the claim that the Soviets
must have known that KAL 007 was a civilian plane. It was quite possible that Soviet air defenses had inadvertently confused the track of
KAL 007 with that of a U.S. Cobra Ball intelligence flight in the same
general area on the evening of August 31.[12]

Moscow's reaction was anger and disbelief in U.S. characterizations
of the Korean airliner's reason for straying over Russian territory dot-
ted with secret military installations and noted on international avia-
tion maps as a forbidden zone for civilian overflight. The Soviet
leadership charged that the airliner had been on a U.S. intelligence
mission. The CIA reported in the president's daily intelligence briefing on September 2 that throughout most of the time interval when
Soviet air defenses were attempting to track the "intruder" and deciding what to do about it they may have thought they were tracking a
U.S. RC-135 reconnaissance plane monitoring a Soviet ICBM test.[13] This

supposition was not an unlikely hypothesis given the well-known weaknesses of Soviet air defenses (painfully demonstrated several years later in the Gorbachev era when a German civilian flew a Cessna through Soviet air defenses and landed it in Red Square).

The Soviet leadership maintained the official position that KAL 007 was a deliberate intelligence provocation and that U.S. public denunciations of the Soviets for the shootdown were a deliberate escalation of East–West tension.[14] One consequence of KAL 007 was to add to the high priority already assigned to Operation RYAN. According to Christopher Andrew and Oleg Gordievsky, Party Chairman Andropov spent the last months of his life after the KAL 007 shootdown "as a morbidly suspicious invalid, brooding over the possible approach of a nuclear Armageddon."[15] After the collapse of the Soviet Union the Russian government made public transcripts of the September 2, 1983, Politburo meeting to discuss the incident. Those high officials in attendance, especially Defense Minister Dmitri Ustinov, believed that Soviet actions the previous day had been appropriate and resented U.S. depiction of their actions as barbaric. Although the actual impact of the shootdown on day-to-day U.S.–Soviet foreign relations was slight, the Soviet perception of anti-Soviet rhetoric in Washington, together with Soviet concerns about SDI and INF modernization, raised the level of Kremlin anxiety about American intentions in the autumn of 1983 to levels not seen for many years.

THE SEPTEMBER SATELLITE WARNING INCIDENT

On September 26, 1983, a false alarm occurred in a Soviet early-warning installation that could have, given the previously described mood of the Politburo in 1983 and the tense atmospherics of U.S.–Soviet political relations, become more than a footnote in history books. The incident took place in a closed military facility south of Moscow designed to monitor Soviet early-warning satellites over the United States. On September 26 at this installation, designated Serpukhov-15, a false alarm went off, signaling a U.S. missile attack.[16]

According to Stanislav Petrov, a lieutenant colonel who observed and participated in the incident, one of the Soviet satellites sent a signal to his command bunker in the warning facility that a missile had been launched from the United States and was headed for Russia. Soon the satellite was reporting that five Minuteman ICBMs had been launched. The warning system was white hot with indicators of war. However, Petrov decided that the satellite alert was a false alarm less than five minutes after the first erroneous reports came into his warning center. He based this decision partly on the fact that Soviet ground-based radar installations showed no confirming evidence of enemy

missiles headed for the Soviet Union. Petrov also recalled military briefings he had received stressing that any enemy attack on Russia would
involve many missiles instead of a few.[17]

Under the circumstances, Petrov's decision was a courageous one.
He was in a singular position of importance and vulnerability in the
command structure. He oversaw the staff at his installation that monitored satellite signals and he reported to superiors at warning-system
headquarters who, in turn, reported to the Soviet General Staff. The
immediate circumstances were especially stressful for him because
reported missile launches were coming in so quickly that General Staff
headquarters had received direct, automatic notification. At the time
the Soviet version of the U.S. "football," or nuclear suitcase linking
political leadership with nuclear commands, was still under development. This made prompt alert directly to the General Staff necessary.

Soviet investigators first praised and then tried to scapegoat Petrov
for the system failures. The false alarm was actually caused when the
satellite mistook the sun's reflection off the top of clouds for a missile
launch. The computer program designed to prevent such confusion
had to be rewritten.[18] The September warning incident took place weeks
after the KAL 007 shootdown and shortly before the start of a NATO
military exercise that may have been the single most dangerous incident contributing to the war-scare atmosphere in 1983. The September
satellite warning incident has another implication, carrying forward
into post–Cold War Russia. The Russian satellite and early-warning–
command and control network is undoubtedly less reliable now (in
2002) than it was in 1983 under more resourceful Soviet support.

ABLE ARCHER

According to several accounts the most dangerous single incident
in 1983 related to military stability between the superpowers was the
Soviet reaction to NATO command-post exercise Able Archer. The exercise took place from November 2 through 11 and was designed to
practice the alliance's procedures for nuclear release and alert. Unfortunately it took place within a context overshadowed by Soviet fears
of U.S. and NATO plans for initiating a war in Europe and/or a nuclear
war between the superpowers.[19]

As Able Archer got under way, Soviet and allied Warsaw Pact intelligence began routine monitoring of the exercise. NATO was, of course,
observing and reacting to the Soviet monitoring of Able Archer. Soon
the British and U.S. listening posts detected that "something was going badly wrong."[20] Intelligence traffic from the other side suggested
that the Soviets might be interpreting Able Archer not as an exercise
but as a real prelude to a decision for war. Soviet "paranoia" at Moscow Center during this time might have been fueled by the awareness

that Moscow's own contingency plans for surprise attack against NATO used training exercises to conceal an actual offensive.[21]

According to Christopher Andrew and Oleg Gordievsky, there were two aspects of Able Archer that caused particular concern in Moscow. First, message formats and procedures used in previous exercises were different from the ones being used now. Second, the command-post exercise simulated all phases of alert, from normal day-to-day readiness to general alert.[22] Thus, Able Archer seemed more realistic to Soviet monitors than earlier exercises had. In addition, thanks to Operation RYAN and the increasingly sensitive Soviet nose already out of joint and predisposed to find sinister meaning behind standard operating procedures, Able Archer rang unusual alarm bells in KGB and GRU intelligence channels. Thus, KGB reports at one point during the exercise led the Center to believe that there was a real alert of NATO forces in progress, not just a training exercise.

On November 6 Moscow Center sent the London KGB residency a checklist of indicators of Western preparations for nuclear surprise attack. The checklist included requirements to observe key officials who might be involved in negotiations with the United States preparatory to a surprise attack, important military installations, NATO and other government offices, and communication and intelligence centers. Several days later, KGB and GRU residencies in Western Europe received "flash" (priority) telegrams that reported a nonexistent alert at U.S. bases. The telegrams suggested two probable reasons for the "alert": concerns about U.S. military base security following a terrorist attack against a U.S. Marine barracks in Lebanon and U.S. army maneuvers planned for later in the year. But the telegrams also implied that there might be another reason for the putative U.S. "alert" at these bases: the beginning of plans for a nuclear surprise first strike.[23]

Soviet reactions to Able Archer apparently had gone beyond warnings and communications within intelligence bureaucracies. During the NATO exercise some important activity took place in Soviet and Warsaw Pact military forces. Elements of the air forces in the Group of Soviet Forces, Germany, and in Poland, including nuclear-capable aircraft, were placed on higher levels of alert on November 8–9.[24] Units of the Soviet Fourth Air Army went to increased levels of readiness and all of its combat flight operations from November 4 through 10 were suspended. Soviet reactions may have been excessive and driven by selective perception, but they were not posturing. According to 1983 Deputy Director of Intelligence Robert M. Gates, writing in reflection after the end of the Cold War,

After going through the experience at the time, then through the postmortems, and now through the documents, I don't think the Soviets were crying wolf. They may not have believed a NATO attack was imminent in November, 1983, but they did seem to believe that the situation was very dangerous. And U.S. intelligence had failed to grasp the true extent of their anxiety.[25]

EAST GERMAN INTELLIGENCE

The Soviets may not have been crying wolf, but they were crying Wolf. Even prior to Able Archer, the KGB enlisted allied intelligence services, especially the highly regarded East German foreign intelligence directorate (HVA) of Colonel–General Markus Wolf, in its Operation RYAN intelligence gathering and reporting. According to Ben B. Fischer of the CIA's history staff, Wolf created an entire early-warning system that included required reports keyed to a KGB catalogue of indicators of U.S. or NATO preparations for war, a large situation center for monitoring global military operations with a special link to the KGB headquarters, a HVA headquarters staff dedicated to RYAN, and special alert drills, annual exercises, and military training for HVA officers that simulated a surprise attack by NATO.[26]

Of special interest is that East German wariness about a possible nuclear attack continued after the war-scare atmosphere had apparently calmed down in Moscow. Acting in his capacity as head of foreign intelligence and deputy director of the East German Ministry for State Security, Wolf tasked the entire ministry in June 1985 to conduct an aggressive search for indicators of planning for a nuclear missile attack. His Implementation Regulation of June 5 directed that the operational and operational–technical service units of the ministry engage in "goal oriented operational penetration of enemy decision-making centers." Top priority, he stated in the same message, are "signs of imminent preparations of a strategic nuclear-missile attack (KWA)," as well as other imperialist state plans for military surprise.[27] In addition, the East German political leadership had built a large complex of bunkers (*Fuhrungskomplex*, or leadership complex) near Berlin designed to save the military, political, and intelligence elites from nuclear war.[28]

Markus Wolf was more skeptical than alarmists in Moscow about the urgency for RYAN, but he carried out orders to increase surveillance and collect indicators pertinent to a possible surprise attack for reasons of alliance solidarity, fraternal intelligence sharing, and bureaucratic self-protection. Although the foreign intelligence services of East Germany and the Soviet Union often cooperated for obvious reasons, their specific reactions to Cold War situations of threat were by no means always identical. Wolf's reputation as an intelligence icon (allegedly the model for John Le Carre's fictional spymaster Karla, although Le Carre denies it) and his tenacious competency at intelligence (respected by friends and enemies alike) made him the least likely intelligence officer in the entire Soviet Bloc to overreact to indicators of crisis or possible war. Wolf's reputation, to the contrary, was that of an intelligence supervisor who was careful, methodical, and politically astute in his judgments about allies and adversaries.[29] Wolf contends, in fact, that his service eventually provided a definitive estimate that no threat of war was imminent, based in part on NATO documents obtained by one of his agents who worked at the alliance's Brussels headquarters.[30] He was careful not to dispute any of Moscow Center's pessimistic assumptions about NATO intentions in real time, however.

THE SOVIET NUCLEAR DETERRENT

Nuclear forces have quantitative and qualitative attributes. Numbers of warheads and launchers matter, but so too do the operational characteristics of forces and the military–strategic assumptions on which they are deployed. By 1983 the Soviet Union had long since attained parity in numbers of deployed systems and the capability for assured retaliation after surviving a first strike. On the other hand, there were important qualitative differences between U.S. and Soviet force structures related to assumptions made by American and Soviet political and military leaderships about the requirements for deterrence and for war if necessary.

Speaking broadly, the Soviet view of deterrence was different from the American one, and involved some additional subtleties. Soviet military writers distinguished between deterrence as *sderzhivanie* (forestalling or avoiding) and deterrence as *ustrashenie* (intimidation).[31] Deterrence in the Soviet view was not a deterministic outcome of force balances. It was as dependent on political factors as on military factors.[32] Thus, military–strategic parity, or an essential equivalence in deployed force structures, was not in itself a sufficient condition for military stability. The imperialist camp led by the United States and NATO was a political threat by virtue of its existence and regardless of particular fluctuations in its patterns of military spending. Therefore, Soviet survival in the nuclear age could not be trusted to force balances alone. How the forces would operate in time of crisis or threat of war had to be taken into account.

This stance on the part of many Soviet military thinkers was quite logical from their perspective. One must remember that, notwithstanding their disclaimers about the historical inevitability of socialist victory, some Soviet leaders by the 1980s recognized that their economy had failed. As dedicated Marxists they knew what might follow from that: If the economy could not be saved, then neither could national defense and the communist grip on Soviet power. Somehow resources had to be freed up for economic growth and renewal, but this required a favorable threat assessment. This combination of a reduced threat assessment and economic restructuring was not attempted seriously by the Kremlin leadership until Gorbachev became Party chairman in 1985.

In the early 1980s the Soviet leadership was in a bind. The need for reduced defense expenditures and for economic restructuring was obvious, but the perceived threat from the West was not judged to have been diminished compared to previous decades: quite the contrary. The projected Carter defense buildup, followed by Reagan's even larger increases and hostile rhetoric, convinced the Soviet leadership that there were no immediate prospects for U.S.–Soviet detente. The explicitness of Carter military doctrine (PD-59) on the requirement for protracted nuclear war fighting (for deterrence) had resonated in Moscow in the same way as the INF deployment decision a year earlier had. For present purposes, the point is not whether any of these U.S. or NATO decisions was correct or incorrect in itself. It is the cumulative effect of these decisions as seen from Moscow and in the context of Soviet threat perception that is pertinent to our discussion.

Soviet force structure in 1983 also affected its view of the requirements of deterrence and of nuclear crisis management. The makeweight of Soviet strategic retaliatory forces was its ICBM force: In 1983 all of these were deployed in underground silos. In order to guarantee their survival against a U.S. first strike (which might, in the view of Soviet military planners, come as a "bolt from the blue" or from escalation after conventional war fighting in Europe), these land-based missiles would have to be launched before U.S. warheads exploded against their assigned targets.[33] This meant, in American military jargon, that Soviet ICBMs would have to be "launched on warning" (LOW)- or "launched under attack" (LUA)."[34] Only launch on warning could guarantee that sufficient numbers of Soviet ICBMs would survive a well-orchestrated U.S. first strike. Soviet leaders could not rely upon retaliation after ride out to do so. According to some expert analysts, the United States also did not plan to rely mainly on retaliation after ride out in order to fulfill the requirements of its retaliatory strike plans.[35]

According to Western experts, the Soviet armed forces were eventually tasked to prepare for a continuum of retaliatory options, from preemption to retaliation after ride out. However, leaders' decisions about a preferred option in actual crisis or wartime would have been constrained by capabilities available at the time. During the latter 1960s and early 1970s, improved capabilities for rapid launch and better warning, communication, and control systems made it possible for Soviet leaders to place more reliance upon launch on warning and to be less dependent on preemption.[36] The option of preemption was not discarded. The variety of accidental or deliberate paths by which a nuclear war might be initiated left the Soviet leadership no choice, in their view, but to have contingent preparedness for a spectrum of possibilities.

Differences between U.S. and Soviet force structures would also have implications for the willingness of either side to rely upon LOW as its principal retaliatory option. U.S. retaliatory capabilities in 1983 were spread more evenly among three components of a strategic triad: intercontinental ballistic missiles, submarine-launched ballistic missiles, and long-range bombers, compared to Soviet forces. The most survivable part of the U.S. deterrent was its fleet ballistic missile submarine force, virtually invulnerable to first-strike preemption. The U.S. bomber-delivered weapons, including air-launched cruise missiles (ALCMs), gravity bombs, and short-range attack missiles, were slow flyers compared to the fast-flying ICBMs and SLBMs. Nevertheless, the highly capable U.S. bomber force, compared to its Soviet counterpart, forced the Soviets to expend considerable resources on air defense and complicated their estimates of time-on-target arrivals for U.S. retaliatory forces.

The effects of force structure and doctrine combined created some significant pressures for Soviet reliance upon prompt launch to save the ICBM component of their deterrent. Doctrine suggested that crises were mainly political in their origin and were to be avoided, not managed. The onset of a serious crisis was a threat of war. The U.S. view that brinkmanship could be manipulated to unilateral advantage during a crisis struck most Soviet leaders before and after Khrushchev as a highly risk-acceptant strategy. The Soviet leadership, after Khrushchev's enforced retirement, did engage in rapid nuclear force building in order to eliminate American strategic nuclear superiority, but they also eschewed "adventurism" in the forward deployments of nuclear weapons and in the use of nuclear forces as backdrops. Because they were pessimistic about "managing" a crisis once confrontation was forced upon them (in their view), Soviet leaders would have to include in crisis preparedness a capability for, and perhaps a bias toward, prompt launch to save the strategic rocket forces. Pessimism about crisis management combined with an ICBM-heavy deterrent constrained Soviet leaders' choices once general deterrence (the basic Hobbesian condition of threat created by the international system of plural sovereignty and the security dilemma) turned to immediate deterrence (a situation in which one state has made an explicit military threat against another or others).

ANALYSIS

How might the strategic nuclear deterrent relationship between the Soviet Union and the United States in 1983 have been influenced by expected war outcomes if deterrence failed, given the factors already discussed? In order to answer this question, we first consider how stable the 1983 relationship was by comparing the outcomes that would have resulted from any breakdown of deterrence. The following list summarizes and compares the numbers of U.S. and Soviet retaliatory warheads and equivalent megatonnage (EMT) expected to survive a first strike in 1983:

Russia	United States
Surviving WH—1,831	Surviving WH—1,947
Surviving EMT—894	Surviving EMT—436
Reserve WH—668	Reserve WH—1,064
Reserve EMT—216	Reserve EMT—234

These numbers show that neither side could have launched a first strike without receiving a retaliatory blow that inflicted socially unacceptable and economically catastrophic damage. In addition, despite very different force structures, the two states' overall retaliatory capabilities are very similar. The degree of similarity is emphasized in the following summary of the ratio of U.S. to Soviet survivors:

Deliverable WH	1.06
Deliverable EMT	0.49
Reserve WH	1.59
Reserve EMT	1.08

Note that a ratio of unity (1.0) means the two sides are equal. Ratios higher or lower than 1.0 indicate results favorable to the United States or to the USSR, respectively.

The ratio of U.S. to Soviet survivors is one possible measure of the stability of their nuclear deterrent relationship in 1983, but not the only one. Another possible measure compares the metastability of that relationship. A metastable relationship is one that simultaneously reduces the incentive for both sides to strike first. To measure this, we will calculate a Soviet first-strike advantage, a U.S. first-strike advantage, and the ratio between the two advantages. The "advantage" for each state is the difference between the number of warheads available for striking first and the number available for retaliation after accepting a first strike.

Soviet First-Strike Advantage	9,507.25
U.S. First-Strike Advantage	8,134.89
Metastability Index	1.17

The metastability index is the ratio of Soviet to U.S. first-strike advantage. A metastability index of 1.0 is a best case: The two sides' first-strike advantages are equal and cancel one another out. The closer to 1.0 the metastability index, the greater the degree of first-strike stability. The more the index deviates from 1.0 (either higher or lower), the lesser the degree of stability. A metastability index of 1.17 says that, in 1983, the U.S. and Soviet first-strike advantages were very similar: Therefore, there was little incentive to strike first in order to obtain a relatively preferred outcome. Of course, this is a very static measure and does not capture some of the true differences between the basic concept of first-strike stability and the more nuanced concept of crisis stability. Crisis stability involves issues that go beyond first-strike stability, including the perceptions and expectations of policy makers and their principal military advisors. The next section offers a proposal for comparing the 1983 war-scare crisis with other possible "war scares" of the Cold War in order to develop some comparative historical perspective on the problem of crisis stability.

OTHER WAR SCARES

Do the preceding conclusions apply only to the situation in 1983? Undoubtedly, the situation at the top of the Soviet leadership was unsettled, feeding expectations that, if not paranoid, were certainly suspicious with regard to U.S. intentions. Comparison with other periods of tension and crisis might help to establish whether the analytic part of our methodology has applicability across different cases before and after the Cold War. Let us, for example, take 1962, 1991, and 1995 as candidate benchmark "war-scare" years.

The reasons for these choices are as follows. The Cuban missile crisis of 1962 is self-evidently the most dangerous single thirteen days of the Cold War. The failed coup of August 1991 led to the demise of the Soviet Union and solidified the end of the Cold War. From August 19 through 21, the world waited nervously for the outcome of the power struggle between Boris Yeltsin and democratic forces and the "Emergency Committee for the State of Emergency" of usurpers in Moscow. During the crisis the exact chain of command by which Kremlin leaders would authorize nuclear release was uncertain and fogged from outside observers, including the U.S. president and NATO. Gorbachev was a temporary prisoner in his dacha in Foros in the Crimea, and the other two nuclear briefcases or "footballs" used by leaders to authorize nuclear retaliatory launch were in the possession of the defense minister and the chief of the General Staff. On August 19, Defense Minister Dmitri Yazov ordered the armed forces, including strategic nuclear forces, to increased combat readiness. According to Peter Vincent Pry, "During the August 1991 coup, the United States was in grave danger without knowing it. A NATO or Strategic Air Command exercise, or the generation of U.S. forces to counter Moscow's escalation to Increased Combat Readiness, might have provoked the Committee (the coup plotters) to launch a preemptive nuclear strike."[37]

The situation in 1995 was somewhat different. There was no legitimacy crisis in Russia, but another kind of risk of accidental or inadvertent war presented itself. On January 25, 1995, a U.S.–Norwegian scientific experimental rocket launched from Andoya Island off the Norwegian coast was identified by Russian early warning as a possible threatening launch vehicle headed for Russia. The initial launching position and early trajectory of the meteorological rocket resembled, from the perspective of operators at the Russian missile-attack warning system, a possible U.S. submarine-launched ballistic missile fired off the northern coast of Russia and arriving within ten minutes or so over Russian territory. Russia's General Staff had in fact anticipated that a likely form of any U.S. surprise nuclear strike would begin with submarine-launched ballistic missiles fired from the Norwegian and/or Barents seas. The General Staff was especially concerned about the possibility of an SLBM electromagnetic pulse (EMP) precursor strike disabling radar warning systems, cutting off strategic communications, and disabling computers. Russian President Boris Yeltsin for the first time opened his "football" or briefcase with communications codes used to authorize a nuclear launch. After some minutes it was determined that the rocket's trajectory would not actually impact Russian territory and a mistaken prompt launch by Russian rocket forces was avoided.[38]

Each of these cases offers anecdotally interesting and somewhat disconcerting evidence of a higher than normal risk of accidental or inadvertent nuclear war. But each case has unique political and military aspects. Some method permitting comparison across cases is called for. To accomplish this, we will use various measures of the "trigger happiness" or degree of dependency of the United States and the Soviet Union or Russia on launch on warning or force generation in the four cases: 1962 Cuban missile crisis, 1983 war scare, 1991 failed coup, and 1995 mistaken scientific rocket. Each of these situations will be interrogated for the numbers of surviving and retaliating (arriving) warheads in each of four conditions: generated forces–launch on warning, generated forces–ride out attack, day-to-day alerted forces–launch on warning, and day-to-day alerted forces–ride out attack. Both the numbers of surviving warheads and the relative percentages of dependency on (sensitivity to) force generation or launch on warning are computed in Table 6.1.

All Soviet and post-Soviet Russian forces were more dependent than their U.S. contemporary counterparts on launch on warning, whether the Soviet or Russian forces were on generated or day-to-day alert. And

Soviet or Russian forces riding out an attack were more dependent on generated alert during these crises than U.S. forces were. On the other hand, Soviet or Russian forces launched on warning were less dependent on generated alert than their U.S. counterparts in three of four crisis situations. Only in the Cuban missile crisis of 1962 were Soviet forces more dependent than those of the other side on generated alert.

The significance of these findings across various cases is as follows. The findings do not change the inescapable statistics of the Cold War nuclear balance. Neither the United States nor the Soviet Union (or later Russia) could launch a nuclear surprise attack without receiving historically unprecedented and socially unacceptable retaliation. But crisis behavior of leaders is conditioned not only by scientific facts, but also by subjective expectations about the likely behavior of the other side. In each of these situations, strategic warning of a tense situation that might, with unknown probability, lead to an actual outbreak of war was already on the table. What mattered next was the expected reaction by each side to tactical warning of an actual attack in progress, or to indicators considered tantamount to confirmation of an attack.

The results summarized in Table 6.1 and in other information presented in this study suggest that, at the cusp of decision about how hard or how soft tactical warning would have to be, Soviet and Russian leaders were far too dependent on early-alerted nuclear forces and, even more so, on launch on warning in order to guarantee retaliatory strikes against desired target sets. It deserves reemphasis that it is in the unknown but potentially deadly conjunction of images of the enemy and actual capabilities that the difference between a war and a crisis can be found. Neither theorists nor policy makers can derive any complacency from the fortuitous escape from disaster repeated four times.

Another issue raised by these findings is the operational propensity of the Russian nuclear command and control system. There is considerable evidence from Russians that the strategic nuclear command and control system may be tilted toward the prevention of decapitation and loss of control by enemy first strikes. Less emphasis, if any, is given to the avoidance of accidental or inadvertent nuclear war or escalation. We are not speaking here of technical-use control devices such as Permissive Action Links (electronic locks that must be unlocked by codes before launch vehicles or warheads can be activated). Instead, we are now addressing the military ethos in the minds of principal commanders who control the use of, or have custody of, nuclear forces. According to Peter Vincent Pry, although the president of the Russian Federation is the only person who can legally order the launch of nuclear weapons, the General Staff "controls all of the electronic, mechanical, and operational means for waging nuclear war."[39]

Table 6.1
Surviving and Arriving Re-Entry Vehicles: Four Scenarios and Four Time Periods

	U.S. 1962	USSR 1962	U.S. 1983	USSR 1983	U.S. 1991	USSR 1991	U.S. 1995	Russia 1995
Gen. LOW	2,630	412	8,011	9,504	9,375	9,228	6,726	5,786
Gen. ROA	2,517	344	6,273	4,425	7,390	4,373	5,511	3,329
Day LOW	920	87	5,299	6,332	5,929	6,405	3,768	3,751
Day ROA	807	13	3,561	909	3,944	822	2,553	536
% depend Gen. Alert (LOW)	186	373	51	50	58	44	78	54
% depend Gen. Alert (ROA)	212	2,471	76	387	87	432	116	521

This situation by itself is not necessarily disquieting. The United States also has arranged means by which retaliation will still take place in the event that the top political leadership and even the major military commands are destroyed in surprise nuclear attacks. These kinds of arrangements are called "delegation of authority" and "devolution of command."[40] However, in the U.S. case orderly political succession in peacetime or even during a crisis is ensured. In addition, the U.S. nuclear command and control system is designed to shift gradually from an emphasis on negative control (prevention of accidental or unauthorized nuclear release or launch) to positive control (guaranty that authorized alerting and launch commands will be readily obeyed).

Table 6.1 (*continued*)

	U.S. 1962	USSR 1962	U.S. 1983	USSR 1983	U.S. 1991	USSR 1991	U.S. 1995	Russia 1995
% de-pend LOW (Gen)	4	20	28	115	27	111	22	74
% de-pend LOW (ROA)	14	552	49	597	50	679	48	600

Source: NIE 11-5-58, *Soviet Capabilities in Guided Missiles and Space Vehicles*, 65–70; NIE 11-8/1-61, *Strength and Deployment of Soviet Long Range Ballistic Missile Forces*, 121–138; NIE 11-3/8-82, *Soviet Capabilities for Strategic Nuclear Conflict, 1981–1991*, 483–490, all in Donald P. Steury, ed., *Intentions and Capabilities: Estimates on Soviet Strategic Forces, 1950–1983* (Washington, D.C.: CIA History Staff, Center for the Study of Intelligence, 1996). See also NIE 11-3/8-91, *Soviet Forces and Capabilities for Strategic Nuclear Conflict Through the Year 2000*, in Benjamin B. Fischer, ed., *At Cold War's End: U.S. Intelligence on the Soviet Union and Eastern Europe, 1989–1991* (Washington, D.C.: Central Intelligence Agency, 1999), 359–368.

Note: This table involves calculations from a model developed by Dr. James Scouras, Strategy Research Group. He is not responsible for its use here.

The Russian nuclear command and control system apparently emphasizes positive compared to negative control, even apart from times of crisis. Some Western experts believe that Russian officers charged with the day-to-day management of nuclear forces could, from the main General Staff underground command post at Chekov, initiate a nuclear attack even in the absence of authorized commands from the Russian president or senior officers.[41] Noted Russian analyst and nuclear arms-control expert Alexei Arbatov warned in a 1992 article that the monopoly of the military in devising the control system and operational plan resulted "in a concept which guards not against an accidental strike due to a mistake, a nervous breakdown, or a technical problem, but against failure to respond to an attack promptly and on a massive scale. . . . This is a reflection of a typically militaristic mentality— the main goal is to crush the enemy; deterrence is just a sideline."[42]

The point of these citations is not to imply that Russians are, or ever were, war acceptant to an extent that Americans or others are not:

Russians, above all others in this century, have paid the costs of war. The issue raised here is the possible consequences of system design combined with crisis stimulation to produce the equivalent of a "normal accident."[43] As in other large and complex organizations, standard operating procedures and organizational routines built into the nuclear command and control system, as well as the operational habits and expectations of operators, create biases and predispositions that could be dysfunctional in a crisis.[44] If, in addition, leading Russian military theorists expect that any Western attack might be preceded by strategic-information warfare against computers and communication systems, cyberglitches could be mistaken for the first wave of enemy attacks during a period of tension.

CONCLUSIONS

The United States and the Soviet Union in the early 1980s failed miserably at one of the essential tasks required for success in military persuasion: perceptions management. The Reaganauts were busy with a full court press against the Soviet Union, including large increases in defense spending and aggressive rhetoric designed to identify the Soviet Union as a demonic aberration in history, doomed to eventual failure. The Soviet leadership felt trapped between the limitations imposed by its failing economy and a more aggressive, confrontational U.S. defense and foreign policy supported by technology innovation that was out of Moscow's reach. Each side failed to understand correctly that the other was pessimistic, not optimistic, about the existing state of their relationship. Each misjudged the other as risk acceptant, when in fact both sides were risk averse. The Soviet leadership was moribund and its economy was on a descent that would not cease until the union did, but American leaders in the early 1980s anticipated a stronger and more internationally competitive Soviet adversary for the remainder of the decade. The Soviet and American minds were being driven by realities of their own mental construction and imagination, and in directions opposed to their own best interests.

Was the 1983 war scare real or imaginary, and how serious was it? These are important questions for students of Cold War history and of contemporary strategy and arms control. Not all aspects of the issue can be dealt with here. Significant anecdotal evidence, combined with modeling of some aspects of U.S. and Soviet likely operational performance in 1983, supports the case that Soviet fears of an outbreak of war in 1983 were real, and in some cases justified, given their political and military–strategic outlooks. U.S. intelligence needed to have done a better job of "seeing the other," and not for the first time in 1983. A series of apparently discrete events between 1979 (NATO's INF modernization decision) and November 1983 (Able Archer) cumulated unexpectedly in a "positive feedback loop" of negative expectations. Soviet foreign and military intelligence, tasked by their uptight political masters, reported back to Moscow Center those indicators and pessimistic appraisals that seemed to confirm initial suspicions that the West was up to something, and data analysis shows that this misperception by both sides could have been linked with a realistic concern on the part of Soviet military planners that their first strike might be their last. Nor are these patterns necessarily confined to 1983. Modeling of situations in 1962, 1991, and 1995 shows disturbingly similar Soviet and Russian dependencies on prompt launch and early force generation in a crisis.

APPENDIX: SOVIET AND U.S. STRATEGIC NUCLEAR FORCES, 1983

Soviet Forces	Launchers	Warheads per Launcher	Total Warheads
SS-11/3	550	1	550
SS-13/2	60	1	60
SS-17/3	150	4	600
SS-18/4/5	308	10	3,080
SS-19/3	330	6	1,980
SS-24 (fixed)	0	10	0
subtotal fixed land	1,398		6,270
SS-24 (rail)	0	10	0
SS-25 (road)	0	1	0
subtotal mobile land	0		0
subtotal land based	1,398		6,270
SS-N-6/3	384	1	384
SS-N-8/2	292	1	292
SS-N-18/3	224	7	1,568
SS-N-20	200	10	2,000
SS-N-17	12	1	12
SS-N-5	9	1	9
subtotal sea based	1,121		4,265
Bison	43	4	172
Tu-95 Bear B/G ALCM	100	2	200
Tu-95 Bear B/G Bomb	100	2	200
subtotal air breathing	243		572
Total Soviet Forces	2,762		11,107

U.S. Forces	Launchers	Warheads per Launcher	Total Warheads
Minuteman II	450	1	450
Minuteman III	250	3	750
Minuteman IIIA	300	3	900
Titan	45	1	45
subtotal land based	1,045		2,145
Poseidon C-3	304	10	3,040
Poseidon C-4	192	8	1,536
Trident C-4	72	8	576
subtotal sea based	568		5,152
B-52G gravity	41	4	164
SRAM		8	328
B-52G gravity	46	4	184
ALCM/SRAM		20	920
B-52H gravity	90	4	360
SRAM		8	720
B-52D	31	4	124
subtotal air breathing	208		2,800
Total U.S. Forces	1,821		10,097

NOTES

The author gratefully acknowledges Dr. Ben B. Fischer, Central Intelligence Agency, for sources pertinent to this study and for additional helpful suggestions; Dr. Raymond L. Garthoff, Brookings Institution, for important critical comments and corrections; and Dr. James Scouras for assistance in developing historical databases. None of these persons is responsible for any arguments or opinions.

1. Christopher Andrew and Oleg Gordievsky, *KGB: The Inside Story* (New York: HarperCollins, 1990), 583.

2. Christophe Andrew and Oleg Gordievsky, eds., *Comrade Kryuchkov's Instructions: Top Secret Files on KGB Foreign Operations, 1975–1985* (Stanford, Calif.: Stanford University Press, 1993), 68–90, provides a full account of RYAN.

3. See Reference no. 373/PR/52, Attachment 2, *The Problem of Discovering Preparation for a Nuclear Missile Attack on the USSR*, in ibid., 74.

4. Ibid., 77–81.

5. Ibid., 76.

6. My appreciation of the Soviet perspective here owes much to helpful comments from Raymond Garthoff. See also Raymond L. Garthoff, *Detente and Confrontation: American–Soviet Relations from Nixon to Reagan* (Washington, D.C.: Brookings Institution, 1985), 864–872.

7. Robert M. Gates, *From the Shadows: The Ultimate Insider's Story of Five Presidents and How They Won the Cold War* (New York: Simon and Shuster, 1996), 262.

8. Andrew and Gordievsky, *Comrade Kryuchkov's Instructions*, 76. Soviet fears of the preemptive value of Pershing II seemed excessive from the U.S. and NATO perspective. The range of the Pershing II given by U.S. official sources would not have permitted prompt attacks against main military command bunkers in or near Moscow. However, Soviet military planners might have feared that, once in place, Pershing II missiles could be enhanced and given extended ranges, bringing Moscow and its environs within their reach.

9. Gates, *From the Shadows*, 264.

10. Statement of Soviet scientists on SDI, quoted in Andrei A. Kokoshin, *Soviet Strategic Thought, 1917–91* (Cambridge: MIT Press, 1998), 182.

11. Gates, *From the Shadows*, 268.

12. Seymour M. Hersh, *"The Target Is Destroyed": What Really Happened to Flight 007 and What America Knew About It* (New York: Vintage Books, 1987), 147–150, 246–247.

13. Ibid., 267.

14. Andrew and Gordievsky, *KGB*, 597.

15. Ibid., 598.

16. My account of this episode is taken from David Hoffman, "I Had a Funny Feeling in My Gut: Soviet Officer Faced Nuclear Armageddon," *Washington Post*, February 10, 1999, p. A19.

17. Ibid.

18. Ibid.

19. Accounts of Able Archer appear in Andrew and Gordievsky, *KGB*, 599–600; Gates, *From the Shadows*, 270–273. See also Gordon Brook-Shepherd, *The Storm Birds: Soviet Postwar Defectors* (New York: Wiedenfeld and Nicolson, 1989), 328–335.

20. Brook-Shepherd, *The Storm Birds*, 329.

21. Andrew and Gordievsky, *KGB*, 599.

22. Ibid.

23. Ibid., 600.

24. Peter Vincent Pry, *War Scare: Russia and America on the Nuclear Brink* (Westport, Conn.: Praeger, 1999), 41.

25. Gates, *From the Shadows*, 273.

26. Ben B. Fischer, "Intelligence and Disaster Avoidance: The Soviet War Scare and U.S.–Soviet Relations," in *Mysteries of the Cold War*, ed. Stephen J. Cimbala (Aldershot, England: Ashgate, 1999), 89–104, especially p. 98. I gratefully acknowledge Ben Fischer for calling this important aspect of Operation RYAN to my attention.

27. Council of Ministers of the German Democratic Republic, Ministry for State Security, Deputy of the Minister, *Implementation Regulation to Order no. 1/85 of February 15, 1985: Comprehensive Use of Capabilities of the Service Units of the MfS for Early and Reliable Acquisition of Evidence of Imminent Enemy Plans, Preparations, and Actions for Aggression*, Berlin, June 5, 1985.

28. Fischer, "Intelligence and Disaster Avoidance," 98.

29. Markus Wolf, *Man Without a Face: The Autobiography of Communism's Greatest Spymaster* (New York: Times Books, 1997), is a first-person account of his amazing career.

30. Markus Wolf, *Spionage Chef im geheimen Krieg: Erinnerungen* (Dusseldorf and Munich: List Verlag, 1997), 332, cited in Fischer, "Intelligence and Disaster Avoidance," 101.

31. Raymond L. Garthoff, *Deterrence and the Revolution in Soviet Military Doctrine* (Washington, D.C.: Brookings Institution, 1990), 24–25.

32. William E. Odom, *The Collapse of the Soviet Military* (New Haven, Conn.: Yale University Press, 1998), 1–15, is excellent on this point. See also Garthoff, *Deterrence and the Revolution in Soviet Military Doctrine*, 16–22.

33. Ghulam Dastagir Wardak, compiler, and Graham Hall Turbiville, Jr., gen. ed., *The Voroshilov Lectures: Materials from the Soviet General Staff Academy*, vol. 1 (Washington, D.C.: National Defense University Press, 1989), 69–75.

34. In theory, according to some U.S. distinctions, launch "on warning" would take place in response to multiple indicators that an attack had been launched but prior to the actual detonations of warheads on U.S. soil. Launch "under attack" would be delayed until after actual detonations had occurred. Skeptics can be forgiven for assuming that launch under attack was a euphemism in declaratory policy for action policy that was likely to be launch on warning. Launch on warning would be necessary to save the ICBM force from prompt destruction: The difference between LOW and LUA might, at most, affect some components of an already partly alerted U.S. bomber force.

35. Bruce G. Blair, *The Logic of Accidental Nuclear War* (Washington, D.C.: Brookings Institution, 1993), 177, passim.

36. Garthoff, *Deterrence and the Revolution in Soviet Military Doctrine*, 78.

37. Pry, *War Scare*, 81.

38. This summary of the January 1995 incident is taken from ibid., 214–221.

39. Ibid., 152.

40. Paul Bracken, *The Command and Control of Nuclear Forces* (New Haven, Conn.: Yale University Press, 1983), passim.

41. Pry, *War Scare*, 152.

42. Cited in ibid., 155.

43. Charles Perrow, *Normal Accidents: Living with High-Risk Technologies* (New York: Basic Books, 1984), develops this concept.

44. This case is argued with regard to U.S. systems in Scott D. Sagan, *The Limits of Safety: Organizations, Accidents and Nuclear Weapons* (Princeton, N.J.: Princeton University Press, 1993). See especially his discussion of the U-2 "stray" into Soviet airspace during the Cuban missile crisis (pp. 135–146).

PART III

FUTURE PROBLEMS

7

Friction and Nuclear Deterrence

Nuclear weapons readily lend themselves to military persuasion—only too much so. Policy makers can see immediately two things about nuclear weapons, especially in large quantities. First, nukes can be intimidating, especially against an adversary who does not have them. Second, if the act of nuclear intimidation or military persuasion by means of nuclear threat fails, the costs of war will almost certainly pass the limit of social and political acceptability. This paradox of nuclear military persuasion, that it is persuasive because it so awfully risky, lies behind the seductive appeal of deterrence and other forms of military psychology based on nuclear weapons.

The end of the Cold War and the peaceful collapse of the Soviet Union have led to some expert and lay judgments that military history has been repealed. Political leaders such as Mikhail Gorbachev, last president of the Soviet Union, and eminent scholars asserted that nuclear weapons had severed the necessary relationship between war and politics that the Prussian philosopher of war, Carl von Clausewitz, had placed at the center of his military thought. But the reasons why the Cold War ended peacefully and in favor of the West are more complicated than the singular role of nuclear weapons or nuclear deterrence alone.[1] In addition, nuclear and other deterrence as practiced during the Cold War was marked by a dangerous and unavoidable component of what Clausewitz referred to as "friction," and so, too, will it be in the future.[2]

This chapter asks about the impact on nuclear deterrence (as a form of military persuasion) of friction. Friction is the difference between expected outcomes and actual results. The first part of the chapter discusses Clausewitz's concept of friction, albeit very briefly and in general terms. In the second part of the chapter we consider different kinds of deterrence and the difference between deterrence and coercive diplomacy, two of the most frequently discussed forms of military persuasion related to nuclear weapons. In the third section we discuss the operational aspects of friction as it might affect nuclear offenses and antimissile defenses.

CLAUSEWITZ AND THE CONCEPT OF FRICTION

One of Clausewitz's more interesting and thought-provoking ideas about military art was the concept of friction. This seminal concept has been cited repeatedly by writers on military art and strategy as a pivotal notion that must be comprehended by all great captains and students of military history. As Colin Gray has noted, "If Clausewitz had written only about friction in war, his place among the heroes in the Valhalla of strategic theory would be secure."[3] Despite this acknowledgment by military theorists and historians of the significance of friction for Clausewitzian (or other) interpretations of war, the concept has received comparatively little attention from modern social scientists.

This fact is regrettable, and no one would be more disappointed than Clausewitz. He was not writing a museum piece for display among historical curiosities. Unfinished in Clausewitz's lifetime and organized for publication by his wife after his death in 1831, *On War* is a living and breathing treatise on the nature of war and its attributes for commanders and for policy makers. If only warriors and not policy makers understand what Clausewitz has to say about war eternal as well as about war in particular, much of the intended value of Clausewitz's insights will be lost. Related to the requirement for policy makers as well as military leaders to comprehend the major insights of *On War* is the recognition that Clausewitz did not intend a static theory resembling his bust at Carlisle Barracks. A late twentieth-century Clausewitz would insist on taking into account what has been learned since the initial publication of *On War* from military history, from politics, and from other social science research applicable to war. If Clausewitz was anything he was one of the first and most durable examples of a behavioral scientist in the study of war. In that spirit, the present study takes that concept of friction from its originator and applies it to help understand aspects of international security in the recent past and present. Having done so, we should be better prepared to understand the future too.

The subject of friction in war is most explicit in Book 1, Chapter 7 of Clausewitz's widely read and highly regarded *On War*.[4] The Prussian military philosopher begins by pointing out that a person who has not experienced war cannot comprehend why the conduct of battle is so difficult. The tasks that have to be accomplished in war seem very simple, but that semblance is deceptive: "Everything in war is very simple, but the simplest thing is difficult. The difficulties accumulate and end by producing a kind of friction that is inconceivable unless one has experienced war."[5]

So far it might be thought that Clausewitz was expressing an idea related to the physics of motion or the mechanics of machine breakdown. Far from it. Friction affects the material components of a war plan, to be sure, but its most unpredictable aspect is the relationship of friction to people: the troops who fight and the commanders who command them. Of the military machine, Clausewitz notes that "none of its components is of one piece: each part is composed of individuals, every one of whom retains his potential for friction."[6] In theory, discipline keeps the behavior of individuals fully consistent with the expectations of commanding officers. In practice, as Clausewitz explains, "A battalion is made up of individuals, the least important of whom may chance to delay things or somehow make them go wrong."[7]

Friction is not alone a cause of disparity between the aims of commanders and the unfolding of events in battle. Friction is compounded by other factors and forces, including the environment of danger that characterizes war and the physical exertion required in battle. The most unpredictable element is introduced by the relationship between friction and chance in war.[8] Chance in contact with friction "brings about effects that cannot be measured, just because they are largely due to chance."[9] One example given by Clausewitz of friction related to chance is the weather and its effects on the outcome of battle. He then offers a simile that is as memorable as it is appropriate: "Action in war is like movement in a resistant element. Just as the simplest and most natural of movements, walking, cannot easily be performed in water, so in war it is difficult for normal efforts to achieve even moderate results."[10] In the same passage, Clausewitz disparages the views of theorists "who have never swum."

Clausewitz did not limit his discussion of friction to the happenings of battle. In a letter to his future wife, editor and publisher Marie von Bruhl, in September 1806, Clausewitz expressed his frustration with the decision-making process within the Prussian high command. As he explained, the Prussian army at the time had "three commanders-in-chief and two chiefs of staff." His mentor, Gerhard von Scharnhorst, was frustrated in this situation because "he is constantly confronted by obstacles of convenience and tradition, when he is paralyzed by

constant friction [*Friktion*] with the opinions of others."¹¹ The three commanders-in-chief were the Duke Karl of Brunswick, nominally in command of the army; King Frederick William III, who decided to
accompany the army in the field; and Prince Hohenlohe-Ingelfingen,
who was given command of one half the army.¹² The concerns of
Clausewitz were justified: Less than three weeks later France defeated
Prussia at the battles of Jena and Auerstadt, thus destroying the Prussian army of Frederick the Great. After France later defeated what remained of Prussia's armies in the battle of Friedland in June 1807, she
knocked Prussia temporarily out of the ranks of the powers and reduced her to a satellite within the French empire.¹³

In a later elaboration of the concept of friction, in 1812 Clausewitz
wrote to the Prussian crown prince (later Frederick William IV), whom
he had been tutoring while also teaching at the Prussian war academy.
In this correspondence Clausewitz listed eight sources of "tremendous
friction" that make even the simplest plans difficult to realize in war:

1. insufficient knowledge of the enemy.
2. rumors (information gained by remote observation or spies).
3. uncertainty about one's own strength and position.
4. the uncertainties that cause friendly troops to tend to exaggerate their own difficulties.
5. differences between expectations and reality.
6. the fact that one's own army is never as strong as it appears on paper.
7. the difficulties in keeping an army supplied.
8. the tendency to change or abandon well-thought-out plans when confronted with the vivid physical images and perceptions of the battlefield.¹⁴

In addition, in his discussion on danger in war in Book 1, Chapter 4
of *On War*, Clausewitz notes that "danger is part of the friction of war.
Without an accurate conception of danger we cannot understand war."¹⁵
Clausewitz's concluding observations on Book 1 include the following summation on the topic of friction: "We have identified danger,
physical exertion, intelligence, and friction as the elements that coa-
lesce to form the atmosphere of war, and turn it into a medium that
impedes activity. In their restrictive effects they can be grouped into a
single concept of friction."¹⁶

The preceding discussion shows that, in his earlier thinking as well
as that later appearing in his posthumously published *On War*, Clausewitz was viewing friction as a multidimensional concept, fundamental both to the art of war and to the relationship between war and
policy. Were Clausewitz alive and writing about friction today, he
would also be aware of the research developments in social and be-

havioral science since the 1840s (when *On War* was published by his widow) and of the additional military history written since then. We should do as he would: build on his foundation laid down in the first half of the nineteenth century, but not rest there.

MILITARY PERSUASION IN ACTION: DETERRENCE, COERCIVE DIPLOMACY, AND FRICTION

Deterrence is used in academic and policy-making circles to refer both to a process and to a condition or situation; that is, a state party to a dispute may be practicing deterrence or not, or a disputant may be deterred or not. Deterrence is a psychological process by which an actor influences one or more other actors to behave in accord with the desires of the first actor. In military affairs, usually conducted by governments or "state actors," deterrence is thought to rest on the ability of the influencer (or deterrer) to manipulate both threats and reassurances in a way that maximize its influence over the behavior of the party being threatened. As Alexander L. George has noted, "Deterrence, which relies on threats, is better conceived as part of a broader influence theory that combines threats with positive inducements and diplomatic efforts to explore the desirability and feasibility of working out a mutually acceptable accommodation of conflicting interests."[17]

George emphasizes that the successful practice of deterrence is not necessarily guaranteed by careful study of the theory. In state-to-state behavior one is dealing with an opponent whose very aim is to confound one's own military or diplomatic strategy. Therefore, the most skillful combination of threats and reassurances may fall short if it assumes on the part of the adversary a set of motives and expectations that are not present. One must comprehend the "otherness" of the opponent, and this requires some understanding of his cultural and social parameters as well as his politics and military art. In addition, deterrence cannot substitute for or be practiced in ignorance of the hard realities of national interest and geopolitics. A state's threat to defend a vital interest is simply more credible, other things being equal, than its willingness to defend an interest of secondary importance to its security. As George has indicated, "Early deterrence theory was defective in that it placed too much emphasis on various gimmicks for enhancing the credibility of commitment—such as the 'threat that leaves something to chance,' playing the game of 'chicken,' etc.—and failed to recognize that credibility is based on the magnitude and nature of the national interests at stake."[18]

Deterrence is related to but distinct from coercive diplomacy. Coercive diplomacy or compellence is the use of force or threats of force to persuade an opponent to stop an action already begun or undo that action and its effects.[19] During the Cuban missile crisis of 1962, for example, President Kennedy used coercive diplomacy in order to get the Soviet premier initially to halt further shipments of nuclear-capable missiles to Cuba and eventually to remove the missiles from Cuba and return them to the Soviet Union. Coercive diplomacy when skill-fully practiced employs only the amount of force, or the degree of threat of force, necessary to demonstrate resolve to the opponent and to make credible one's threat to employ a military strategy. As Gordon A. Craig and George have explained, "Coercive diplomacy needs to be distin-guished from pure coercion. It seeks to *persuade* the opponent to cease his aggression rather than bludgeon him into stopping. In contrast to the crude use of force to repel the opponent, coercive diplomacy em-phasizes the use of threats and the exemplary use of limited force to persuade him to back down."[20]

It has been established that deterrence relies for its success either on threats of denial (physically or otherwise preventing the opponent from accomplishing his military object) or of punishment. Nuclear deter-rence rests mainly on the threat of punishment and that threat has two parts: capability and credibility.[21] Capability implies the means to re-taliate once having been attacked or in the expectation of an attack. Credibility implies that the deterree understands the threat being made and believes that if the specified behavior is engaged in the deterrer will actually carry out the threat. Capability is easier to show than credibility, on the evidence. It seemed relatively simple for the Cold War superpowers to demonstrate that they could not only blow them-selves up simultaneously or sequentially, but much of the exterior world besides. This capability endured for most of the Cold War as a constant. It did not necessarily follow that, in the variable circumstances of a specific crisis or attack, deterrence would work as expected to.

There is some controversy over whether deterrence is truly a strat-egy or an experiment in applied psychology. Successful deterrence means that a war does not have to be fought, but success is defined in a very short-term manner. In the Agadir crisis several years before the start of World War I, the outbreak of war among the major powers was avoided, so Germany was presumably deterred by the denouement of that crisis. However, Germany (at least the kaiser) was also frustrated and enraged and resolved not to yield the next time around. So being deterred in the short term can light the fuse for failed deterrence later.

Deterrence in history also suffers from a lack of evidence of its ef-fects. One cannot prove that deterrence "worked" when one state failed to attack another: There are many reasons why a state contemplating an attack might stay its hand. Deterrence is also latent as well as mani-fest. A latent deterrence system exists among all states dependent on self-help for military security: The possibility of war in general is ever present, although the specific causes for war and the lineup of enemies may vary. Manifest deterrence takes place when a state or other actor has issued a specific threat against another, has defined conditions for compliance, and has explained what will happen if compliance is not forthcoming. It follows that states that cannot or will not communicate cannot play at deterrence: They can engage in other mischief though, including aggression.[22]

During the Cold War it was assumed by most Western policy makers and military analysts that technology favored the offense over the defense in the case of nuclear weapons. The defender's task was judged as especially problematic if it aspired to defend cities instead of retaliatory forces. The ABM Treaty of 1972 was regarded by U.S. arms-control advocates, but apparently not by Soviet military or political leaders, as an acknowledgment that this state of affairs could never be changed. Soviet leaders continued to work on the development of antinuclear strategic defenses, and deployed an ABM system around Moscow subject to treaty constraints. In 1983 President Ronald Reagan called on the U.S. defense technology community to produce a multitiered missile-defense system that could protect the American homeland even against large-scale Soviet attacks. After the Cold War the U.S. research and development program was scaled back to one favoring a smaller defense system for limited strikes by rogue states or accidental launches.

This rejection of defense and embrace of offensive retaliation as a necessary evil or as a desirable condition simplified arms-control negotiations but also nullified much of traditional military strategy. Traditional strategy for conventional deterrence or for prevailing in war regarded offenses and defenses as competitive and interactive war forms. Historically, a temporarily superior form of attack had eventually produced its antithesis: a countervailing form of defense. Nuclear weapons seemed to exist apart from this action–reaction dynamic, although it was possible that the years between 1945 and 1990 offered too short a time interval to tell. Some argued in the 1980s that eventually space- and terrestrially-based nonnuclear weapons based on new physical principles, would unlock the deadlock of deterrence based on assured retaliation. This futuristic technology remained out of reach at century's end, and Congressional advocates of limited national missile defense for the U.S. homeland plumped for ground-based, kinetic-kill interceptor and other technologies closer to hand.

The potential for first-strike stability and for central deterrence is partly related to the prevailing technology environment: offense dominant, defense dominant, or mixed. Central deterrence exists if, in a two-sided relationship, neither side can calculate "in cold blood" that a first strike would pay. First-strike stability requires, in addition to the standards for central deterrence, that neither side be tempted to launch its forces preemptively on the assumption that it is under attack or about to be attacked. Table 7.1 summarizes possible relationships between technology environments and optimism or pessimism about central deterrence and first-strike stability.

Some prominent military thinkers now hold that nuclear weapons may give pride of place to a "revolution in military affairs" led by improved electronics, information, and communications technologies.[23] Nuclear weapons would not be defeated so much as circumvented. The United States and other high-technology societies that were first to exploit advanced information technologies for military purposes would, in this view, have a rich deterrent in the form of "dominant battlespace awareness." This meant being able to see and interpret the entire battlefield and to deny the opponent a clear vision of it, perhaps by confusing or distorting the opponent's own information systems themselves. Some visionaries foresaw techniques for cyberwar that could bypass the actual destruction of armies and missile silos by holding hostage or incapacitating enemy communications, computers, electric power grids, banking records, or other social and economic necessities for modern life. Cyberwar might make possible both "counterforce" and "countervalue" attacks against nuclear command and control systems and against civilian infrastructure without firing a single shot in anger.

In summary thus far, both conventional and nuclear deterrence can rely on punishment or denial, on offensive or defensive technology, and on offensively or defensively oriented military doctrines. We will ignore for purposes of this discussion the fact that politicians and others use the terms "offensive" and "defensive" as pejorative and approbative references to the strategies of their enemies and allies. The terms have familiar meaning to readers of this study. The preceding considerations are necessary prologue to the more specific arguments that follow. They establish that friction in war or deterrence depends upon the specifics of strategy and force structure as well as upon the generalities to which theorists are naturally attracted. What kind of friction relative to nuclear deterrence might be of interest to theorists and to military operators in the next century, based on experience?

FRICTION IN OPERATIONS

In the discussion that follows I consider friction in offensive and defensive force operations. Models will be used in order to try to pin down some of the more abstract but policy-relevant aspects of offen-

Table 7.1

First-Strike Stability and Central Deterrence in Three Environments

	Offense Dominant	Defense Dominant	Offense–Defense Competitive
Central deterrence	STRONG Assured retaliation by offenses	STRONG Replaced by denial of attack objectives	UNCERTAIN Retaliatory threats may not be credible
First strike stability	STRONG No advantage to going first; both destroyed	STRONG No advantage to going first; both survive	UNCERTAIN Survival may be dependent upon first strike

Source: Adapted from Glenn A. Kent and David E. Thaler, *First Strike Stability and Strategic Defenses* (Santa Monica, Calif.: RAND, 1990), 4. I have reworded some cell entries in keeping with my purposes but not changed the thrust of the Kent–Thaler model.

sive or defensive force operations. There is an obvious asymmetry here. We know a great deal about the behavior of launchers and reentry vehicles for offensive forces based on considerable testing during the Cold War and later. But the state of defensive technology is comparatively immature and extrapolations about defenses are, of necessity, less confident.

Offensive Force Operations

Accounts of U.S. or Soviet strategy for nuclear war published during the Cold War years had an antiseptic, unreal quality, something like Clausewitz's reference to "war by algebra." Statistical estimates of the outcomes of nuclear wars were necessary substitutes for real thing. The danger was that models of nuclear war might distort probable outcomes by ignoring friction and assuming best-case performances for missiles, bombers, and command systems never tested in combat conditions. Contributors to the academic literature on nuclear strategy and arms control during the Cold War tended to assume away the significance of operational issues. The large and redundant force structures of the nuclear superpowers, it was presumed, would make irrelevant any comparisons among postattack states of affairs.

The assumption of nuclear-operations irrelevancy was not necessarily correct even for the years of the Cold War. It becomes even more important to consider offensive and defensive operational issues, including those related to friction, when American and Russian forces are greatly reduced from their Cold War levels.

Because political relations remained uncertain of direction in the 1990s, U.S. and Russian nuclear war planning remained on a Cold War gyroscope, albeit with some modifications that reflected the implausibility of global nuclear war. The reality for military planners in Washington and in Moscow was that, although the intentions of the two governments with respect to one another might have changed dramatically, the nuclear capabilities of Russia and America still loomed large. Thus, the U.S. decision-making process related to nuclear deterrence in the first post–Cold War decade adapted only in part to the requirements of the new world order.

This partial adaptation was reflected in the almost automated forward march of START nuclear arms-reduction talks. The first President Bush and President Clinton had agreed with Russia to START II reductions of strategic nuclear warheads down to ceilings of 3,000 to 3,500 along with some important specific counting rules (elimination of MIRVed ICBMs, for example). But START II was delayed in ratification by Russia and never actually implemented on account of both sides' reservations about various aspects of the agreement. President George W. Bush stated in November 2001 that he preferred to have the United States and Russia engage in further nuclear arms reductions by taking parallel decisions outside of a formal treaty framework, although he did not rule out the possibility of a treaty-based, sub-START regime. Bush administration officials estimated the United States could reduce its deployed strategic nuclear weapons down to 1,700 to 2,200 warheads. Russian President Vladimir Putin said the same month that his country's planners intended to reduce their numbers of equivalent weapons to 1,500 or fewer.

The Bush administration also indicated in its Nuclear Posture Review (NPR) released in January 2002 that major changes were planned in the relationship between offensive nuclear forces and other elements of U.S. deterrence policy. The NPR called for a "New Triad" composed of (1) offensive strike systems, both nuclear and nonnuclear; (2) defenses, both active and passive; and (3) a revitalized defense infrastructure. Common to all elements of the New Triad were improved command and control and intelligence systems.[24] The NPR stated that the United States "will no longer plan, size or sustain its forces as though Russia presented merely a smaller version of the threat posed by the former Soviet Union."[25] The NPR was one part of a Bush strategy revision to drastically reduce U.S. dependence on nuclear weapons by increasing capabilities for high-technology conventional warfare and by deploying missile defenses.[26]

These promising hopes for reducing the sizes of deployed forces are dependent on the confidence that both Washington and Moscow can have in the capabilities of their remaining forces. Even if their respective launchers and warheads are no longer aimed at one another's territory (nowadays a matter of several minutes to adjust), neither the United States nor Russia wants to doubt its retaliatory capability even after absorbing a surprise attack. Planners will continue to use their survivability against one another's arsenals as the "worst case" test case. How would friction in offensive force operations reduce the numbers of surviving and retaliating U.S. or Russian forces under various post–Cold War arms-control regimes?

Friction can be said to affect offensive force operations as a gradient between the maximum number of weapons originally deployed, on one end of the scale, and the minimum number of weapons actually fired back at enemy targets. Between these high and low extremes are intervening variables. Some deployed weapons are not on line at the time of attack. Some weapons deployed and on line are not yet alerted. Among weapons deployed, on line and alerted, not all will survive attack. Finally, some fraction of weapons deployed, on line, alert, and surviving a first strike will fail to arrive at their intended targets due to a variety of technical malfunctions or errors (gravitational anomalies, incorrect navigation fixes, unstable accelerometers, and so forth).

Let us make use of a model for estimating how many actual surviving and retaliating warheads would be available to the United States or to Russia after absorbing a first strike under plausible conditions of attack (the attack takes place after a political crisis has begun so that forces are alerted above normal peacetime operating tempos, but variation exists in the extent to which force components require prompt launch for survivability). Figures 7.1 through 7.4 summarize the expected numbers of surviving and retaliating warheads for Russian and American START III compliant forces at two levels: 2,500 and 1,500 ceilings.

The results summarized in Figures 7.1 through 7.4 show that there are significant differences in the numbers of surviving and retaliating warheads for each side, and especially for the Russians, based on the level of alertness and launch doctrines chosen by Washington and Moscow. As the total numbers of deployed warheads for each state shrink from between 6,000 and 8,000 to between 1,500 and 2,500, redundancy in survivable forces no longer compensates for diminished survivability of one or more force components. Now survivability will have to be guaranteed by higher alertness, by prompt launch, or by deployment patterns (mobile land-based missiles or submarine-launched missiles) that are proof against first strike even under the

Figure 7.1
U.S. START III (2,500) Strategic Forces

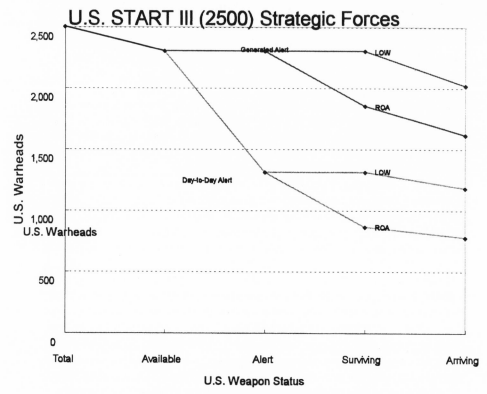

most favorable conditions for the attacker. Russia's heavier dependency on ICBMs compared to the Americans and Russia's anemic submarine and bomber fleets will create some additional inclinations toward launch on warning for the ICBM force.

In addition, there is the possibility of friction in the divergent expectations imposed by U.S. arms-control policy, on one hand, and presidential guidance for the development of actual nuclear war plans. Clinton administration policy guidance laid down in 1997 required that the United States maintain a number of deployed and survivable warheads sufficient to destroy some 2,260 highly valued targets in Russia. Approximately 1,100 of these targets were thought to be nuclear forces or installations that support nuclear forces. In order to guarantee that the United States could retaliate after absorbing a first strike and meet destruction requirements (80% or more) against this target set, the survivability of at least 1,800 warheads had to be guaranteed

Figure 7.2
U.S. START III (1,500) Strategic Forces

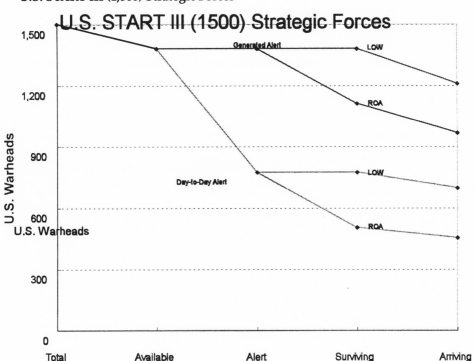

under all circumstances. In addition, military planners said they needed to maintain 2,200 warheads on alert. A summary of the requirements inferred by expert analysts with regard to Clinton targeting requirements appears in Table 7.2.

Clearly, policy guidance and targeting requirements will have to be "downsized" in order to mesh with the expectations of further arms reductions, especially if the United States and Russia prefer to reduce START III accountable force ceilings to 1,500 deployed warheads instead of 2,500 (as the Russians may prefer because of economic constraints on their force modernization). Whether targeting guidance and arms control can be synchronized will also depend upon Russian and Chinese reactions to any U.S. decision to deploy national missile defenses in this decade.

The larger context of these results, however, is more reassuring. Even friction-constrained retaliatory forces at START III levels will inflict destruction beyond historical precedent on either society. It remains

Figure 7.3
R.F. START III (2,500) Strategic Forces

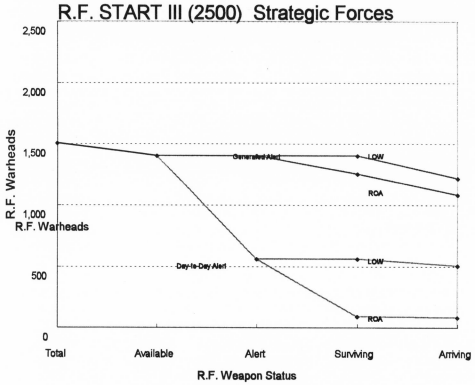

as it did during the Cold War. The cost of being number one or number two in strategic nuclear forces is that the United States and Russia, absent friendly political relations, invite massive destruction on themselves in the name of making deterrence credible. There was no escape from this nuclear straitjacket during the Cold War. Will post–Cold War defenses get Houdini out of this jacket, and what part might friction play in their operations?

Defenses

Offensive technologies are mature compared to anti-nuclear-missile defenses (BMD, ballistic missile defenses). During the Cold War the Soviets deployed a limited, early-generation ABM (anti-ballistic missile, early nomenclature for BMD) system around Moscow, causing some U.S. partisans of BMD to demand an arms race in defenses as

Figure 7.4
R.F. START III (1,500) Strategic Forces

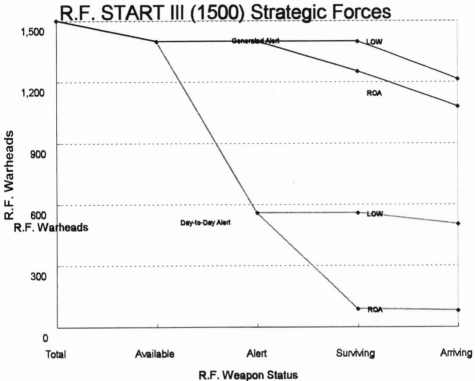

R.F. START III (1500) Strategic Forces

well as in offenses. The United States deployed a one-site BMD system (Safeguard) to defend ICBM fields at Grand Forks, North Dakota, until 1974. Neither the Soviet nor the U.S. technologies of the Cold War years could have coped with a large-scale attack. The Soviets feared in the 1980s that President Ronald Reagan's Strategic Defense Initiative would produce a technological leap ahead in missile defense for the United States that would undermine the Soviet deterrent. But the technology to make the president's dream a Cold War reality was not at hand. Under the first President Bush and President Clinton, the United States reduced its research and development objectives for NMD to defense against limited strikes. The Clinton administration, goaded by the Rumsfeld Report issued in 1998 on ballistic missile threats, moved within striking distance of a decision to deploy a limited NMD system in 2005. A summary of the steps in the development of the U.S. national missile defense technology appears in Table 7.3.

Table 7.2
U.S. Strategic Nuclear Targeting, 1997 Presidential Guidance

Requirement	Number
Total Targets (Russia, China, other)	at least 3,000
High Value Targets	2,560
Russia	2,260
—Nuclear Forces and Sites	1,100
—OMT (Other Military Targets, or conventional forces and their bases and installations)	500
—Leadership (Major military command centers, communications and supporting infrastructure)	160
—War-Supporting Industry (factories for arms production, equipment storage facilities, etc.)	500
China (limited nuclear options for attacking nuclear forces, leadership and major war-supporting industry)	300
Secondary Targets (additional targets in China, plus Iran, Iraq, and North Korea)	450–500

Source: Based on Bruce Blair, "Going Backwards: Number of US Nuclear Targets Has Grown since 1993," *Manchester Guardian*, June 16, 2000. Available at: http://www.cdi. org/issues/proliferation/goingbckbb.html. This table extrapolates from Blair's article and includes some deductions not in the original.

President George W. Bush fulfilled a campaign promise in 2001 by placing additional emphasis upon technology development for eventual deployment of a U.S. national missile defense system. In December 2001 Bush announced the United States would withdraw from the ABM Treaty in order to permit continued development and deployment of missile defenses. Meanwhile, the Department of Defense continued to pursue several technology-development projects that might lead to defenses capable of intercepting attacking rockets or warheads in various stages of their flight: boost phase, midcourse, and terminal. The DOD's Quadrennial Defense Review called for greater emphasis on nonnuclear systems for deterrence and defense, including missile defenses. This opened the door to large reductions in the numbers of deployed and/or stored U.S. nuclear weapons.

A notional BMD system based on nonnuclear exoatmospheric intercept might involve different kinds of friction. First, space- and earth-based radars would have to track incoming reentry vehicles and the warheads they dispensed. Second, interceptors would have to accelerate very rapidly in order to attain the velocities necessary for non-

Table 7.3
Phases in National Missile Defense

NMD Program	Mission	Defense
Phase I (1987–1989)	Enhance deterrence of Soviet first strike	Thousands of interceptors, ground and space based
Global Protection against Limited Strikes (GPALS) (1989–1992)	Protect against accidental or unauthorized launch	Hundreds of interceptors, ground and space based
Technology Readiness (1993–1995)	Prepare technology to reduce deployment time	Ground-based system; deployment not a consideration
Deployment Readiness— "3 + 3" (1996–1999)	Integrate systems; prepare for deployment three years after a future decision	Tens of interceptors, ground based only
NMD Acquisition (1999–2005)	Prepare for initial deployment in 2005	Tens of interceptors, ground based only

Source: Ballistic Missile Defense Organization, *Fact Sheet no. Jn-00-04*, January 2000, p. 1.

nuclear kill by impact with incoming warheads. Third, command, control, and communications would have to synchronize threat detection with the appropriate pattern of response. C3 would be even more important if the defenses involved a preferential firing doctrine instead of one that was random subtractive. Also related to C3 is the necessity for political leadership to take a timely decision to fire. Fourth, offensive countermeasures to defeat the defense might include chaff or other devices to blind or confuse radar tracking. Fifth, the "footprint" or area covered by the missile might not be as extensive as planners hoped: Targets outside of the footprint would be vulnerable. Friction in any or all of these components of the defense might add to "leakage" or the overall rate at which attackers succeed in penetrating the defense. The following list summarizes the possible sources of friction in missile defenses:

Detection	Detection might not take place in time for response or mischaracterize innocent event as attack.
	Large-scale or sneaky attack might overwhelm or confuse defenses.
Interception	Extreme accuracies and velocities required for exo/nonnuclear kill.
	Firing doctrine must be appropriate to the attack.
Command and control	Policy makers must react quickly and decisively to indications of attack, which might be ambiguous.
	C3 system must provide for feedback on intercept failures to correct follow-on forces.
Enemy countermeasures	Chaff, decoys, and other devices might confuse detection and tracking.
	Enemy might use nonstandard methods of attack (e.g., low-trajectory ballistic or cruise missiles).
Footprint	Not all areas within the footprint of the defender are equally important in terms of military assets, population, or other values.
	Enemy method of attack may outsmart defensive firing doctrine, making some areas within the footprint vulnerable.

These illustrations do not cover the entire range of possible sources of friction in defenses any more successfully than the earlier short resume of problems in offenses. And we have the additional disadvantage of dealing in hypothetical technologies instead of actual forces deployed and (occasionally) alerted. Despite these handicaps in discussing defenses, some discussion of friction even in defenses based on very simple concepts, and tasked against very limited attacks only, might be useful now.

The question of most importance to Russian and U.S. policy makers in this hypothetical situation is this: Will defenses be so competent as to negate or impose significant penalties on the second or retaliatory strike by either side? If so, that side fears loss of its deterrent and is all the more motivated toward a crisis-time decision for preemption or launch on warning. The concern is an immediate one for Russia, given the U.S. decision in December 2001 to withdraw from the ABM Treaty in order to clear the way for missile-defense site construction beginning in the summer of 2002. In Figures 7.5 and 7.6 we interrogate this issue from the Russian perspective. In these two illustrations we play U.S. defenses based on current NMD technology (ground-based, exoatmospheric intercept, nonnuclear hit to kill) against surviving Russian forces at initially deployed levels of 2,500 and 1,500 warheads.

Defenses were assigned plausible attrition rates against retaliating warheads from ICBMs, SLBMs, and bomber-delivered weapons.

The data summarized in Figures 7.5 and 7.6 are based on models of hypothetical offense–defense exchanges, but they show something important. Even very competent defenses combined with first strikes cannot reduce the numbers of U.S. or Russian survivors to an "acceptable" level of retaliation from the standpoint of societal disaster. But defenses combined with first strikes could limit offensive retaliation to countersocietal attacks only. There is no overturning of mutual deterrence based on offensive retaliation evident here, but there could be friction attendant to the combining of offensive missile and defensive antimissile technologies by one side against another that deployed offenses only.

Figure 7.5
Russian Survivors and Penetrators: R.F. START III (2,500) Strategic Forces

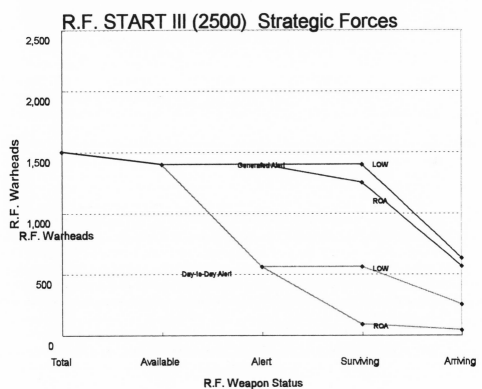

Figure 7.6
Russian Survivors and Penetrators: R.F. START III (1,500) Strategic Forces

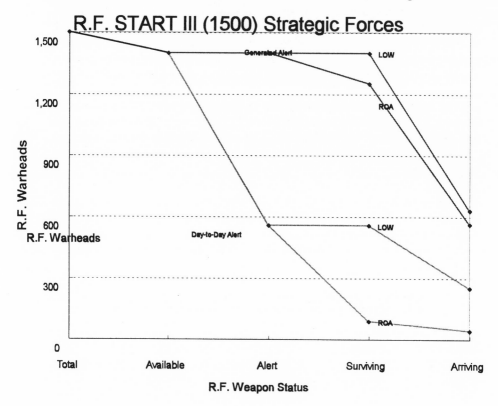

Of course, much remains uncertain about the evolution of U.S. or Russian missile-defense technology. U.S. and Russian antinuclear strategic defenses would also have implications not only for one another's deterrents, but for those of other powers, including China, Britain, and France. Thus friction characterizes not only the problem of defense-technology development, but also the arms-control and political relationships between the United States and Russia, between Russia and Europe, and between the United States and its NATO allies. Russian President Putin has already taken advantage of these uncharted political waters by putting forward a proposal in June 2000 for a Euro missile-defense system, including Russia and NATO. We are in for an interesting decade on the politics and technology of missile defense.

CONCLUSIONS

The logic of deterrence, including nuclear deterrence, is one of psychological persuasion backed up by the sharp end of military power. Friction limits how influential or effective deterrence can be. Friction affects both the physical and the social–political aspects of war and crisis decision making. In the case of nuclear deterrence as military persuasion, there is more than circumstantial evidence that friction affects peacetime and crisis decision making. In addition, the attempt to use nuclear weapons as a means of influence is prone to slippage to the extent that the other side's intentions are wrongly construed or its capabilities misestimated. Deterrence depends entirely on seeing the "other" correctly. If our arguments about deterrence as a form of military persuasion and friction are correct, then deterrence is likely to work less well in the post–Cold War international environment than hitherto. Missile defenses will not remove friction from the equation of deterrence as military persuasion, and they may very well increase the degree and danger of friction by contributing to arms races, proliferation, or crisis uncertainty.

APPENDIX: U.S. AND RUSSIAN STRATEGIC NUCLEAR FORCES

U.S. Strategic Forces

System	Warheads per Launch Vehicle	START III (2,500)	START III (1,500)
Minuteman II	1		
Minuteman III	3		
Minuteman III	1	500/500	300/300
Peacekeeper	10		
Total ICBM		500/500	300/300
Poseidon C3	16x10		
Poseidon C4	16x8		
Trident C4	24x8		
Trident D5	24x8		
Trident D5	24x5		
Trident D5	24x4	336/1,344	
Trident D5	14x4		196/784
Total SLBM		336/1,344	196/784
B52G	12 ALCM		
B52H	20 mixed		

B52H	20 ALCM		
B52H	8 ALCM	62/496	32/256
B1B 16 bombs			
B2 16 bombs			
B2 8 bombs	20/160	20/160	
Total Bomber		82/656	52/416
Total Triad		918/2,500	548/1,500

R.F. Strategic Forces

System	Warheads per Launch Vehicle	START II START III
SS-19	1	105/105
SS-19	6	
SS-25 mobile	1	251/251
SS-27 mobile	1	60/60
SS-27 mobile	3	
SS-27 silo-based	1	60/60
SS-27 silo-based	3	
Total ICBM		476/476
Delta IV (SS-N-23) or equivalent	16x4	112/448
Total SLBM		112/448
Bear H	6 ALCM	66/396
Blackjack	12 ALCM	15/180
Total Bomber		81/576
Total Triad		669/1,500

NOTES

Charts and appendix for this chapter are based on force-exchange models and data developed by Dr. James Scouras, Strategy Research Group. He bears no responsibility for their use here, nor for any arguments.

1. William E. Odom, *The Collapse of the Soviet Military* (New Haven, Conn.: Yale University Press, 1998), 388–404; Edward A. Kolodziej, "The Pursuit of Order, Welfare and Legitimacy: Explaining the End of the Soviet Union and the Cold War," in *Mysteries of the Cold War*, ed. Stephen J. Cimbala (Aldershot, England: Ashgate, 1999), 19–48; Peter Rainow, "The Strange End of the Cold War: Views from the Former Superpower," in ibid., 49–69.

2. Carl von Clausewitz, *On War*, ed. and trans. Michael Howard and Peter Paret (Princeton, N.J.: Princeton University Press, 1976), 119–121.

3. Colin S. Gray, *Modern Strategy* (Oxford: Oxford University Press, 1999), 94.

4. Clausewitz, *On War*, 119–121.

5. Ibid., 119.

6. Ibid.

7. Ibid.

8. For useful comments on the relationship between friction and chance in *On War*, see Gray, *Modern Strategy*, 41.

9. Clausewitz, *On War*, 120.

10. Ibid.

11. Clausewitz to Marie von Bruhl, September 29, 1806, cited in Peter Paret, *Clausewitz and the State: The Man, His Theories and His Times* (Princeton, N.J.: Princeton University Press, 1976), 124. I am grateful to Barry D. Watts for calling this reference to my attention. See Barry D. Watts, *Clausewitzian Friction and Future War*, McNair Paper 52 (Washington, D.C.: Institute for National Strategic Studies, National Defense University, 1996), 7–8.

12. Watts, *Clausewitzian Friction and Future War*, 8. See also Peter Paret and Daniel Moran, ed. and trans., *Clausewitz "From Observations on Prussia in Her Great Catastrophe," Historical and Political Writings* (Princeton, N.J.: Princeton University Press, 1992).

13. Watts, *Clausewitzian Friction and Future War*, 8.

14. Paret, *Clausewitz and the State*, 197–198; also cited in Watts, *Clausewitzian Friction and Future War*, 10.

15. Clausewitz, *On War*, 114.

16. Ibid., 122.

17. Alexander L. George, "The Role of Force in Diplomacy: A Continuing Dilemma for U.S. Forreign Policy," in *The Use of Force after the Cold War*, ed. H. W. Brands with Darren J. Pierson and Reynolds S. Kiefer (College Station: Texas A&M University Press, 2000), 59–92, especially pp. 73–79.

18. Ibid., 76.

19. Compellence is explained in Thomas C. Schelling, *Arms and Influence* (New Haven, Conn.: Yale University Press, 1966), passim.

20. Gordon A. Craig and Alexander L. George, *Force and Statecraft: Diplomatic Problems of Our Time* (New York: Oxford University Press, 1983), 189.

21. Gray, *Modern Strategy*, ch. 11, especially p. 309, offers some interesting retrospective and contemporary appraisals of U.S. nuclear strategy and strategy debates.

22. My distinction parallels that drawn by Patrick M. Morgan between "general" and "immediate" deterrence. See Patrick M. Morgan, *Deterrence: A Conceptual Analysis*, 2d ed. (Beverly Hills, Calif.: Sage, 1983), 27–48. A related distinction of significance is made by Alexander L. George with regard to the type of peace that deterrence is intended to help achieve: precarious peace, conditional peace, or stable peace. Precarious peace implies an acute conflict relationship between parties in which general deterrence must be reinforced by frequent and timely resort to immediate deterrence (i.e., specific threats and/or reassurances). Conditional peace, on the other hand, points to a less intense conflict relationship in which general deterrence plays the predominant and usually effective part in discouraging crises. In contrast to both, a stable peace is a relationship between parties in which neither considers threatening or using force to resolve disagreements. See George, "The Role of Force in Diplomacy," 73–74.

23. For views on the RMA and information-based warfare, see John Arquilla and David Ronfeldt, "A New Epoch—and Spectrum—of Conflict," in *In*

Athena's Camp: Preparing for Conflict in the Information Age, ed. John Arquilla and David Ronfeldt (Santa Monica, Calif.: RAND, 1997), 1–22. See also, on definitions and concepts of information warfare, Martin Libicki, *What Is Information Warfare?* ACIS paper 3 (Washington, D.C.: National Defense University, 1995); Martin Libicki, *Defending Cyberspace and Other Metaphors* (Washington, D.C.: National Defense University, Directorate of Advanced Concepts, Technologies and Information Strategies, 1997); Alvin Toffler and Heidi Toffler, *War and Anti-War: Survival at the Dawn of the 21st Century* (Boston: Little, Brown, 1993), 163–207; John Arquilla and David Ronfeldt, *Cyberwar Is Coming!* (Santa Monica, Calif.: RAND, 1992); David S. Alberts, *The Unintended Consequences of Information Age Technologies: Avoiding the Pitfalls, Seizing the Initiative* (Washington, D.C.: National Defense University, Institute for National Strategic Studies, Center for Advanced Concepts and Technology, 1996).

24. Donald H. Rumsfeld, Secretary of Defense, *Nuclear Posture Review Report: Forward* (Washington, D.C.: U.S. Department of Defense, 2002). Available at: http://www.fas.org/sgp/news/2002/01/npr-foreward.html.

25. Ibid.

26. James Dao, "Pentagon Study Urges Arms Shift, from Nuclear to High-Tech," *New York Times,* January 9, 2002. Available at: http://www.nytimes.com/2002/01/09/international/09PENT.html?todaysheadlines.

8

Military Persuasion and Small Wars

Small wars and military peace operations are not identical, either in
their objectives or in the preferred methods for conducting them. But
they share at least one important commonality: Psychological strategy
is as important, if not more important, than actual combat. Small wars
and peace operations are won or lost in the minds of participants and
observers. Victory or defeat is tabulated not by body count but by the
sum of allegiance or disaffection that the various combatants or peacekeepers can call upon. War, or antiwar in the case of peace operations,
is about cultural and social privations and priorities. Most often in the
1990s, small wars were ethnonationalist or religious conflicts resulting
from the decline of legitimacy in failed or failing states, but there were
many other causes too numerous to mention here. The complexity of
causes made the design of peace wars, intended to terminate small
wars growing out of various causes, all the more difficult.

  This chapter considers the demands made upon U.S. and allied forces
in peace operations and small wars. First, we review existing concepts
having to do with small wars, including so-called unconventional wars
and low-intensity conflicts. This conceptual thicket cries out for some
clarity, and we offer a small contribution in this regard. Second, we
discuss some U.S. armed forces doctrine for organizing and conducting military "operations other than war" (OOTW).[1] Third, we consider
the special complexities of urban conflict, since the next century may
see more warriors and peace operators tasked to work in urban environments. Fourth, we discuss the problem of conducting small wars
or peace operations with allies, using U.S. relations with NATO as il-

lustrative. Fifth, we consider the problem of U.S. public, media, and congressional support for small wars and peace operations, especially for those with the potential to turn into larger wars through inadvertence or deliberate escalation.

CONCEPTS OF AMBIGUOUS WAR

Military planners and scholars have been frustrated by the lack of a conceptual framework for understanding how the internal wars of the post–Cold War era are different from the revolutionary wars of the Cold War. Donald M. Snow has outlined some of the important ways in which contemporary internal wars differ from traditional insurgencies.[2] First, traditional insurgencies are fought with the object of capturing control over the political system; for many of the new internal wars, this object is absent or secondary. Criminal organizations and narco-terrorists, for example, prefer a weak state, not a strong one, and are comparatively indifferent to who rules as long as they can escape effective control. Second, contemporary internal wars are often marked by lack of restraint when compared to Cold War insurgencies. Insurgent tactics emphasize winning over the "hearts and minds" of a politically ambivalent population. Internal wars of the 1990s (for example, in Bosnia and Rwanda) were marked by "ethnic cleansing" and other massacres with no apparent object other than killing itself.

A third apparent difference between Cold War insurgencies and post–Cold War internal wars, according to Snow and others, is that many internal wars are concentrated in the economically least developed states or in politically failed states. Failed states are those in which the government has suffered a terminal loss of legitimacy and effectiveness. Loss of legitimacy means that the state is no longer regarded as authoritative (i.e., entitled to rightful rule). Lack of effectiveness in a failed state is often apparent in the shift of control to local centers of real power and resistance: warlords, clans, criminal syndicates, ethnonational rebels, and others from a list difficult to exhaust.[3] Although a weak or failing state may give the appearance of sovereignty and strength, its durability rests solely on context. As the weak state increases its level of context seeking in vain to substitute for lost legitimacy and effectiveness, resistance to context also increases. Eventually the state fails of its own apparent incompetence, as even its coercive powers dissolve or are overthrown by its enemies.[4]

It may be useful to distinguish between small wars and peace wars. Small wars may be peace wars and vice versa, but the similarities between the two have more to do with the types of forces engaged or equipment used than they do with the purpose of fighting. Small wars are military conflicts in which at least one side employs irregular forces and unconventional methods of battle. Often this side is something other than a politically accountable state authority.[5] Small wars have variable purposes and even more variable methods, especially on the irregular side: terrorism, insurgency, guerrilla warfare, and so forth. The unconventional and usually weaker side in a small war against a state authority wins if it is not defeated as a political force in the society: Absent a decisive political setback, it can live to fight another day and gather new recruits to replace the ones lost.

Peace wars are those military deployments or threats of intervention that are intended to accomplish some political purpose other than victory in battle, but which may require capability for military combat as well as noncombatant missions. I prefer the term "peace wars" because it emphasizes the two-sided demands placed upon military operators in these situations: They are simultaneously diplomats or politicians as well as warriors. These missions, however honorable in intent, (1) force military commanders into political, cultural, and social contexts over which they have partial and often inadequate control relative to their assigned mission; and (2) within those contexts may require that commanders and forces be forced to play an undesirable, unaccustomed, or unpopular political part. U.S. forces in Somalia from 1991 to 1994 found themselves in the first situation; French paratroops in Algeria from 1956 to 1958 ended up in the second situation.

Involvement in small or peace wars by outside powers, especially great powers involved in another state's civil wars, often brings into play the "Gulliver effect." The Gulliver effect is the discrepancy between a state's ability to destroy things, on one hand, and its ability to persuade or coerce its opponent with the use of minimum or no force, on the other. It is not a static measure of winning or losing. The Gulliver effect is a loss of strength gradient that, on account of the domination of small or peace wars by political, social, cultural, and other nonmilitary factors, creates a lower than expected military effect on the part of a larger power against a smaller one. The more prolonged the conflict, the more the potential for Gulliver effects. It is worth noting that, at least in democratic societies, Gulliver-type loss of political and military strength in the field can originate from causes on the home front, as the Americans and French in Vietnam and the Soviet Union in Afghanistan and in Chechnya discovered.

ORGANIZING FOR
UNCONVENTIONAL CONFLICTS

The U.S. Department of Defense recognizes that its responsibilities now include preparedness for so-called unconventional conflicts, including revolutionary and counterrevolutionary warfare, terrorism, antidrug operations, and peace operations, inter alia. In part this recognition has found its way into manuals and other publications giving the accepted version of military doctrine and practice. For example, specific kinds of Operations Other Than War included in a mid-1990s version of Army doctrine were (1) support to domestic civil authorities, (2) humanitarian assistance and disaster relief, (3) security assistance, (4) noncombat evacuation operations, (5) arms-control monitoring and verification, (6) nation assistance, (7) support to counterdrug operations, (8) combating terrorism, (9) peacekeeping and peace enforcement operations, (10) show of force, (11) support for insurgency or counterinsurgency, and (12) attacks and raids.[6]

Current U.S. joint (multiservice) military doctrine assumes that most peace operations will take place in "complex contingencies." A complex contingency operation is one that responds to a complex emergency. The United Nations defines a complex emergency as "a humanitarian crisis in a country, region or society where there is a total or considerable breakdown of authority resulting from internal conflict and which requires an international response that goes beyond the mandate (or) capacity of any single agency and/or the on-going United Nations country program."[7]

Experts on complex emergencies emphasize that complex emergencies must be distinguished from natural disasters. According to Mark Duffield,

So-called complex emergencies are essentially political in nature: they are protracted political crises resulting from sectarian or predatory indigenous responses to socioeconomic stress and marginalisation. Unlike natural disasters, complex emergencies have a singular ability to erode or destroy the cultural, civil, political and economic integrity of established societies.[8]

According to the U.S. *Joint Task Force Commander's Handbook for Peace Operations* (1997 edition), complex contingencies have the following characteristics:

- Increased use of asymmetrical means by belligerents
- Dominance of political objectives
- Presence and involvement of nongovernmental, private, voluntary, and international organizations, media, and other civilians in the military operations area, and impacting upon military activities
- Usually takes place in a failed state, which also implies: undisciplined factions, absence of law and order, numerous parties to the conflict, large scale violations of human rights, risks of armed opposition to peace forces, and other problems[9]

Operations Other Than War constitute an elastic category. As such, they invite controversy about the boundary line between "war" and "other than war." When, for example, does U.S. support for the counterinsurgency or counterterror operations spill over from nonwar (NW) into de facto involvement in a war? The object of insurgents is to blur the line between peace and war until such a time as they are ready to wage open, conventional warfare to their advantage. This is not merely a problem of terminology. Confusion about whether the United States is actually at war invites inconsistency between policy objectives and military operations. A working solution to the boundary problem is depicted in Table 8.1.

Table 8.1
OOTW and Types of Military Operations

Combat or Noncombat	Type of Military Operation	General U.S. Goals	Examples
Combat	War	Fight and Win	Large-Scale Combat Operations: Attack, Defend, Blockade
Combat and Noncombat	MOOTW	Deter War and Resolve Conflict	Peace Enforcement, Counterterrorism; Show of force, raid, strike; Peacekeeping; Nation Assistance; Counter-insurgency
Noncombat	MOOTW	Promote Peace and Support Civil Authority	Freedom of navigation; Counterdrug; Humanitarian assistance; Protection of shipping; U.S. civil support

Source: U.S. Joint Chiefs of Staff, *Joint Doctrine for Military Operations Other Than War*, Joint pub. 3-07 (Washington, D.C.: Joint Chiefs of Staff, 1995), I-2.

Since word processors make it possible to produce new doctrinal manuals at nearly the speed of light nowadays, the citations in this chapter may be superseded by the time this book has gone to press, but clearly, doctrine on this topic is important, since doctrine tells the troops how to implement or operationalize the goals of policy makers and higher-level commanders. Equally clear is that doctrine on this topic is a moveable feast, subject to the vicissitudes of changes in U.S. government administration. And even the best doctrine must speak in glittering generalities. It is up to the field commanders and the plethora of other actors with whom they must work on site to bring stability and postintervention responsive government into war-torn areas. As bitter experience in Sierra Leone in May 2000 showed only too clearly, international and regional military forces cannot by themselves create a legacy of peaceful expectations for conflict resolution. Multinational intervention forces can only influence some of the environmental parameters conducive or unfavorable to lasting pacific settlement of conflicts.

THE "WHERE" OF PEACE OPERATIONS AND SMALL WARS: A SPECTRUM OF QUAGMIRES

Urban Warfare

The last quarter of the twentieth century has shifted the milieu for many intrastate conflicts from rural to urban environments. Twenty-first-century fighting in cities might follow neither the Maoist nor the Leninist pattern of revolutionary war nor prior experience in conventional campaigns against cities. New technologies, forms of organization, and causes of fighting in cities will stress existing templates of military planners and political leaders. For example, future urban revolutionaries may prefer dispersed and decentralized command systems that are harder to identify, target, or destroy compared to cells centralized under a single directorate. According to Gerard Chaliand, an expert on unconventional conflicts,

The new factor in contemporary terrorism as compared with national liberation movements (some of which also resort to terrorism) is the emergence of little groups with no organized links with the masses and no movement worthy of the name to draw up a political program. There has been a massive increase in the number of minuscule groups that see indiscriminate terrorism as both tactic and political line.[10]

Future urban warfare may require more than peace or stability operations against lightly armed, indigenous paramilitary forces. General Charles Krulak has described the diversity of future urban military operations as a "three-block war": U.S. forces might be conducting a humanitarian operation in one part of a city, peacekeeping or peace enforcement in another, and fighting a mid-intensity battle in a third sector.[11] Lieutenant Colonel Robert F. Hahn and Bonnie Jezior of the U.S. Army After Next Urban Warfare Project argue that U.S. military planners must exploit new technologies for situation awareness, precision fire, mobility, and other uses if they are to cope with the complexity of urban warfare in the next century.[12] These recommendations will collide with existing U.S. and allied military doctrine that emphasizes the avoidance of fighting in built-up areas. Although cities can sometimes be made to surrender by siege or be bypassed and isolated, these favorable outcomes cannot always be assumed.[13]

Both the political and the military operational settings for fighting in urban areas are full of potholes. Combat will be taking place in conditions that impede communications, hamper movement of friendly forces, permit maximum concealment to enemy regular and irregular forces, and commingle noncombatants with combatants. Adversaries will definitely exploit all the opportunities for friction that these political and military conditions make possible. As the analysis of the battle of Grozny in January 1995 by Timothy L. Thomas suggests, urban warfare in the age of information can combine the friction of unconventional and conventional military operations, as well as the frustrations of first-, second-, and third-wave warfare in a single military campaign.[14] The environment of urban warfare is especially unforgiving. Urban combat is three dimensional in nature: (1) It makes insatiable demands on casualty evacuation and resupply, (2) urban structures block line-of-sight radio communications and create other difficulties that force units to fight in a highly decentralized, separated manner, and (3) situation awareness is limited because the terrain imposes so many constraints on intelligence gathering and troop movement.[15] According to Lieutenant Colonel John F. Antal,

The history of conventional combat in the 20th century proves that single arm solutions in complex, urban terrain almost always fail, particularly if they are hastily prepared and poorly planned. Roof-to-roof, house-to-house, cellar-to-cellar city fighting against a determined foe is grisly business, a business that requires a tough, competent combined arms solution.[16]

Urban Warfare Plus: Russia in Chechnya

When Russia invaded its rebellious province Chechnya in December 1994 it was expected in Moscow that Chechen resistance would rapidly give way to superior Russian forces. Previously Russian security organs had failed to topple the government of rebel Chechen President Dzhokar Dudayev by working with indigenous forces to attempt a coup. Frustrated by its inability to dislodge Dudayev by other means, Russia escalated and sent in its army and air force. Russia's initial military campaigns in Chechnya were poorly prepared and met with disaster. Instead of fighting for several months, Russian forces were bogged down in Chechnya for two years. Russia was forced to negotiate a peace settlement in August 1996 calling for the removal of Russian forces from Chechnya by the end of the year and leaving the political future of Chechnya open ended.[17]

Although the combat organization, training, and performance of Russia's forces in Chechnya were unimpressive, these weaknesses were made worse by Russia's failure to correctly forecast how Chechen society and culture would hobble its war effort. Russia's own experience in the previous century against Imam Shamil and other Chechen resistance fighters was ignored.[18] The more recent Soviet combat experience against Afghan resistance yielded little in the way of lessons learned for an overconfident Russian defense ministry in 1994. The ineptitude of Russian combat tactics in Chechnya was compounded by the inability of President Boris Yeltsin and his entourage to make a persuasive case for the legitimacy of the military campaign. Russians by and large were skeptical of the entire affair, or opposed, or tuned out.

Russia lost the battle of moral influence, as the renowned Chinese military philosopher Sun Tzu would have called it (see Chapter 1), for several reasons. First, the leadership of the Russian armed forces was bitterly divided over the prudence of using the security forces of Russia, especially those of the defense ministry, to impose order on Chechnya. Second, the Russian media covered the war like a proverbial blanket and gave a great deal of publicity to Russian and Chechen opponents of the war. Third, Chechens successfully used psychological warfare, including deception operations, to favorably depict their cause and to attempt to intimidate and deceive their opponents.

For example, a commander of Russia's North Caucasus Military District complained that the Ministry of Defense had almost totally ignored any preparations for psychological warfare in Chechnya. As a result, the Dudayev forces had nearly demoralized the 19th Motorized Rifle Division by sending radio messages to individual officers by name and threatening their wives and children if those officers took part in any attack on Grozny. Another example is the use of Ukrainian nationalists in Chechen deception operations. Ukrainians dressed in Russian uniforms led unsuspecting Russian comrades to Dudayev as prisoners of war. Other Ukrainians disguised themselves as members of Doctors without Borders (Medecins sans Frontieres) or the Red Cross in order to question refugees and obtain other intelligence for Chechen forces.[19] Chechen "psyop" information activities against Russia also exploited perceptions management in order to present favorably the case against Russian military intervention to Russian and other news media. These and other problems that marked Russia's conduct of its disastrous military self-invasion in Chechnya are summarized by the principles of military effectiveness that they violated in the following list:[20]

Principle of War or Military Art	Deficiency in Russian Performance
Objective	The stated objective was to preserve territorial integrity of Russia and reestablish constitutional order in Chechnya. Use of the military was premature and no real crisis resolution was attempted. Military tactics of massive firepower and killing of civilians alienated population.
Offensive	Russians launched a hastily prepared offensive in December 1994 with untrained troops and ambivalent commanders. The initial assault on Grozny moved along three different and mutually unsupported axes.
Mass	Massed force and indiscriminate firepower were not appropriate for situation. Air, artillery, and tanks were of limited value in low-intensity conflict. In addition, the principle of mass requires that forces are closely coordinated: Many Russian units, in contrast, failed to cooperate.
Economy of force	Sloppy employment and distribution of forces resulted from poor planning and lapses in control. Russians were unable to isolate and target actual Chechen fighters or to crush Chechen center of gravity. Instead, Russian forces set mass fires and destruction of civilian areas.
Maneuver	Chechen knowledge of territory kept Russians off balance. Russians often operate with a "firebase" mentality. Russians lack flexibility in adapting tactics to changed situation: For example, when unexpected resistance impeded original plan to seize Grozny, Russians continued frontal assault.
Unity of command	Dissension was evident among all levels of command and between field commanders and Moscow. Ground forces, air forces, and interior troops operated as separate forces and distrust one another. No concept of professional solidarity was evident.
Security and intelligence	Chechens were apparently aware of every major Russian military action in advance (except for air)

	from December 1994 through August 1996. Russians were unaware of Chechen plans for hostage seizures and unable to identify sources of intelligence leaks.
Surprise	Russians expected to catch Chechens unaware in December 1994, but failed. Chechen tactics in Grozny surprised Russians.
Simplicity	Russian forces drawn from a large number of different security agencies were unfamiliar with one another's operational modes. The training, coordination, and leadership needed to combine these forces into a cohesive whole were absent.

Superficially, it might appear that this critique is obsolete in view of the apparently more favorable outcome for Russia in its second war against Chechen rebels in 1999–2000. Acting President Vladimir Putin, already having been anointed as the chosen successor of Russian President Boris Yeltsin, vaulted into the latter's job in 1999 on the strength of his determination to redo the war of 1994–1996 but get it right the second time. Getting it right got down to a two-part campaign. First, Russian commanders used the Russian air force and heavy artillery to shell Chechen resistance in Grozny and other major centers into submission. Outside of cities they used equally devastating firepower against villages suspected of being occupied by Chechen fighters. These "clear and hold" operations paid no heed to the problem of "collateral damage" (the loss of life of innocent noncombatants and the devastation of their property). When the Russians were done bombing Grozny in Chechnya II in the winter of 2000, it resembled Stalingrad in 1942–1943.

Second, and probably more important to the temporary success of Russia's 1999–2000 campaign in Chechnya, the Putin administration had its political ducks in order prior to and during the actual fighting, as the Yeltsin gang failed to do five years earlier. Putin succeeded in rousing the hostile ethnic feelings on the part of many Russians against Chechens that have been a part of Russian history for centuries. He turned public opinion in favor of decisive military action by taking advantage of two issues: the incursion into neighboring Dagestan in August 1999 by Chechen rebels, and a series of sanguinary hotel bombings in Moscow that were not so subtly blamed by the government on Chechen terrorists.

Buoyed by favorable public opinion that had been missing in 1994, the Russian military also applied some lessons learned in 1994–1996 to the later conflict. Command and control were improved, resulting in improved coordination among the military and internal security units tasked to do the actual fighting. In turn, the scorched earth–artillery and air war fought by the Russians caught the Chechens outgunned and outmanned: Russia tasked some 100,000 troops for the theater of operations. Russian armed forces also avoided futile attempts to take urban areas such as Grozny by storm, as they had tried to do in January 1995, before pounding resistance into the ground with long-range artillery and air strikes. Finally, Chechen resistance in 1999–2000 did not appear to be as coordinated or as determined as it had been in the earlier conflict. Many noncombatant Chechens appeared to be dismayed by the possibility of another war against Russia given the setback to their standard of living inflicted by the last war. Chechen field commanders feuded among themselves and antagonized some elements of the population in Chechnya and, especially, in Dagestan.

Then, too, some of the motivation for the Russian generals to get it right the second time in Chechnya was personal or a mixture of personal and professional: a matter of wounded pride. For example, General Anatoliy Kvashnin was chief of the Russian Armed Forces General Staff in 1999. He had long memories. In 1995, before Russian troops under his overall command were defeated and forced to withdraw from Grozny, he had predicted,

We will beat the Chechens to pulp so that the present generation will be too terrified to fight Russia again. Let Western observers come to Grozny and see what we have done to our own city so that they shall know what may happen to their towns if they get rough with Russia. But you know, in 20 or 30 years, a new generation of Chechens that hasn't seen the Russian army in action will grow up and they will again rebel, and we'll have to smash them down all over again.[21]

The first part of the prediction was not borne out, at least not in 1994–1996. Whether it would work in 1999–2002 was a matter of dispute at the time of this writing. The comment that Western observers should come and see "what we have done to our own city" is an interesting one: It suggests that part of Russia's determination to fight again in Chechnya was based on resentment of NATO's air war against Serbia and Putin's desire to show international as well as internal audiences a more militarily impressive facade.

It remained the case as the year 2001 drew to a close that Russia, having brought its immediate military campaign in Chechnya to a close, was very far from having won the protracted war. Chechen resistance remained strong, if scattered and sporadic, in the southern part of the troubled republic. Resistance fighters holed up in mountain redoubts in southern Chechnya licking their wounds, reorganizing and reequipping, and awaiting another crack at Russia's legions. For Chechen resistance fighters, Russia symbolized both imperialism and defilement of their religion and way of life based on that religion. For Russians, Chechens symbolized criminality and banditry on a large scale, capable of destabilizing Russia. The continuing clash of these negative stereotypes alone made it unlikely that the military persuasion of cultural conflict and social antagonism would cease, even if all regular Russian military units were fully withdrawn from Chechnya.

ALLIES TOGETHER OR SEPARATELY?

Command and Control

Fighting or peace soldiering with allies is one way to blunt the fear of casualties and the risks of wider war, but alliances introduce other complexities, including the question of shared military command. Napoleon is reported to have commented on at least one occasion that fighting with allies was even worse than fighting without them. In the 1994 version of its annual report to the Congress, the U.S. Department of Defense was careful to acknowledge the difficulty of command and control for multinational operations and to offer itself a plausible way out:

The issue of command and control will always be a key factor in deciding whether to deploy U.S. forces as part of a U.N. peace operation. As a practical matter, if significant combat operations are contemplated, and if American involvement is planned, it is unlikely that the United States would agree to place its forces under the operational control of a U.N. commander. In these situations, the United States would prefer to rely either on its own resources, on those of a capable regional organization such as NATO, or on an appropriate coalition such as that assembled for Operation Desert Storm.[22]

The 1994 Clinton administration policy statement on U.S. participation in multilateral peace operations established three sets of criteria.[23] The first set of factors would be considered in deciding whether to vote in support of a U.N. peace operation (Chapter VI or Chapter VII). The second set of even more restrictive standards would apply when the participation of U.S. personnel in peace operations is being considered. Third, additional and more rigorous factors would be taken into account if the peace operation is a peace-enforcement (Chapter VII) exercise likely to involve combat. These criteria reflected a post-Somalia and more cautious view of military intervention, at least outside of Europe, compared to that with which the Clinton administration operated in its first several years.[24]

In the aftermath of NATO's air war (Operation Allied Force) against Yugoslavia in 1999, Clinton officials were less fastidious in their public pronouncements about the criteria for humanitarian intervention than they appeared to be in the 1994 guidelines. National Security

Advisor Samuel Berger indicated that future interventions could be undertaken if a sufficiently grave violation of human rights existed, if the United States and its allies possessed the military capability to do something about it, and if other options seemed to have exhausted themselves. It was not clear that Kosovo was more than sui generis in its implications for further U.S. decision making about the uses of force for humanitarian rescue or for peace and stability operations. Much would depend upon the political outcomes in Kosovo subsequent to NATO's seventy-eight days of air war.

NATO in Kosovo: Marching More, or Less, in Step

Some critics of U.S. and NATO performance in the air campaign against Yugoslavia blamed the need for interallied consensus for inept war plans, unwillingness to authorize a ground campaign in Kosovo if necessary, poor communication of signals to the Serbs about probable terms of settlement, and other political and military land mines over which the bombing campaign allegedly tripped. It is not clear that lack of interallied consultation caused most of the hiatus between political and military objectives in Operation Allied Force, however. One apparent cost of alliance management of the war did appear in the area of intelligence. NATO's consultative process for planning the air war leaked important information to the Serbs in the first two weeks of the conflict: Numbered among the suspects were the intelligence services of NATO's newly acquired members who were formerly Soviet allies in the Warsaw Treaty Organization during the Cold War. The leaks could not be proved to come from a particular source, but NATO did narrow the circle of target planners and reviewers after several weeks of war and fewer leaks resulted.

With regard to the successful or unsuccessful practice of military persuasion, a more telling critique of Operation Allied Force was offered by Ivo Daalder and Michael O'Hanlon.[25] Daalder and O'Hanlon note that NATO embarked upon its air campaign on March 24, 1999, with the expectation that Yugoslav President Slobodan Milosevic would rapidly capitulate to NATO's political demands: Halt all repression of Albanians in Kosovo by withdrawing Serb military and police forces from the troubled province, agree to an international military presence (presumably NATO plus coalitions of the willing) in Kosovo, and the safe return of all refugees and displaced persons already having been driven out of Kosovo by Milosevic's military and police forces. However, NATO had attempted this version of a coercive air war without following through and planning for what might happen if, as it turned out, Milosevic was not successfully coerced within a few days or weeks by the air war. Then what? NATO had planned solely for

military operations in support of diplomatic negotiations. As Daalder
and O'Hanlon note,

NATO had no "plan B." The allies viewed force simply as a tool of diplomacy,
intended to push negotiations one way or another. They were unprepared for
the possibility that they might need to directly achieve a battlefield result. . . .
In the end, far from repudiating perhaps the key element of the so-called Powell
doctrine—the notion of decisive force—NATO's war against Serbia was a vivid
reminder that when using military power, one must be prepared for things to
go wrong and be ready to escalate.[26]

On the other hand, Milosevic's reasoning about how far NATO might
be willing to press the issue was as flawed as NATO's image of
Milosevic. He expected that as NATO came to the brink of war it would
back down or risk dividing the alliance. Milosevic also assumed that if
NATO did opt for war Russia would use its diplomatic influence to
stop the war before too much damage was done. Russia might also be
willing to supply some of its newer air-defense missiles to Belgrade in
order to increase the risks for American and allied NATO air power
(Russia, in the event, chose not to do so). Another flawed aspect of the
Yugoslav leader's image of Western democracies was that they were
weak and decadent: He once told the German foreign minister, "I can
stand death—lots of it—but you can't."[27]
To give credit where credit is due, NATO did hang together sufficiently to accomplish most of its political missions. It did so after revising its air strategy in late April and bringing up for discussion, with
some dissent, the possibility of a previously forbidden ground option:
an actual invasion of Yugoslavia to liberate Kosovo. But the outcome
of alliance spin control was at best tolerable. Russians across the political spectrum denounced Operation Allied Force and saw it as an
advertisement of their military impotence, especially because NATO
went ahead without the approval of the U.N. Security Council. In addition, there was great division within the U.S. public over the necessity and desirability of the air war against Serbia. Many Americans
could not understand why NATO had gone to war for the first time in
its history over the internal affairs of a country that had committed no
acts of aggression against the United States or its NATO allies.
Even after the fact there was some confusion about what, exactly,
the basic assumptions of the NATO air campaign had been with regard to the ability of bombing to influence the calculations of the Serbian
leadership. After about one month of war, allied officers began referring
to a "strategic campaign plan" that was called the "3M strategy" by
targeteers. The term "3M" referred to money, MUP (Serbian Interior Ministry), and media. These were defined as Yugoslavia's centers of gravity,

or critical points of potential vulnerability. Bombing would be coordinated with covert operations, psychological warfare, and information operations (all aspects of military persuasion, in other words) in order to obtain the capitulation of the Serbian and Yugoslav regimes.[28] This strategy was also referred to as "crony" targeting, because it included electric power, dual-use industries, and media facilities that were thought to be important to elites who were members of Milosevic's political and military power bases. Whether the "3M" or "crony" targeting had a decisive impact upon the Yugoslav leadership's eventual decision to terminate the war remains an unanswered question.[29]

NATO in Bosnia: Peacekeeping or Peace Enforcement?

One of the earliest tests of the post–Cold War cohesion of NATO and the willingness of the United States and its NATO allies to support multilateral peace operations occurred in the former Yugoslavia beginning in 1991. The breakup of that multinational state into Serbia, Croatia, Bosnia-Herzegovina, and Slovenia resulted in a variety of uncivil wars involving "ethnic cleansing" and other atrocities. Bosnia itself was eventually torn apart by civil strife. A U.N. peacekeeping force was established and NATO, in support of U.N. efforts, was tasked to help isolate the battlefields from outside intervention and to maintain as level a playing field as possible among combatant factions. Toward these ends, NATO used its maritime forces to enforce an embargo against the shipment of arms from outside sources into the Yugoslav cauldron. NATO also established a "no fly" zone over portions of former Yugoslavia, especially over parts of the former Bosnia-Herzegovina, to support U.N. efforts to restore peace there.

It became clear by the summer of 1995 that traditional peacekeeping based on the assumption that disputant parties are ready to stop fighting was insufficient as a mechanism for conflict termination in Bosnia. The U.N. forces were a lucrative target set for angry sharpshooters not yet disarmed. Accordingly, NATO resolved its differences of opinion and intervened with massive and effective force to establish an at least temporary freezing of the military status quo. By means of the Dayton peace agreement of December 1995, NATO deployed some 60,000 troops, of which about 20,000 were Americans, in Bosnia-Herzegovina with an objective somewhere between traditional peacekeeping and peace enforcement.

NATO's Operation Joint Endeavour tasked its Implementation Force (IFOR) to disarm combatant factions and by other means to support an enforced pause in the fighting among Bosnian factions. At the same time, NATO's diplomacy had obtained the necessary political and diplomatic acquiescence of Slobodan Milosevic's Serbian government to ensure the cooperation of Bosnian Serbs. IFOR's mandate was for one year, after which it was supplanted by a smaller NATO contingent Stabilization Force (SFOR) with a mandate permitting more military support for the rebuilding of consensus-based political institutions in Bosnia. SFOR's mission was originally scheduled to expire in 1998, but the actual termination date for the mission was left dependent upon conditions.

NATO's Joint Endeavour combined peacekeeping and peace-enforcement duties with humanitarian assistance in a single, complex contingency operation. Peacekeeping, according to the U.S. DOD, refers to military or paramilitary operations that are "undertaken with the consent of all major parties to a dispute" and are primarily designed to "monitor and facilitate implementation of an agreement . . . and support diplomatic efforts to reach a long-term political settlement."[30]

Peace enforcement, on the other hand, involves the application or threat of military force "to compel compliance with resolutions or sanctions" designed to "maintain or restore peace and order."[31] The U.S. Department of Defense terminology is more or less similar to the difference between Chapter VI and Chapter VII operations according to the U.N. Charter. Chapter VI operations are carried out "with the *consent* of belligerent parties in support of efforts to achieve or maintain peace, in order to promote security and sustain life in areas of potential or actual conflict." Operations authorized under Chapter VII, on the other hand, are conducted in order to "restore peace between belligerent parties *who do not all consent* to intervention and may be engaged in combat activities."[32]

The distinction between peacekeeping and peace enforcement is not semantic only.[33] The availability of consent on the part of local belligerent parties may determine the likelihood of success or failure of an intervention. The difficulty is that consent is not a hard line but a vanishing and reappearing fog of indistinct political and military attributes.[34] The range of the zone of intervention is wide: On one sided it is bounded by traditional U.N. Chapter VI peacekeeping, and on the other by large-scale but limited wars like Desert Storm. In-between lies a no-man's-land with plentiful opportunities for self-deception and wishful thinking on the part of outside interveners and their militaries: "It becomes clear that once one moves into the zone of intervention, anything can happen. It is therefore unrealistic and dangerous to make decisions about the nature of an operation and expect it to conform to one's wishes. It won't."[35]

NATO could argue with some merit that Joint Endeavour had established its competency as a collective security organization in addition to its traditional mission of collective defense. Skeptics when this intervention was first proposed had to concede NATO's first-round success in dampening conflict. This success was conditional. NATO could not guarantee the transition from military to political and social stability among suspicious and antagonistic political communities. Military stability in Bosnia was the necessary but less than sufficient condition for enduring peace among previously warring factions.

The same gap between the military conditions necessary for post-conflict stability and the wider social and political matrix that determined whether stability would hold good after NATO's forces departed was also apparent in NATO's 1999 war against Yugoslavia. After eleven weeks of bombing the regime of Yugoslav President Milosevic agreed to accept a postwar peacekeeping force directed by NATO in Kosovo. The immediate tasking for Operation Joint Guardian was to oversee the safe repatriation of Albanian Kosovar refugees who had been victims of Milosevic's ethnic cleansing in 1998 and 1999. However, NATO's approximately 50,000-strong Kosovo Force (KFOR) was also tasked to demilitarize the Kosovo Liberation Army and to protect remaining Serbs in Kosovo from the wrath of displaced Albanians. NATO's period of military stabilization would also be required to permit the secure rebuilding of infrastructure destroyed by Milosevic's armed forces (VJ) and special policy (MUP). NATO's postconflict transitional occupation of Kosovo was made easier by the enforced electoral departure of President Milosevic from the post of federation president in the autumn of 2000 and by the decision of Yugoslavia's successor government to turn Milosevic over to international tribunals for trial as a war criminal.

Professor Lawrence Freedman has suggested that peace and other operations apart from war be defined as "stability support" operations, and in offering this terminology he also makes an important distinction between "wars of survival" and "wars of choice."[36] Wars of survival are those undertaken against a rising hegemon that threatens an entire region or larger area with conquest and who poses an obvious threat to vital interests. Wars of choice are created by the internal problems of weak states, including civil war and communal violence. Publics understand the necessity for costs, including possible high casualties and economic privations, in undertaking wars of survival, but they do not readily understand or accept the rationale for wars of choice, and the level of sensitivity for even moderate casualties and other costs is apt to be extremely high.[37] The next section considers this factor of expectations about the human costs of war or military peace operations.

CASUALTIES AND EFFECTS

Greater sensitivity to casualties may be a feature of "post-heroic" warfare, according to some military theorists and historians.[38] Other experts feel that the U.S. policy process is, on account of cultural traditions or media saturation, exceptionally vulnerable to the political impact of casualties. One French commander of U.N. forces in Bosnia reportedly stated, "Desert Storm left one awful legacy. It imposed the idea that you must be able to fight the wars of the future without suffering losses. The idea of zero-kill as an outcome has been imposed on American generals. But there is no such thing as a clean or risk-free war. You condemn yourself to inactivity if you set that standard."[39] The conclusion of the air campaign against Yugoslavia in 1999 without a single U.S. or allied air fighter killed in action will further solidify a public and media expectation of zero friction in modern warfare. The unwillingness of the United States and NATO to even threaten a ground offensive into Kosovo, despite the deterrent effect this threat might have posed to Serbian President Milosevic, reflects the influence of sensitivity to the fear of casualties in framing military options.

In place of a ground campaign, NATO added spin control to its use of air power. At the conclusion of Operation Allied Force in June 1999, Secretary of Defense William Cohen contended that NATO "severely crippled the (Serb) military forces in Kosovo by destroying more than 50 per cent of the artillery and one third of the armored vehicles." General Henry Shelton, chairman of the U.S. Joint Chiefs of Staff, estimated that NATO air forces had destroyed "around 120 tanks, . . . about 220 armored personnel carriers [and] . . . up to 450 artillery and mortar pieces."[40] Later investigations, including some conducted by the U.S. military and NATO, questioned whether the air campaign had even made a dent in Serbian military power. Pilots flying at 15,000 feet to maximize their safety against Serbian air defenses achieved consistently high accuracy only against fixed targets, such as bridges and military installations. Hitting tanks, armored personnel carriers, and other mobile targets from that distance was much more difficult. A U.S. Air Force study at first suppressed and then leaked to the media estimated that 14 tanks instead of 120 had been destroyed by NATO bombing, 18 armored personnel carriers not 220, and 20 artillery pieces not 450.[41]

On the other hand, the sensitivity of Americans to U.S. armed force should not be overstated. Immediately after the deaths of eighteen U.S. Army Rangers in October 1993 in Somalia, the majority of Americans were in favor of sending reinforcements to capture Somali warlord Aideed.[42] U.S. public sensitivity to combat casualties has a direct relationship to at least two other variable: (1) public perceptions of the significance of the conflict, and (2) the expectation that U.S. political and military objectives will be accomplished in a timely manner and at acceptable cost. Of course, the U.S. political leadership plays an important role, especially the president, in mobilizing or failing to drum up public support for military intervention. The irony is that the presi-

dent may have a harder sell for nonwar operations in which significant casualties are possible than for traditional wars, since public understanding of the latter is apt to be more intuitive.

Evidence for this assertion became immediately available in the aftermath of the terrorist attacks of September 11, 2001, on the World
Trade Center in New York and the Pentagon in Washington, D.C.
American public furor was aroused in support of retaliation against
the al-Qaeda terrorist network charged with carrying out the attacks.
President Bush was determined to pursue the terrorists to their lair in
Afghanistan, to remove the Taliban regime from power in that troubled
land, and to chase down the Taliban and al-Qaeda leaderships to the
bitter end. Polls showed that Americans saw the terrorist attacks as a
second Pearl Harbor and would give the president wide latitude in
prosecuting the war, including a conflict with significant numbers of
U.S. casualties. In the event, the United States successfully carried out
its war plan based on a unique combination of high technology (long-
range, precision strike by air-delivered bombs and missiles, supported
by highly integrated systems for ISR [intelligence, surveillance, and
reconnaissance]) and allied ground forces from the Northern Alliance
intertribal coalition opposed to the Taliban. U.S. special-operations
forces and CIA operatives worked with friendly indigenous forces to
establish and maintain control of territory and military assets.

September 11, 2001, and its aftermath are exceptional. Unconventional warfare, including covert operations of various sorts, by its very
nature demands things that do not televise well. It sometimes requires
that U.S. policy makers get in bed with disreputable characters among
the leaders of other state or nonstate actors. The U.S. government may
be required to disown its prior authorship of operations gone afoul of
their original intent, or to conceal the role of allies.[43] Leaders may have
to dissemble for reporters or for Congress while an operation is in the
planning and hopeful stages in order to avoid compromising security.
All these possible requirements for the successful conduct of covert
operations sit poorly in the minds of many, not only in the U.S. Congress and media, but also entrenched in U.S. intelligence bureaucracy.

U.S. military service intelligence, including that pertinent to unconventional warfare and special operations, is as steeped in a legalistic
paradigm as is its civilian counterpart. The jurisprudential paradigm
for deciding how and whether to engage in unconventional warfare is
an understandable temptation.[44] Any officer or policy maker who lived
through the 1970s investigations of U.S. intelligence or the 1980s Iran–
Contra flap has developed forgivable protective instincts and a necessary reflex for a backside-covering paper trail. Unfortunately, those
behaviors and legalisms that are self-protective in courtrooms or congressional hearings are not necessarily those that are strategically use-

ful in a timely manner. Peace operations and other operations "other than war" will not escape the constraints of U.S. legalism and formalism in policy making. This means, in all likelihood, that a successful endgame for U.S. participation in peace operations will require the drawing of a clear line between peacekeeping and peace enforcement and staying clear of the netherworld between the two conditions.

There is worse. Operations "other than war" can quickly and inadvertently become warlike. Outside interveners in civil wars need a clear statement of mission and some reasonable expectations about the endgame. One Rand study published in 1996 concluded that, with respect to U.S. and Russian use of armed forces since the end of the Cold War,

Intervention decisions have been made in both countries from time to time for no more profound reason than the absence of any better ideas. Both the United States and Russia are configured toward unstructured and often shortsighted policy planning, with a tendency to commit forces without clearly articulated aims. In particular, ad hoc and impromptu assessments of "what is at stake" often decide what ultimately gets placed on the U.S. intervention calendar.[45]

CONCLUSIONS

Peace support operations and small wars call forth diverse military tasks as well as nontraditional mind-sets, and thus take on some aspects of military persuasion. Symbolism and the management of perceptions become as important as tactics and strategy. Forces sent into failed or "failing" states are described as having the mission to restore a peace, preserve a peace, or establish a peace not yet agreed to. Peace support forces may have international, regional, or singular-state political backing. Endgames for peace operations are variously described and, like the descriptions of their purposes, often ambiguously so. Humanitarian disasters, especially those widely televised, often turn into peace operations or even more ambitious military involvements. The necessity for using armed forces in support of peace and against political anarchy that makes possible mass slaughter is as clear as is the difficulty of actually getting it done. The symbolism of soldiering for peace is a necessary but not sufficient condition for military operational success in the event.

Not all small wars are peace wars and vice versa. Peace wars have as their object the minimizing of casualties, the disarming and separation of combatant forces, and the cessation of fighting. Small wars have various objectives, but historically have tended to be more one-sided and unforgiving than peace operations: Russia's war against Chechnya in 1994–1996 qualifies as a small war but doubtfully as a peace operation, despite Russia's willingness to so classify it. Despite these differences in purpose or in choreography, small wars and peace wars are both limited in aim and in methods employed. Therefore, each kind of conflict demands a coordination or synthesis of policy and strategy that draws heavily on a state's bank account of symbolic reassurance and gratification. Since small wars and peace wars are often not perceived as being fought for a state's vital interests, and since in the U.S. case they are often fought far from home, maintaining public support for the cause requires policy leadership of an unusual kind. These conflicts also demand for their successful conduct atypical soldiers: those who can routinely think "out of the box." This finding has implications for the training and education of postmodern militaries.

NOTES

1. Some prefer MOOTW, for Military Operations Other Than War, but we prefer OOTW because it preserves the idea that political variables are more important in these situations.

2. Donald M. Snow, *Uncivil Wars: International Security and the New Internal Conflicts* (Boulder, Colo.: Lynne Rienner, 1996), 144–146.

3. On the concept of failed states, see K. J. Holsti, *The State, War, and the State of War* (Cambridge: Cambridge University Press, 1996), 119–122.

4. I. William Zartman, "Introduction: Posing the Problem of State Collapse," in *Collapsed States: The Disintegration and Restoration of Legitimate Authority*, ed. I. William Zartman (Boulder, Colo.: Lynne Rienner, 1995), 1–11. See also Holsti, *The State, War, and the State of War*, 116–117.

5. Charles E. Calwell, *Small Wars: A Tactical Textbook for Imperial Soldiers* (1906; reprint, London, 1990), cited in Colin S. Gray, *Modern Strategy* (Oxford: Oxford University Press, 1999), 276.

6. Daniel J. Kaufman, "The Army," in *America's Armed Forces: A Handbook of Current and Future Capabilities*, ed. Sam C. Sarkesian and Robert E. Connor, Jr. (Westport, Conn.: Greenwood Press, 1996), 49–50. I have combined two of the items into one from the original list.

7. Bradd C. Hayes and Jeffrey I. Sands, *Doing Windows: Non-Traditional Military Responses to Complex Emergencies* (Washington, D.C.: Department of Defense C4ISR Cooperative Research Program, 1999), 2.

8. Mark Duffield, "Complex Emergencies and the Crisis of Developmentalism," *IDS Bulletin* 4 (1994): 38, cited in Hayes and Sands, *Doing Windows*, 3–4.

9. Joint Warfighting Center, *Joint Task Force Commander's Handbook for Peace Operations* (Ft. Monroe, Va.: Joint Warfighting Center, 1997), iii.

10. Gerard Chaliand, *Terrorism: From Popular Struggle to Media Spectacle* (London: Saqi Books, 1987), 117.

11. Charles C. Krulak, "The Three Block War: Fighting In Urban Areas," presentation at the National Press Club, October 10, 1997, Washington, D.C., cited in Robert F. Hahn II and Bonnie Jezior, "Urban Warfare and the Urban Warfighter of 2025," *Parameters* 2 (Summer 1999): 74–86, especially p. 75.

12. Hahn and Jezior, "Urban Wafare and the Urban Warfighter of 2025."

13. For a discussion of the complexity of urban operations and an innovative proposal, see Robert H. Scales, Jr., "The Indirect Approach: How U.S. Forces Can Avoid the Pitfalls of Future Urban Warfare," *Armed Forces Journal International* 3 (October 1998), reprinted in Robert H. Scales, Jr., *Future Warfare Anthology* (Carlisle Barracks, Pa.: U.S. Army War College, 1999), 173–186.

14. Timothy L. Thomas, "The Battle for Grozny: Deadly Classroom for Urban Combat," *Parameters* 2 (Summer 1999): 87–102.

15. John F. Antal, "A Glimpse of Wars to Come: The Battle for Grozny," *Army*, June 1999, pp. 29–38.

16. Ibid., 37.

17. Pontus Siren, "The Battle for Grozny: The Russian Invasion of Chechnia, December 1994–December 1996," in *Russia and Chechnia: The Permanent Crisis*, ed. Ben Fowkes (New York: St. Martin's Press, 1998), 87–169.

18. Anatol Lieven, *Chechnya: Tombstone of Russian Power* (New Haven, Conn.: Yale University Press, 1998), 303–323.

19. Timothy L. Thomas, "The Caucasus Conflict and Russian Security: The Russian Armed Forces Confront Chechnya III. The Battle for Grozny, 1–26 January 1995," *Journal of Slavic Military Studies* 1 (March 1997): 50–108, especially pp. 60–64.

20. Adapted from Major Raymond C. Finch III, *Why the Russian Military Failed in Chechnya* (Fort Leavenworth, Kans.: Foreign Military Studies Office, 1998). Available at: http://leav-www.army.mil/fmso/fmso.htm.

21. Quoted in Pavel Felgenhauer, "Chechnya: No End in Sight," *Moscow Times*, December 7, 2000, from Center for Defense Information, *CDI Russia Weekly no. 131*, December 8, 2000.

22. Les Aspin, Secretary of Defense, *Annual Report to the President and the Congress* (Washington, D.C.: U.S. Government Printing Office, 1994), 67.

23. U.S. Department of State, *The Clinton Administration's Policy on Reforming Multilateral Peace Operations* (Washington, D.C.: U.S. State Department, 1994).

24. See Donald M. Snow, "Peacekeeping, Peace Enforcement, and Clinton Defense Policy," in *Clinton and Post–Cold War Defense*, ed. Stephen J. Cimbala (Westport, Conn.: Praeger, 1996), 87–102.

25. Ivo H. Daalder and Michael E. O'Hanlon, *Winning Ugly: NATO's War to Save Kosovo* (Washington, D.C.: Brookings Institution, 2000).

26. Ibid., 105.

27. David Halberstam, *War in a Time of Peace: Bush, Clinton, and the Generals* (New York: Scribner, 2001), 420.

28. William M. Arkin, "Smart Bombs: Dumb Bombing?" *Bulletin of the Atomic Scientists* 3 (May–June 2000): 46–53. Available at: http://www.bullatomsci.org/issues/2000/mj00/mj00arkin.html.

29. Ibid.

30. Joint Warfighting Center, *Joint Task Force Commander's Handbook for Peace Operations*, xiv.

31. Ibid.

32. U.N. Chapter VI and VII citations are from Christopher Bellamy, *Knights in White Armour: The New Art of War and Peace* (London: Hutchinson, 1996), 156. Italics added.

33. Donald M. Snow objects to the locution "peace enforcement" as an oxymoron. Snow argues that the critical line is between "peacekeeping," which occurs with the consent of previously combatant parties, and "peace imposition," which involves a settlement imposed over the objections of one or more combatants by outsiders. See Snow, *Uncivil Wars*, 132–133.

34. Chris Bellamy's discussion of this point is very insightful. See *Knights in White Armour*, 155–161, passim.

35. Ibid., 160. We have defined the zone of intervention a little more narrowly than Bellamy, who puts major coalition wars at the other end of the spectrum, but the concept is useful either way.

36. Lawrence Freedman, "Bosnia: Does Peace Support Make Any Sense?" *NATO Review* 6 (November 1995): 19–23.

37. Ibid., 20. See also Bellamy, *Knights in White Armour*, 30–35.

38. Edward Luttwak, "Toward Post-Heroic Warfare," *Foreign Affairs* 3 (May–June 1995): 109–122. See also, on the nature of "unheroic" and "post-heroic" military leadership and command styles, John Keegan, *The Mask of Command* (New York: Penguin Books, 1987), ch. 3, 311–351.

39. General Philippe Morillon, quoted in Keith B. Payne, *Deterrence in the Second Nuclear Age* (Lexington: University Press of Kentucky, 1996), 14, n. 23.

40. See *Newsweek*, May 15, 2000, p. 23, for quotes from Cohen and Shelton.

41. Ibid.

42. We are grateful to Professor Peter Viggo Jakobsen for calling this point to our attention.

43. Roy Godson, *Dirty Tricks or Trump Cards: U.S. Covert Action and Counterintelligence* (Washington, D.C.: Brassey's, 1995), 158–180.

44. The temptation is for scholars as well as for soldiers, with the result that there is little written about the strategic character of special operations, covert action, or other unconventional means. A useful corrective appears in Colin S. Gray, *Explorations in Strategy* (Westport, Conn.: Greenwood Press, 1996), 163–188.

45. Jeremy R. Azrael, Benjamin S. Lambeth, Emil A. Payin, and Arkady A. Popov, "Russian and American Intervention Policy in Comparative Perspective," in *U.S. and Russian Policymaking with Respect to the Use of Force*, ed. Jeremy R. Azrael and Emil A. Payin (Santa Monica, Calif.: Rand, 1996). Available at: http://www.RAND.org/publications/CF/CF129.

9

Nuclear Weapons and Cyberwar: Persuasive Deadlock?

A TALE OF TWO INCIDENTS

The American aircraft carrier USS *Kitty Hawk* was operating in the Sea of Japan on October 17, 2000, on normal peacetime patrol. The political world was calm. No military threats were apparent. Suddenly Russian fighter aircraft appeared, literally out of blue sky, and streamed toward the American carrier. As bemused or incredulous sailors on the *Kitty Hawk* watched, the Russian combat aircraft closed with the carrier and directly overflew it at low altitude: within several hundred feet of the carrier's high profile. Having "buzzed" the major U.S. symbol of America's uncontested control of the seas, the Russians departed quickly before the *Kitty Hawk* could scramble its fighters or other U.S. forces might be invited into the action.

The Pentagon at first denied that the Russians had flown directly over the *Kitty Hawk*, but later acknowledged that Russian planes had done so and within such close range. The Russians had found an interesting way to force the Pentagon's hand. In November, black-and-white photographs taken by the Russian planes were e-mailed from a Russian regional military command directly to the U.S. Navy! According to Pentagon spokesman Kenneth Bacon, the Russians "did take some pictures. They did e-mail the pictures to the Navy and to the ship actually, and I would refer you to the Navy for those pictures."[1] The Navy was not releasing the pictures.

Russian officials contended the pictures proved that the *Kitty Hawk* was taken by surprise by the Russian aerial chest thumping. U.S. officials denied this. The U.S. postepisode version was that the Russian aircraft (four SU-24 Fencers and SU-27 Flankers) were tracked almost from the time of their takeoff from their bases in the Russian Far East. The carrier, according to one U.S. Navy spokesman, took a "calculated risk" that the flights bore no hostile intent.[2] In addition, press sources revealed that the October 17 Russian flyover was only one of three similar and recent episodes in which Russian combat aircraft had over-flown the *Kitty Hawk*: Other incidents occurred on October 12 and November 9. No U.S. official protest was filed with Russia over these incidents, but the Pentagon acknowledged that the *Kitty Hawk* would be changing its alert procedures as a result of the Russian fly-bys.[3] Reportedly, one reason for the lack of immediate response by the *Kitty Hawk* on October 17 was that the carrier was refueling at the time and not traveling with enough speed to launch aircraft. Naval historians could be forgiven for recalling what had happened to Japan at the Battle of Midway: Some of its carriers were caught by U.S. dive and torpedo bombers with planes on deck and in the process of being bomb loaded and fueled.

Fortunately for the sailors and airmen involved, these provocative dustings of American ego took place in a time of post–Cold War political quiescence between America and Russia. No military confrontation between the two states had taken place since the collapse of the Soviet Union: Indeed, military-to-military cooperation between Russia and NATO was under way in peace operations in Bosnia and Kosovo. Russia and the United States shared certain early-warning information about ballistic missile launches and were planning to increase their cooperation in this regard by setting up a joint warning center. In a move more symbolic than substantive, but nonetheless in the proper direction, the United States and Russia agreed in the mid-1990s to "detarget" one another's territories out of the prestored electronic memories in their long-range ballistic missiles.

In a period of political and military hostility between the United States and Russia, however, incidents such as this could have had very serious effects on the two states' day-to-day relations. And in time of crisis when tensions are high and the alert levels of military forces have been raised, incidents such as the *Kitty Hawk* buzzing have the potential to turn a crisis into war. The *Kitty Hawk* buzzing should remind students of history of another October incident: On October 27, 1962, an American U-2 spy plane accidentally strayed into Soviet airspace over the Chukchi Sea off eastern Siberia. October 27, 1962, was one of the tensest days of the Cuban missile crisis, the most serious U.S.–Soviet clash of the entire Cold War. Soviet air defenses were scrambled to meet the stray U-2, and in response American fighters were sent to escort the wandering spy plane back into U.S. airspace before Russian fighters reached it and shot it down. Fortunately the U-2 exited Russian airspace before American and Russian fighters got into a shooting match that might have sparked a crisis slide into nuclear war.

As for the Russian use of psychological strategy over the *Kitty Hawk*, it was not entirely clear who authorized the buzzing: local air commanders acting on their own or commanders carrying out the tacit or explicit instructions of more senior military officials. The exact chain of responsibility in incidents of this sort is often unclear, and thus contributory to confusion on the part of the crisis-time disputants. For example, Soviet Premier Nikita Khrushchev revealed to President John F. Kennedy that some Soviets suspected that the stray U-2 might have been a deliberate provocation by the Americans. It often happens that states and leaders attribute malevolence and design to miscreance by other states that is in fact coincidental or serendipitous. Fortunately the Soviet leadership did not react beyond the scrambling of tactical aircraft on October 27, 1962, despite the high alert rates of both sides' militaries.

Suppose, instead, that the Russian aircraft had been buzzing the *Kitty Hawk* at the same time that the decrepit Russian nuclear early-warning system temporarily and mistakenly "detected" the launch of a U.S. submarine-launched ballistic missile from waters off the coast of Norway toward Russia. This temporary and mistaken detection of what Russian warning-system operators suspected might be an American submarine missile launch actually took place in January 1995. A Norwegian scientific test rocket designed to study the aurora borealis and other natural phenomena was launched on January 25 from the Andoya Island rocket range. Norway had previously fired many hundreds of missiles for scientific research since 1962, and the Norwegian government was always careful to provide prenotification to Russia in order to avoid misunderstanding. Norway sent notice to Russia on December 21, 1994, and again on January 16, 1995, specifying the type of rocket, where it would land, and the probable dates and windows (time intervals) when launch would take place (dates were always approximate due to weather). However, the Norwegian prenotification somehow got lost in Russia's foreign or defense ministry. Neither the Russian General Staff nor the operators of early-warning and air-defense systems were aware that a Norwegian test rocket launch was scheduled between January 15 and February 5.[4]

When the scientific rocket lifted off on January 25, operators of the Russian missile attack warning system detected the launch and alerted higher command levels that a nuclear attack might be in progress. General Staff officers alerted President Boris Yeltsin by activating the KAZBEK system that linked the highest commanders of the Russian armed forces with the political leadership. KAZBEK included activation of the nuclear briefcases or "footballs" assigned to President Yeltsin,

Defense Minister Pavel Grachev, and Chief of the General Staff Mikhail Kolesnikov. For the first and only time, Yeltsin's military aide opened the president's "briefcase" (*chemodanchik*), explaining to the president the display he was seeing (equivalent to the display on the "big board" at the main command post of the General Staff). Yeltsin and Kolesnikov followed the trajectory of the Norwegian rocket for some minutes before it became apparent that its trajectory would not take its eventual landing point into Russian territory. The next day the Russian president was addressing an audience in Lipetsk on economic issues but diverted to impromptu remarks on the nearness of World War III:

Yesterday I used my attache case for the first time. . . . I called the defense minister and the relevant services and asked them what kind of missile it was and where it had come from. Within a minute I had the information—the entire flight of the missile had been monitored from start to finish. . . . *They* (those who launched the missile) *clearly did not expect us to detect the missile on our radar*. Maybe someone has decided to test us out?[5]

Yeltsin's suspicion, even after the fact, that the West had not intended for Russia to detect the launch speaks volumes about the perceptions that some Russian political and military leaders held at the time about U.S. and allied intentions with regard to Russia. It points to the significance of expectations in crisis management and to the importance of perspective taking: seeing the other side as they see themselves. In addition, note the symbolism of the ever-present nuclear briefcase, reminding all observers of the awesome power available to the Russian president on behalf of the state: literally the power of life and death over much of humanity. The compartmentalized communication channels among the president and his principal military advisors not only expedite rapid discussion and evaluation. They also represent or symbolize exclusivity in the right of members of this small circle to take the most portentous decisions within minutes.

By itself, the misjudged Norwegian rocket launch did not bring Russia to the brink of war. And by itself, neither did the buzzing of the USS *Kitty Hawk* by Russian aircraft. But if we can imagine that, in a crisis between the two states, incidents such as these might occur simultaneously or in close sequence, one can deduce that a fog of assessment and panic might be created that resulted in accidental escalation or inadvertent war. Unexpected paths to war have happened between governments in ancient and modern times. For example, tensions between India and Pakistan in December 2001, and January 2002, growing out of terrorist attacks in Indian-held Kashmir and on the Indian parliament, caused both states to mobilize their entire militaries and make ready for action missiles and aircraft capable of delivering nuclear weapons.

Cyberwar is the high-tech version of military persuasion. Interest in cyberwar increased after the one-sided outcome of the Gulf War of 1991 persuaded many policy makers and military specialists that attacks on C4ISR systems might be the key to future victory in a major war. Optimism about cyberwar was prompted by the U.S. military interest in systems for long-range, precision strike that minimized collateral damage and friendly casualties. Entrepreneurial innovation in the 1990s also created a bow wave of interest in off-the-shelf technologies that could serve as military force multipliers. Cyberattacks were also thought to appeal to some small states and nonstate actors, since the price of admission was so much lower than that required for modern armies, navies, and air forces.

Proponents of a new age of information warfare failed to hear the voice of Cassandra or history: War, regardless of its time, place, or level of technology, is a competition of wills and minds. Cyberwar is a fruitful approach to war, or to the limitation and prevention of war, to the extent that it influences the enemy's will as well as his capacity for war. And the military persuasion of cyberwar is a war within a war: If the enemy thinks that his information and control systems are not working and that his coordination has been disrupted, then to an extent it has. Or, in reverse, if the enemy can be deceived into accepting as valid false information that we have fed into his computers and control systems, and if he further chooses to act on that information, cyberwar has aided our cause. But this is nothing new in concept, only in technology: Operation Overlord for the invasion of Normandy involved just such a deception plan, and it bought precious time by delaying the movement of German panzers to the major locus of attack.

This chapter brings up another aspect of cyberwar that should make optimists cautious, if not concerned. Nuclear and other weapons of mass destruction are still out there, and in large numbers. And nuclear deterrence, like cyberwar, is also a military persuasion: It depends upon a clever mixture of certainty and ambiguity communicated between two states, especially in time of crisis when they are suspicious of one another. It requires that each reassure the other that it has no intention of launching an unprovoked attack. Each must also persuade the other that, if attacked, it can retaliate and inflict damage unacceptable to the attacker. Sending this mixed message in time of trouble is sufficiently challenging for people who have repeatedly practiced it, as the Americans and Russians did during the Cold War. The post–Cold War spread of nuclear weapons and ballistic delivery systems empowers other actors with more lethal weapons coupled to command systems of unknown fidelity. This mixture of dumb weapons, uncertain nuclear command systems, and smart cyberwar holds interesting possibilities for collapsing deterrence by bits and bytes.

INFORMATION WARFARE AND NUCLEAR DETERRENCE

Will the information revolution make nuclear weapons obsolete? Military analysts and academic experts in security studies have described a post–Cold War world dominated by a revolution in military affairs based on advanced conventional weapons and nearly complete knowledge of the wartime environment.[6] Other experts have suggested that nuclear and other weapons of mass destruction are the past tense of military art: Information-based nonnuclear weapons, in this vision, are the future of war.[7] The George W. Bush administration's Quadrennial Defense Review and Nuclear Policy Review of January 2002 called for a transformation in U.S. military strategy to primary reliance upon conventional instead of nuclear deterrence.[8] The assumption of entirely separate paths for nuclear weapons and for information warfare may be correct in general but incorrect for some kinds of situations, including crises between nuclear-armed states. In nuclear crises or arms races, nuclear power and information strategies may come together to create a new and potentially terrifying synthesis.

For present purposes, information warfare can be defined as activities by a state or nonstate actor to exploit the content or processing of information to its advantage in time of peace, crisis, and war, and to deny potential or actual foes the ability to exploit the same means against itself.[9] This is intended as an expansive and permissive definition, although it has an inescapable bias toward military and security-related issues. Information warfare can include both cyberwar and netwar. Cyberwar, according to John Arquilla and David Ronfeldt, is a comprehensive, information-based approach to battle, normally discussed in terms of high-intensity or mid-intensity conflicts.[10] Netwar is defined by the same authors as a comprehensive, information-based approach to societal conflict.[11] Cyberwar is more the province of states and conventional wars; netwar is more characteristic of nonstate actors and unconventional wars.[12]

There are at least three reasons why the issues of information warfare and its potential impact upon nuclear deterrence are important. First, there is the growing significance of information warfare as a speculative construct for military–strategic thinking, especially in countries with high-technology militaries. Along with this trend is the emergence of technologies that have made policy makers and planners more sensitive to the significance of communications, computers, and networks of information in time of peace, crisis, and war.

Second, there is some appreciation on the part of the U.S. defense community, at least, that infowar may have strategic potential. This means that infowar could, by itself, bring about fundamental or decisive changes in the peacetime balance of power, or in friendly or enemy perceptions of the balance. In addition, in time of war, infowar could be a major if not decisive factor in determining the outcome of a military conflict. The Gulf War of 1991 has been called, not without reason, the first information war.[13] However, compared to what is conceivable or potentially available for future infowarriors, Desert Storm was an early-generation dress rehearsal.[14] The United States and its allies must assume that other states will be able to acquire and to use infowar technologies: Leadership in present-day infowar is no assurance of future preeminence. This warning against infowar complacency is especially timely now, when direct military challenges to U.S. security are seemingly nonexistent. Military–strategic surprise is, by definition, almost never anticipated by the victim.[15]

The assertion that information warfare is an issue of potentially strategic significance for U.S. planners and policy makers is not an endorsement of the idea that the United States is vulnerable to an imminent infodriven Pearl Harbor. The U.S. national information infrastructure (NII) "has yet to suffer a major attack or anything close to it despite numerous smaller attacks."[16] Although some military functions are vulnerable to attacks against part of the NII, a "strategic" disruption of the entire U.S. computer and communications system by hackers would require fictional capabilities not yet available. The more realistic aspect is that partial attacks could distort policy makers' and commanders' perceptual universes or information flows in crises or wartime situations, leading to faulty decision.[17] Even the carrying out of successful attacks is not easy. As Martin C. Libicki has noted,

Can communications be sufficiently disrupted to retard or confound the nation's ability to respond to a crisis overseas? An enemy with precise and accurate knowledge of how decisions are made and how information is passed within the U.S. military might get inside the cycle and do real damage—but the enemy must understand the cycle very well. Even insiders can rarely count on knowing how information is routed into a decision; in an age in which hierarchical information flow is giving way to networked information flow the importance of any one predesignated route is doubtful.[18]

A third reason for the significance of the infowar–deterrence relationship is the continuing reality of nuclear deterrence in the world after the Cold War. Contrary to some expectations, nuclear weapons

and arms-control issues have not vanished over the horizon in a post–
Desert Storm euphoria. There are a number of reasons for this continuing relevancy of nuclear weapons and deterrence for American
policy makers and military planners. First, Russia still has many thou-
sands of nuclear weapons, including those of intercontinental range.
Second, other acknowledged nuclear powers, in addition to the United
States and Russia, show no inclination to abandon nuclear weapons as
ultimate deterrents. A third reason for the continued importance of nuclear
deterrence is the spread of nuclear weapons among formerly "opaque"
proliferators and the potential for additional nonnuclear states to acquire
these and other weapons of mass destruction. India and Pakistan have
now joined the club of declared nuclear states: Iran, North Korea, Iraq,
and others are judged to be nuclear aspiring. Israel is widely acknowledged as an unacknowledged member of the nuclear club.

The general parameters of the problem have been established. The
sections that follow offer three more specific perspectives on the relationship between information warfare and nuclear deterrence: (1) crisis management, (2) preemption, and (3) proliferation. These are not
mutually exclusive categories, and some illustrative material could
just as easily be provided under one heading as under another. Since
no nuclear weapons have been fired in anger since Nagasaki, placement of illustrations or cases is more like a moving finger of historical
analogy than a scientific experiment. For example, it is quite reasonable that the same incident could illustrate pertinent points about crisis management or the risk of preemption, or both.

CRISIS MANAGEMENT AND CYBERWAR

Crisis management, including nuclear crisis management, is both a
competitive and cooperative endeavour between military adversaries. A crisis is, by definition, a time of great tension and uncertainty.[19]
Threats are in the air and time pressure on policy makers seems intense. Each side has objectives that it wants to attain and values that it
deems important to protect. During crisis, state behaviors are especially interactive and interdependent with those of other states. It would
not be too farfetched to refer to this interdependent stream of interstate crisis behaviors as a system, provided the term "system" is not
reified out of proportion. The system aspect implies reciprocal causa-
tion of the crisis time behaviors of "A" by "B," and vice versa.

One aspect of crisis management is a deceptively simple question:
What defines a crisis as such? When does the latent capacity of the
international order for violence or hostile threat assessment cross over
into the terrain of actual crisis behavior? It may be useful to separate
traffic jams from head-on collisions. A traffic jam creates the potential

for collisions but leaves individual drivers with some steering capacity for the avoidance of damage to their particular vehicles. A breakdown of general deterrence in the system raises generalized threat perceptions among salient actors, but it does not guarantee that any particular state-to-state relationship will deteriorate into specific deterrent or compellent threats. Therefore, Patrick Morgan's concept of "immediate" deterrence failure is useful in defining the onset of a crisis: Specific sources of hostile intent have been identified by one state with reference to another, threats have been exchanged, and responses must now be decided upon.[20] The passage into a crisis is equivalent to the shift from Hobbes's world of omnipresent potential for violence to the actual movement of troops and exchanges of diplomatic demarches.

The first requisite of successful crisis management is clear signaling. Each side must send its estimate of the situation to the other in a way that the other correctly interprets. It is not necessary for the two sides to have identical or even initially complementary interests, but a sufficient number of correctly sent and received signals are prerequisite to effective transfer of enemy goals and objectives from one side to the other. If signals are poorly sent or misunderstood, steps taken by the sender or receiver may lead to unintended consequences, including miscalculated escalation.

Clear signaling includes high-fidelity communication between adversaries and within the respective decision-making structures of each side. High-fidelity communication in a crisis can be distorted by everything that might interfere physically, mechanically, or behaviorally with accurate transmission. Electromagnetic pulses that disrupt communication circuitry or physical destruction of communication networks are obvious examples of impediments to high-fidelity communication. Cultural differences that prevent accurate understanding of shared meanings between states can confound deterrence as practiced according to one side's theory. As Keith B. Payne notes with regard to the potential for deterrence failure in the post–Cold War period,

Unfortunately, our expectations of opponents' behavior frequently are unmet, not because our opponents necessarily are irrational but because we do not understand them—their individual values, goals, determination and commitments—in the context of the engagement, and therefore we are surprised when their "unreasonable" behavior differs from our expectations.[21]

A second requirement of successful crisis management is the reduction of time pressure on policy makers and commanders so that no untoward steps are taken toward escalation mainly or solely as a result of a misperception that "time is up." Policy makers and military planners are capable of inventing fictive worlds of perception and evaluation in which "h hour" becomes more than a useful benchmark for decision closure. In decision pathologies possible under crisis conditions, deadlines may be confused with policy objectives themselves: Ends become means, and means, ends. For example, the war plans of the great powers in July 1914 contributed to a shared self-fulfilling prophecy among leaders in Berlin, St. Petersburg, and Vienna that only by prompt mobilization and attack could decisive losses be avoided in war. Plans so predicated on the inflexibility of mobilization timetables proved insufficiently flexible for policy makers who wanted to slow down the momentum of late July–early August toward conciliation and away from irrevocable decision in favor of war.

A third attribute of successful crisis management is that each side should be able to offer the other a safety valve or a "face-saving" exit from a predicament that has escalated beyond its original expectations. The search for options should back neither crisis participant into a corner from which there is no graceful retreat. For example, President John F. Kennedy was able, during the Cuban missile crisis of 1962, to offer Soviet Premier Khrushchev a face-saving exit from his overextended missile deployments. Kennedy publicly committed the United States to refrain from future military aggression against Cuba and privately agreed to remove and dismantle Jupiter medium-range ballistic missiles previously deployed among U.S. NATO allies.[22] Kennedy and his ExComm advisors recognized, after some days of deliberation and clearer focus on the Soviet view of events, that the United States would lose, not gain, by public humiliation of Khrushchev that might, in turn, diminish Khrushchev's interest in any mutually agreed-upon solution to the crisis.

A fourth attribute of successful crisis management is that each side maintains an accurate perception of the other side's intentions and military capabilities. This becomes difficult during a crisis, because in the heat of a partly competitive relationship and a threat-intensive environment intentions and capabilities can change. As Robert Jervis has explained the process by which beliefs that war was inevitable might have created a self-fulfilling Cold War prophecy,

The superpowers' beliefs about whether or not war between them is inevitable create reality as much as they reflect it. Because preemption could be the only rational reason to launch an all-out war, beliefs about what the other side is about to do are of major importance and depend in large part on an estimate of the other's beliefs about what the first side will do.[23]

Intentions can change during a crisis if policy makers become more optimistic about gains or more pessimistic about potential losses during the crisis. Capabilities can change due to the management of military alerts and the deployment or other movement of military forces. Heightened states of military readiness on each side are intended to send a two-sided signal: of readiness for the worst if the other side attacks and of a nonthreatening steadiness of purpose in the face of enemy passivity. This mixed message is hard to send under the best of crisis-management conditions, since each state's behaviors and communications, as observed by its opponent, may not seem consistent. Under the stress of time pressure and military threat, different parts of complex security organizations may be taking decisions from the perspective of their narrowly defined bureaucratic interests. These bureaucratically chosen decisions and actions may not coincide with policy makers' intent, nor with the decisions and actions of other parts of the government.

If the foregoing is accepted as a summary of some of the attributes of successful crisis management, information warfare has the potential to attack or to disrupt crisis management on each of the preceding attributes.

First, information warfare can muddy the signals being sent from one side to the other in a crisis. It can do this deliberately or inadvertently. Suppose one side plants a virus or worm in the other's communications networks.[24] The virus or worm becomes activated during the crisis and destroys or alters information. The missing or altered information may make it more difficult for the cybervictim to arrange a military attack. But destroyed or altered information may mislead either side into thinking that its signal has been correctly interpreted when it has not. Thus, side A may be intending to signal "resolve" instead of "yield" to its opponent on a particular issue. Side B, misperceiving a "yield" message, decides to continue its aggression, meeting unexpected resistance and causing a much more dangerous situation to develop.

Infowar can also destroy or disrupt communications channels that impede successful crisis management. One way infowar can do this is to disrupt communication links between policy makers and force commanders during a period of high threat and severe time pressure. Two kinds of unanticipated problems from the standpoint of civil–military relations are possible under these conditions. First, political leaders may have predelegated limited authority for nuclear release or launch under restrictive conditions: Only when these few conditions obtain, according to the protocols of predelegation, would force commanders be authorized to employ nuclear weapons distributed within their command (see the following discussion of conflict termination for related points about predelegation). Clogged, destroyed, or disrupted communications could prevent top leaders from knowing that force commanders perceived a situation to be far more desperate, and thus permissive of nuclear initiative, than it really was. For example, during the Cold War disrupted communications between the U.S. National Command Authority and ballistic missile submarines once the latter came under attack could have resulted in a joint decision by submarine officers and crew to launch in the absence of contrary instructions.

Second, information warfare during a crisis will almost certainly increase time pressure under which political leaders operate. It may do this actually, or it may affect the perceived time lines within which the policy-making process can take its decisions. Once either side sees parts of its command, control, and communications system being subverted by phony information or extraneous cybernoise, its sense of panic at the possible loss of military options will be enormous. In the case of U.S. Cold War nuclear war plans, for example, disruption of even portions of the strategic command, control, and communications system could have prevented competent execution of parts of the SIOP. The SIOP depended upon finely orchestrated time-on-target estimates and precise damage expectancies against various classes of targets. Partially misinformed or disinformed networks and communications centers would have led to redundant attacks against the same target sets and, quite possibly, unplanned attacks on friendly military or civilian ground zeros.

A third potentially disruptive impact of infowar on nuclear crisis management is that infowar may reduce the search for available alternatives to the few and desperate. Policy makers searching for escapes from crisis denouements need flexible options and creative problem solving. Victims of information warfare may have diminished ability to solve problems routinely, let alone creatively, once information networks are filled with flotsam and jetsam. Questions to operators will be poorly posed, and responses (if available at all) will be driven toward the least common denominator of previously programmed standard operating procedures.

The propensity to search for the first available alternative that meets minimum satisfactory conditions of goal attainment ("satisficing") is strong enough under normal conditions in nonmilitary bureaucratic organizations.[25] In civil–military command and control systems under the stress of nuclear-crisis decision making the first available alternative may quite literally be the last. Or so policy makers and their military advisors may persuade themselves. Accordingly, the bias toward prompt and adequate solutions is strong. During the Cuban missile crisis, for example, a number of members of the ExComm presidential advisory group favored an air strike and invasion of Cuba during the entire thirteen days of crisis deliberation. Had less time been available for debate and had President Kennedy not deliberately structured the discussion in a way that forced alternatives to the surface, the air strike and invasion might well have been the chosen alternative.[26]

Fourth and finally on the issue of crisis management, infowar can cause flawed images of each side's intentions and capabilities to be conveyed to the other, with potentially disastrous results. This problem is not limited to crisis management, as we shall see. A good example of the possible side effects of simple misunderstanding and noncommunication on U.S. crisis management will suffice for now. At the most tense period of the Cuban missile crisis a U-2 reconnaissance aircraft got off course and strayed into Soviet airspace. U.S. and Soviet fighters scrambled and a possible Arctic confrontation of air forces loomed. Khrushchev later told Kennedy that Soviet air defenses might have interpreted the U-2 flight as a prestrike reconnaissance mission or bomber, calling for a compensatory response by Moscow.[27] Fortunately Moscow chose to give the United States the benefit of the doubt in this instance and to permit U.S. fighters to escort the wayward U-2 back to Alaska. The question why this scheduled U-2 mission had not been scrubbed once the crisis began has never been fully answered: The answer may be as simple as bureaucratic inertia compounded by noncommunication down the chain of command by policy makers who failed to appreciate the risk of "normal" reconnaissance under these extraordinary conditions.

All crises are characterized to some extent by a high degree of threat, short time for decision, and a "fog of crisis" reminiscent of Clausewitz's "fog of war" that confuses crisis participants about what is happening. Before the discipline of "crisis management" was ever invented by modern scholarship, historians had captured the rush-to-judgment character of much crisis-time decision making among great powers.[28] The influence of nuclear weapons on crisis decision making is therefore not so dramatic as has been sometimes supposed. The presence of nuclear forces obviously influences the degree of destruction that can be done should crisis management fail. Short of that catastrophe, the greater interest of scholars is in how the presence of nuclear weapons might affect the decision-making process in a crisis. The problem is conceptually overdetermined: There are so many potentially important causal factors relevant to a decision with regard to war or peace.

Despite the risk of explanatory overkill for successful cases of crisis management, including nuclear ones, the firebreak between crises under the shadow of potential nuclear destruction and those not so overshadowed remains important. Infowar can be unleashed like a pit bull against the command, control, communications, computers, intelligence, surveillance, and reconnaissance of a potential opponent in conventional conflicts with fewer risks compared to the case of a nuclear-armed foe. The objective of infowar in conventional warfare is to deny enemy forces battlespace awareness and to obtain dominant awareness for oneself, as the United States largely was able to do in the Gulf War of 1991.[29] In a crisis with nuclear weapons available to the side against which infowar is used, crippling the intelligence and command and control systems of the potential foe is at best a necessary and certainly far from a sufficient condition for successful crisis management or deterrence. Under some conditions of nuclear crisis management, crippling the C4ISR of the foe may be simply unwise. What do we think the Russians will do when their bunkers go bonkers? The answer lies only partly in hardware: The mind-sets of people, their training, and their military–strategic culture must also be factored in.[30]

With or without nuclear weapons, it bears repeating that states are not simply seeking to avoid war once they have entered into a crisis: They are trying to accomplish their objectives without war, if possible, or to position themselves during the crisis so that if war occurs they will be favorably disposed to fight it. These two objectives are in tension at the margin. Nuclear weapons and the complexity of modern command and control systems make this tension more acute. Other aspects of these systems are noted later, but especially pertinent to crisis management are several attributes of nuclear weapons and delivery systems in addition to their high lethality. First, once launched they cannot be recalled. Second, no defenses against large nuclear attacks are presently feasible. Third, governments and their command and control apparatuses are more fragile than forces. Governments and military commanders steering through a nuclear crisis are aware as never before that they are plausible specific and prompt targets of enemy war plans and that these attacks, once launched, cannot be blunted. This concentrates the mind wonderfully, but how effectively?[31]

How should we operationalize or measure the possible effects of information warfare on nuclear crisis management? One possible approach is to ask how information warfare related to crisis management might impact upon expected war outcomes should deterrence fail. An example of information warfare related to crisis management would be infowar that affected the quality of one or both sides' warning and alertness. To simulate and model this process, we developed U.S. and Russian START I, START II, and START III compatible strategic nuclear forces (two versions of START III, with ceilings of 2,500 and 1,500 warheads, respectively). We interrogated each of these forces with a model that compared the postattack surviving warheads for the United States and Russia. We then introduced a surrogate variable for infowar that affected either the Russian level of alertness, the U.S. level, or both. The results of this analysis are summarized in Table 9.1.

Table 9.1
Effects of Information Warfare on Alertness (Russian/U.S. First-Strike Surviving Warheads)

	Both Affected	Russia Affected	United States Affected
START I	798/681	798/1,938	1,639/681
START II	495/394	495/1,063	1,069/394
START III (2,500)	404/390	404/925	779/390
START III (1,500)	252/232	252/497	539/232

Source: Author. Force structures are provided in the appendix to this chapter.

Note: The model permits focused comparison of the poststrike surviving warheads and equivalent megatonnage for the United States and Russia and calculates other indicators of interest to the investigator. It was originally developed by Dr. James J. Tritten and has been modified by the author.

The results of this analysis show that attacks on information systems are by themselves unlikely to nullify the deterrent of either side or to eliminate major strike options from their menus for retaliation. It is conceivable that some confusion in command and control or warning systems might prompt an earlier decision for launch based on mistaken judgment. In that case, information attacks would have the effects opposite to those intended by the attacker, and deterrence would have failed.

CYBERWAR AND PREEMPTION

Preemption is the taking of a decision for nuclear first strike in the expectation that the opponent has already ordered its forces into attack. Preemption thus differs from preventive or premeditated war to forestall a possible attack at a future time.[32] Although preventive war was occasionally advocated by high U.S. officials during the Cold War, no American president ever approved a war plan based on that assumption. Preemption was, for the United States and for the Soviet Union, a more serious and continuing concern.[33]

The first requirement for the avoidance of nuclear preemption is that neither side conclude that war is "inevitable" or that the opponent has already begun it. The "war is inevitable" conclusion and the decision that the opponent has already begun a war are related, but not necessarily the same. Leaders with a fatalistic bent might conclude that war was inevitable well before actual troop movements or shooting started. Something of this sort seems to have gripped the Austro-Hungarians and the Germans in the weeks immediately preceding the outbreak of World War I. The judgment that one's possible adversaries have already begun to fight, correct or not, can also lead to a decision for war. In late July 1914, Germany judged Russian mobilization on the basis of Germany's own mobilization planning: Mobilization for Germany was tantamount to war.[34] Russia's mobilization envisioned a concentration of forces near the frontiers in order to hold a defensive position, but not necessarily a decision to attack into enemy territory. Understanding Russia's mobilization through its own conceptual lenses, the kaiser and his advisors judged that war had, in fact, begun, although Russia's tsar was still vacillating.[35]

A second requirement for the avoidance of nuclear preemption is that each side's forces and strategic command, control, and communications be survivable against any conceivable surprise attack. This is a tall order, and only the U.S. and Soviet systems in the Cold War years could aspire to meet the requirement against a large and diverse arsenal. The second part of the requirement, survivable command and control systems, is much harder to attain. Much depends upon the standard of survivability expected of the components of any command and control system: physical infrastructure (bunkers, computers, landlines), organizational hierarchy (chain of command), communications networks (vertical and horizontal or lateral), and, not least, people (personal reliability, professional ethos).[36] One of these components could fail while others performed up to the expected standard, whatever that was. For example, the destruction of physical infrastructure would not necessarily disrupt the entire chain of command nor change the personal reliability of individuals.

The standard of survivability for forces and command systems can be set high or low. At one extreme the simple requirement to strike back with a minimum retaliatory force against the cities of the opponent might satisfy the requirements of policy makers. At another extreme policy makers might demand nuclear forces and command systems sufficient to fight an extended nuclear war through many stages. Richard Ned Lebow and Janice Gross Stein, among others, classify U.S. schools of thought about the military requirements of nuclear deterrence into three groups: (1) mutual assured destruction, (2) nuclear war fighting, and (3) finite deterrence.[37] Table 9.2 summarizes the tenets of the various schools of thought in terms of each school's (1) images of Soviet foreign and security policy objectives, (2) weapons

Table 9.2
U.S. Cold War Views of Nuclear Deterrence

	IMAGE OF SOVIETS	WEAPONS AND C3 REQUIREMENTS	CHARACTER OF U.S.–SOVIET DETERRENCE
Assured destruction	aggressive but cautious	destroy USSR as a modern society	basically strong, but shaky at the margin
War fighting	bold, potentially undeterrable	match or exceed Soviet counter-force capabilities across conflict spectrum	precarious, at risk from Soviet counterforce advantage
Finite deterrence	fearful of nuclear war	several hundred warheads on Soviet cities	overdetermined by excessive numbers of U.S. and Soviet weapons

Source: Based on and adapted from Richard Ned Lebow and Janice Gross Stein, *We All Lost the Cold War* (Princeton, N.J.: Princeton University Press, 1994), 348–368. See also David W. Tarr, *Nuclear Deterrence and International Security* (London: Longman, 1991), ch. 5–7.

and C3 requirements, and (3) presumed character of U.S.–Soviet nuclear deterrence.

The model of minimum deterrence never appealed to U.S. presidents once nuclear weapons and delivery systems became plentiful in number: They wanted options in addition to several hundred retaliatory strikes against cities.[38] On the other hand, despite considerable hubris in declaratory policy, no U.S. forces and command systems ever met the standard of being able to conduct an "extended" large-scale nuclear war.[39] For the most part, strategists and government officials judged that this was neither necessary nor advisable for deterrence. Most U.S. strategists and policy makers agreed, notwithstanding other differences of opinion, that forces and command systems had to be survivable enough to guarantee "unacceptable" retaliation against a variety of enemy target sets. Arguments about degrees of damage that would meet the standard of "unacceptable" continued throughout the Cold War.[40]

A third requirement for the avoidance of preemption is that the management of nuclear alerts must be competent. This means that the alerting process itself must allow for gradations of military activity, and that such activities must take place according to the guidance previously established by political leaders for the operation of nuclear forces.[41] Alerts also send to the other side, intentionally or not, signals about intent: Is the alert of side A a precautionary measure on account of its fears of side B, or is it an ominous sign that side A is preparing to attack? Alerts are open to ambiguous interpretation. For example, as German forces massed on the western borders of the Soviet Union in the spring of 1941, Soviet and foreign intelligence sources warned the Kremlin of Hitler's plans to attack. Stalin chose to ignore those warnings, and the launch of Operation Barbarossa on June 22, 1941, caught Soviet border forces premobilized and unprepared.[42] Because of security, nuclear alerts may be more opaque than prenuclear ones, with equal possibilities of ambiguity in intelligence assessment of their significance.

A fourth requirement for the avoidance of preemption is the timely and accurate communication of the activities and status of military forces at the sharp end of the spear to higher political and military authorities. Political leaders are, on the evidence, often ignorant of the operational details and standard operating procedures by which their own militaries alert, move, feed, transport, and hide.[43] Two problems here are breadth versus narrowness of vision, and time lines. At the strategic level of command, one is concerned with the "big picture" of fleets, armies, and air wings moving in combined-arms formations. At the tactical level, things are more immediately dangerous and personal. The term "GI" may have survived as slang because it expressed succinctly the worldview of the grunt. Differences in time horizon also matter in ascertaining the status of one's own forces during time of peace, crisis, or war. The time lines of the high command are extended; those of tactical commanders are dominated by the imminent likelihood of being under fire.

The operation of U.S. maritime forces during the Cuban missile crisis offers one illustration of this difference in time and perspective between center and periphery. President Kennedy and his advisors were concerned to avoid if possible a direct confrontation at sea between Soviet and American forces. To that end, they exercised a degree of close supervision over U.S. Navy forces in the theater of operations that some in the Navy chain of command, including the chief of naval operations, found objectionable. From the perspective of Admiral Anderson and some of his tactical commanders, operating a blockade was a dangerous exercise that had to be left to military experts if it was to be carried out successfully. The standpoint of Kennedy and McNamara was that this was no ordinary tactical operation: Shooting between Soviet and American naval forces in the Caribbean could have strategic consequences.[44]

A fifth requirement for the avoidance of nuclear preemption is that flexible options be available to policy makers and force commanders. This requirement has two parts. First, policy makers and their military advisors must be aware of flexible options and believe that they can be carried out under the exigent conditions. Second, those actually holding custody of nuclear weapons or operating nuclear forces must understand the options and be prepared actually to carry them out once told to do so. Each of these requirements is not necessarily easy to meet. Policy makers may not know the availability of options or may be reluctant to order the military into unpreferred choices under duress. For example, Kaiser Wilhelm II, in the late stage of the crisis preceding the outbreak of World War I, ordered his chief of the General Staff, General Helmuth von Moltke, to reverse the direction of the main German mobilization, from west to east (against Russia instead of France). The astonished Von Moltke responded that "it cannot be done." Moltke meant that it could not be done without disrupting the intricate railway timetables for moving forces and supplies that had been painfully worked out according to the prewar Schlieffen plan, based on an assumed prompt offensive westward against France through Belgium.

A second aspect of this requirement is that those holding custody of nuclear weapons, including nuclear force commanders once weapons have been released to them, understand those flexible options of interest to policy makers and are prepared to implement them. Policy makers have sometimes engaged in wishful thinking about available military options. Because flexibility is deemed necessary, it is therefore assumed to be possible. An example of misbegotten assumptions of this sort is provided by the behavior of Russia's high command in the last week of the July 1914 crisis. Foreign Minister Sergei Sazonov sought a partial mobilization including only Russia's western military districts, directed against Austria-Hungary but not against Germany. The intent was to send a message to Austria about Russia's determination not to permit further Austrian aggression against Serbia. Sazonov was unaware that the Russian General Staff had in fact done no serious planning for a partial mobilization under these or similar circumstances of possible multifront war against Germany and Austria. Neither Russia's war minister nor the chief of the General Staff warned Sazonov to this effect. When the tsar—at Sazonov's urging—ordered into effect a partial mobilization, the General Staff and the rest of the military chain of command sat on their hands, hoping it would be

superseded by an order for general mobilization that they were prepared to implement.[45]

Nuclear war plans of the Cold War were equally as elaborate as the
Schlieffen plan, and policy makers' lack of familiarity with them is
well documented. Few presidents received more than a once-and-done
briefing on the U.S. strateguc nuclear war plan (SIOP).[46] Faced with a
serious nuclear crisis or actual war, presidents would have been presented with a short menu of options and advised that other options
could not be improvised on the spot. U.S. presidents and Soviet pre-
miers of the Cold War years thus had political control only over the
actual decision to start a nuclear war, but little effective control over
the military execution of that command once given.

Information warfare might contribute to a failure on the part of policy
makers or the command system to meet each of these requirements
for the avoidance of preemption.

First, infowar might raise first-strike fears based on the mistaken
assumption by one side that the other had concluded that "war is inevitable." It might do this in one of two ways. First, deliberate attack
on the information systems of the other side in a crisis might lead the
victim to conclude mistakenly that war had already begun. The United
States has had some experience with infowar against itself of this sort.
In 1979 and 1980 misplayed tapes or failed computer chips resulted in
false warnings of attack at the North American Aerospace Defense
Command (NORAD). In the June 3, 1980, incident, indicators of attack
from Soviet land- and sea-based missiles spread from NORAD to other
key nuclear command posts. U.S. military commands prepared for
retaliation in case of a valid attack warning: Minuteman launch-con-
trol officers were alerted to be ready for possible launch orders and
bomber crews on bases throughout the United States ran to alert aircraft and started their engines.[47] Fortunately, no crisis was in progress
at the time, and operators were quickly able to calm fears throughout
the nuclear chain of command.

A second way in which infowar might raise first-strike fears is by
confusion of the enemy's intelligence and warning (see also the discussion of this factor in relation to accidental or inadvertent war), but
in unexpected ways. If warning systems and the fusion and analysis
centers to which they are connected overreact to confusion in their
shared information nets, interpreters might conclude that the other
side has already launched a first strike or an "infoattack" preparatory
to preemptive attack. This logic might not, in the abstract, be totally
flawed. From the perspective of traditional military strategy, it makes
sense to attack the enemy's command and control system, including
warning systems, in the early stages of a war. A blinded and misin-

formed opponent can be defeated in battle faster and at lower cost, as U.S. air strikes in the Gulf War of 1991 demonstrated.

Weaknesses in the contemporary Russian warning and information systems for nuclear conflict suggest that the danger of feared attacks against Russia's command and control system is not hypothetical. Russia's military leadership has acknowledged slippage in the reliability of personnel in the Strategic Nuclear Forces, including the Strategic Rocket Forces responsible for land-based, long-range missiles. Inadequate pay and poverty living conditions for the troops are compounded by insufficient funding for replacements and upgrades to computers and electronics that tie together warning systems, communications, and commanders. Cleavage of Ukraine and the Baltics from Russia's western perimeter cost Moscow important warning radar sites, and key satellite tracking stations formerly under Moscow's control now reside in the newly independent states of Georgia, Kazakhstan, and Ukraine. These technical and personnel problems in Russia's warning and response system are compounded by Russia's proclivities in military strategy related to nuclear weapons. Russia's approved military doctrine expressly permits nuclear first use under some conditions, and Russia's Strategic Rocket Forces remain on a hair trigger, launch-on-warning posture capable of nuclear preemption.[48]

Third, infowar might contribute to preemption by complicating the management of alerting operations. Even the alerting of conventional forces on the part of major powers requires many complex interactions among force components. Nuclear forces must be alerted under separate protocols that ensure safety and security of those weapons and that alerted nuclear forces do not invite attack on themselves. Ground-launched and most air-delivered weapons must be moved from storage sites and mated with launch vehicles. Submarines will be surged from port enroute to their holding stations or probable launch positions. As one side's forces and command systems surge to higher levels of activity, the other side's intelligence sensors will be taking in more and more raw information. With strategic nuclear forces and command systems as complicated as those of the Cold War Americans and Soviets, the potential for mischievous misconstruction of alerting operations existed even without present and foreseeable potential for infowar.

What, for example, were the Soviets to make of the massive U.S. military alert of U.S. conventional air, ground, and naval forces during the Cuban missile crisis, poised for an invasion of Cuba if the president so decided? U.S. leaders at the time viewed the preparations as precautionary should the Soviets refuse to remove the missiles and the crisis turn uglier. Soviet leaders understandably saw things differently. They concluded by October 27 that the United States was definitely preparing for an invasion of Cuba. U.S. participants in Cuban missile crisis decision making aver that there were preparations for invasion but no plan for invasion, as such, had been approved. From the Soviet and Cuban standpoint, this might have been distinction without a difference.[49]

Now imagine a rerun of this crisis with more up-to-date information warfare techniques: a "holodeck" version with the same political setting but with technology of the year 2010. In the holodeck version, U.S. planners might insert corruptions into Soviet information networks that simulated an overwhelming attack force about to strike at Cuba, when in fact such a force was far from being fully prepared. And Khrushchev, aided by manipulation of U.S. information systems, might have simulated a full-scale nuclear alert of Soviet forces in order to intimidate Washington. We know now that if the United States had actually invaded Cuba or if the Soviets had actually gone to full nuclear alert in the Cuban missile crisis the probability of a mutually acceptable outcome short of war would have been reduced. U.S. planners were unaware for much of the crisis period of certain tactical nuclear weapons deployed with Soviet ground forces and authorized for use in case of an American invasion of Cuba.[50] And it was helpful to the avoidance of fear of preemption that the U.S. alerting of its nuclear forces, including at least one alert broadcast in the clear, was not matched by as boisterous a military statement from Moscow.[51]

Related to the third factor in avoiding preemption, careful alert management, is the fourth: timely and accurate communication of force status. Leaders must know the status of their own forces and must correctly communicate this to the adversary (unless, of course, they are deliberately attempting to conceal force status because they are actually planning to attack). For example, during the invasion of Czechoslovakia in 1968 by forces of the Warsaw Pact (orchestrated by the Soviet Union), NATO was careful to avoid provocative overflights or troop movements that could be misunderstood as a responsive military intervention. A disquieting example during the Cuban missile crisis was the apparent firing of a test ICBM from Vandenberg Air Force base over the Pacific. Although this missile was not weaponized, Soviet observers could be forgiven if they had assumed otherwise in the middle of the worst crisis of the Cold War. Fortunately, Soviet air defense or other watchers never detected the launch or, if they did, chose not to make an issue of it.[52] One can, on the other hand, overdo the issue of making clear to the opponent the preparedness of one's forces. The U.S. SAC commander who broadcast alerting orders in the clear during the Cuban missile crisis, doubtless to impress his Soviet interlocutors, was trying too hard. Such braggadocio was unintended by his superiors and, under more trying circumstances, could only have contributed to Soviet fears of attack (or of an out-of-control U.S. commander with nuclear weapons, thus overlapping with the problem of accidental or inadvertent war).

A fifth requirement for the avoidance of preemption, the availability of flexible options, might also be put at risk by information warfare. Logic bombs, worms, or viruses that attack information might also deny policy makers and high commanders on the other side an accurate reading on their own command system and forces. It was hard enough to convince Cold War U.S. leaders, on the evidence, that they had options other than those of massive nuclear retaliation. SIOP planners, convinced that nuclear flexibility was the road to defeat in war by overcomplicating the command system, had little or no interest in preparing mini nuclear-strike packages. As a result, in an actual crisis the president might have wanted smaller or more selective options than actually existed on the available menu. Former Secretary of Defense Robert McNamara recalled, with reference to the Cuban missile crisis, that he considered the SIOP options then available irrelevant to the crisis.[53] This is quite a statement, considering that McNamara had just overseen a major overhaul of nuclear war plans with the very object of introducing selective nuclear options.

The issue of flexibility can be misconstrued and that is to be avoided in this context. Flexibility is a two-edged sword. Nuclear flexibility does not imply that any nuclear war would or could be waged at an acceptable cost. It means, to the contrary, that however terrible a smaller nuclear war would be, a larger would be that much worse. This issue should not sidetrack us. The present point is that an infowarrior could "persuade" his opponent that the opponent's information system is full of electronic junk or that his command and control system for nuclear response is about to die off. So persuaded, preemption for fear of death could appeal to leaders even before the other side had made its own irrevocable decision for war.

Preemption for want of information on account of cyberdistortion intended by the other side as intimidation is a possible path to war in an age of information complexity. Even the Cuban missile crisis, taking place in an environment of comparative information simplicity, was dangerous enough in this regard. For example, U.S. leaders at one stage wondered whether Khrushchev was still in control in Moscow.[54] Fear existed that he had been overruled by a more hard-line faction within the Politburo after a relatively conciliatory message from Khrushchev on Friday, October 26 was followed by another message from the Soviet Premier the next day, harsher in tone and more demanding in substance. In Moscow some Soviet leaders feared that Kennedy was a virtual prisoner of hawkish forces that might overthrow his regime unless he acquiesced to an air strike or invasion of Cuba. Fortunately, these mistaken images were not compounded by infowarriors using perceptions management to make them more convincing.

As with the potential impact of information warfare on crisis management, we attempted to operationalize and measure the potential impact of information warfare on preemption. In this case we used as a surrogate variable the calculation that each side would have to make about the probable decrease in force survivability that would result from the other side's preemptive strike prompted by infowar. The results of this analysis are summarized in Table 9.3.

As in the case of nuclear alertness, information attacks do not appear to hold the potential for denying either side its major attack options against several classes of retaliatory targets. However, information attacks might adversely affect warning and response systems, thereby delaying authorized retaliation or denying to the retaliating side the coordination it needs to avoid redundant targeting or missed opportunities.

CONCLUSIONS

Information warfare and nuclear deterrence may lie together peacefully like biblical lions and lambs in the twenty-first century. The preceding arguments do not prove that old-style deterrence can never work in the new world order, including deterrence based on nuclear weapons. But deterrence in the next century will be more conditional, culturally driven, and less technology oriented than it was during the Cold War. States owning weapons of mass destruction and ballistic missiles will present a mosaic of hard-to-read intentions that defy easy

Table 9.3
Effects of Information Warfare on Preemption (Russian/U.S. First-Strike Surviving Warheads)

	Both Affected	Russia Affected	United States Affected
START I	878/973	878/1938	1,639/973
START II	580/532	580/1,063	1,141/532
START III (2,500)	422/463	422/925	779/463
START III (1,500)	289/249	289/497	539/249

characterization by standard intelligence collectors. Deterrence, having been overdetermined in the Cold War, may lead the pack of under-achievers before the twenty-first century is very old.

The impact of information warfare on nuclear deterrence as between the United States and Russia is a short-term consideration but one whose importance should not be exaggerated. Russian suspicions about strategic information warfare include, but are not confined to, issues of nuclear force survivability. Russia can maintain its nuclear deterrent even at levels below START II and has indicated a willingness to do so, assuming parallel U.S. reductions in force, but therein lies a challenge: As the size of arsenals comes down, the quality of their command and control systems, including the assumption that they are proof against cyberwar, matters more. Missile defense adds to Russia's concerns about losing the cyberrace with unwelcome implications for the viability of its nuclear deterrent.

APPENDIX

START I Forces

Russian Forces	Launchers	Warheads per Launcher	Total Warheads
SS-11/3	0	1	0
SS-13/2	0	1	0
SS-17/3	0	4	0
SS-18/4/5	154	10	1,540
SS-19/3	0	6	0
SS-24 (fixed)	60	10	600
subtotal fixed land	214		2,140
SS-24 (rail)	36	10	360
SS-25 (road)	715	1	715
subtotal mobile land	751		1,075
subtotal land based	965		3,215
SS-N-6/3	0	1	0
SS-N-8/2	0	1	0
SS-N-18/2	96	7	672
SS-N-20	120	6	720
SS-N-23	160	4	640
subtotal sea based	376		2,032
Tu-160 Blackjack bomb	70	8	560
Bear-H6 ALCM	130	8	1,040
Tu-160 Blackjack ALCM	70	16	1,120

subtotal air breathing	270		2,720
Total Russian Forces	1,611		7,967
U.S. Forces			
Minuteman II	0	1	0
Minuteman III	0	1	0
Minuteman IIIA	500	3	1,500
Peacekeeper MX	0	10	0
subtotal land based	500		1,500
Trident C-4	192	8	1,536
Trident D-5/W76	0	8	0
Trident D-5/W-88	144	8	1,152
subtotal sea based	336		2,688
B-2 10	16	160	
B-52G gravity	0	0	0
ALCM		0	0
B-52H gravity	95	0	0
ALCM		20	1,900
B-1	97	24	2,328
subtotal air breathing	202		4,388
Total U.S. Forces	1,038		8,576

START II Forces

Russian Forces	Launchers	Warheads per Launcher	Total Warheads
SS-11/3	0	1	0
SS-13/2	0	1	0
SS-17/3	0	4	0
SS-25 silo	90	1	90
SS-19/3	105	1	105
SS-25 Silo	0	1	0
subtotal fixed land	195		195
SS-24 (rail)	0	10	0
SS-25/SS-27 (road)	605	1	605
subtotal mobile land	605		605
subtotal land based	800		800
SS-N-6/3	0	1	0
SS-N-8/2	0	1	0
SS-N-18/2	176	3	528

SS-N-20	120	6	720
SS-N-23	112	4	448
subtotal sea based	408		1,696
TU-95H6	20	6	120
TU-95H16	35	16	560
Blackjack	6	12	72
subtotal air breathing	61		752
Total Russian Forces	1,269		3,248
U.S. Forces			
Minuteman II	0	1	0
Minuteman III	0	1	0
Minuteman IIIA	500	1	500
Peacekeeper MX	0	10	0
subtotal land based	500		500
Trident C-4	0	4	0
Trident D-5/W76	0	4	0
Trident D-5/W-88	336	5	1,680
subtotal sea based	336		1,680
B-52G gravity	0	0	0
B-52H ALCM/ACM	32	0	0
	20	640	
B-52H ALCM/ACM	30	0	0
	12	360	
B-2	21	12	252
subtotal air breathing	83		1,252
Total U.S. Forces	919		3,432

START III (2,500-Warhead Limit)

Russian Forces	Launchers	Warheads per Launcher	Total Warheads
SS-11/3	0	1	0
SS-13/2	0	1	0
SS-17/3	0	4	0
SS-18/4/5	0	10	0
SS-19/3	105	1	105
SS-24 (fixed)	0	10	0
subtotal fixed land	105		105
SS-24 (rail)	0	10	0

SS-25/SS-27 (road)	490	1	490
subtotal mobile land	490		490
subtotal land based	595		595
SS-N-6/3	0	1	0
SS-N-8/2	0	1	0
SS-N-18/2	0	1	0
SS-N-20	120	8	960
SS-N-23	112	4	448
subtotal sea based	232		1,408
Tu-95 B/G gravity	0	2	0
Tu-95 H 16	31	16	496
Tu-160 Blackjack	0	8	0
subtotal air breathing	31		496
Total Russian Forces	858		2,499

U.S. Forces

Minuteman II	0	1	0
Minuteman III	0	1	0
Minuteman IIIA	300	1	300
Peacekeeper MX	0	10	0
subtotal land based	300		300
Trident C-4	150	4	600
Trident D-5/W76	150	4	600
Trident D-5/W-88	132	4	528
subtotal sea based	432		1,728
B-52G gravity	0	0	0
B-52G gravity	0	0	0
ALCM		0	0
B-52H gravity	36	0	0
ALCM		8	288
B-2 15	12	180	
subtotal air breathing	51		468
Total U.S. Forces	783		2,496

START III (1,500-Warhead Limit)

Russian Forces	Launchers	Warheads per Launcher	Total Warheads
SS-11/3	0	1	0
SS-13/2	0	1	0

SS-17/3	0	4	0
SS-18/4/5	0	10	0
SS-19/3	0	1	0
SS-24 (fixed)	0	10	0
subtotal fixed land	0		0
SS-24 (rail)	0	10	0
SS-25/SS-27 (road)	490	1	490
subtotal mobile land	490		490
subtotal land based	490		490
SS-N-6/3	0	1	0
SS-N-8/2	0	1	0
SS-N-18/2	0	1	0
SS-N-20	120	3	360
SS-N-23	112	3	336
subtotal sea based	232		696
Tu-95 H 6/ALCM	5	6	30
Tu-95 H 16	16	16	256
Tu-160 Blackjack	3	8	24
subtotal air breathing	24		310
Total Russian Forces	746		1,496
U.S. Forces			
Minuteman II	0	1	0
Minuteman III	0	1	0
Minuteman IIIA	300	1	300
Peacekeeper MX	0	10	0
subtotal land based	300		300
Trident C-4	0	4	0
Trident D-5/W-76	0	4	0
Trident D-5/W-88	288	3	864
subtotal sea based	288		864
B-52G gravity	0	0	0
B-52G gravity	0	0	0
ALCM		0	0
B-52H gravity	9	0	0
ALCM		12	108
B-2	19	12	228
subtotal air breathing	28		336
Total U.S. Forces	616		1,500

NOTES

1. Kenneth Bacon, in U.S. Armed Forces press release, December 7, 2000, cited in Center for Defense Information, *CDI Russia Weekly 131* (Washington, D.C.: Center for Defense Information, 2000).

2. Ibid.

3. Ibid.

4. Peter Vincent Pry, *War Scare: Russia and America on the Nuclear Brink* (Westport, Conn.: Praeger, 1999), 214–217.

5. Quoted in ibid., 231. Italics added.

6. Dorothy E. Denning, *Information Warfare and Security* (Reading, Mass.: Addison-Wesley, 1999), 21–42, explains the theory of information warfare. Various notions of the RMA are evaluated and critiqued in Michael O'Hanlon, *Technological Change and the Future of Warfare* (Washington, D.C.: Brookings Institution, 2000), 7–31, 106–142. See also Steven Metz and James Kievit, *Strategy and the Revolution in Military Affairs: From Theory to Policy* (Carlisle Barracks, Pa.: U.S. Army War College, 1995), 4.

7. Alvin Toffler and Heidi Toffler, *War and Anti-War: Survival at the Dawn of the 21st Century* (New York: Warner Books, 1993).

8. James Dao, "Pentagon Study Urges Arms Shift, from Nuclear to High-Tech," *New York Times*, January 9, 2002. Available at: http://www.nytimes.com/2002/01/09/international/09PENT.html?todaysheadlines.

9. For an introduction to this topic, see John Arquilla and David Ronfeldt, "A New Epoch—and Spectrum—of Conflict," in *In Athena's Camp: Preparing for Conflict in the Information Age*, ed. John Arquilla and David Ronfeldt (Santa Monica, Calif.: RAND, 1997), 1–22. See also, on definitions and concepts of information warfare, Martin Libicki, *What Is Information Warfare?* ACIS paper 3 (Washington, D.C.: National Defense University, 1995); Martin Libicki, *Defending Cyberspace and Other Metaphors* (Washington, D.C.: National Defense University, Directorate of Advanced Concepts, Technologies and Information Strategies, 1997); Toffler and Toffler, *War and Anti-War*, 163–207; John Arquilla and David Ronfeldt, *Cyberwar Is Coming!* (Santa Monica, Calif.: RAND, 1992); David S. Alberts, *The Unintended Consequences of Information Age Technologies: Avoiding the Pitfalls, Seizing the Initiative* (Washington, D.C.: National Defense University, Institute for National Strategic Studies, Center for Advanced Concepts and Technology, 1996); Gordon R. Sullivan and Anthony M. Coroalles, *Seeing the Elephant: Leading America's Army into the Twenty-First Century* (Cambridge, Mass.: Institute for Foreign Policy Analysis, 1995). A roadmap to information resources related to strategy and other military topics appears in James Kievit and Steven Metz, *The Strategist and the Web Revisited: An Updated Guide to Internet Resources* (Carlisle Barracks, Pa.: U.S. Army War College, Strategic Studies Institute, Army After Next Project, 1996).

10. Arquilla and Ronfeldt, "A New Epoch—and Spectrum—of Conflict," 6.

11. John Arquilla and David Ronfeldt, "The Advent of Netwar," in Arquilla and Ronfeldt, *In Athena's Camp*, 275–294.

12. Ibid.

13. Thomas A. Keaney and Eliot A Cohen, *Revolution in Warfare? Air Power in the Persian Gulf* (Annapolis, Md.: Naval Institute Press, 1995), 188–212. See

also Kenneth Allard, *Command, Control and the Common Defense*, rev. ed. (Washington, D.C.: National Defense University Press, 1996), 273–303. For appropriate cautions, see Jeffrey Cooper, *Another View of the Revolution in Military Affairs* (Carlisle Barracks, Pa.: U.S. Army War College, Strategic Studies Institute, 1994), 8, 36.

14. Martin C. Libicki, "DBK and Its Consequences," in *Dominant Battlespace Knowledge: The Winning Edge*, ed. Stuart E. Johnson and Martin C. Libicki (Washington, D.C.: National Defense University Press, 1995), 27–58.

15. Richard K. Betts, *Surprise Attack: Lessons for Defense Planning* (Washington, D.C.: Brookings Institution, 1982).

16. Libicki, *Defending Cyberspace and Other Metaphors*, 10.

17. David S. Alberts, *Defensive Information Warfare* (Washington, D.C.: National Defense University, Directorate of Advanced Concepts, Technologies and Information Strategies, 1996), 12.

18. Libicki, *Defending Cyberspace and Other Metaphors*, 30.

19. Alexander L. George, ed., *Avoiding War: Problems of Crisis Management* (Boulder, Colo.: Westview Press, 1991).

20. See Patrick M. Morgan, *Deterrence: A Conceptual Analysis* (Beverly Hills, Calif.: Sage, 1983); Richard Ned Lebow and Janice Gross Stein, *We All Lost the Cold War* (Princeton, N.J.: Princeton University Press, 1994), 351–355.

21. Keith B. Payne, *Deterrence in the Second Nuclear Age* (Lexington: University Press of Kentucky, 1996), 57. See also David Jablonsky, *Strategic Rationality Is Not Enough: Hitler and the Concept of Crazy States* (Carlisle Barracks, Pa.: Strategic Studies Institute, U.S. Army War College, 1991), 5–8, 31–37.

22. Lebow and Stein, *We All Lost the Cold War*, 122–123.

23. Robert Jervis, *The Meaning of the Nuclear Revolution: Statecraft and the Prospect of Armageddon* (Ithaca, N.Y.: Cornell University Press, 1989), 183.

24. A virus is a self-replicating piece of software intended to destroy or alter the contents of other software stored on floppy disks or hard drives. Worms corrupt the integrity of software and information systems from the "inside out" in ways that create weaknesses exploitable by an enemy.

25. James G. March and Herbert A. Simon, *Organizations* (New York: John Wiley and Sons, 1958), 140, 146.

26. Lebow and Stein, *We All Lost the Cold War*, 335–336.

27. Graham T. Allison, *Essence of Decision: Explaining the Cuban Missile Crisis* (Boston: Little, Brown, 1971), 141. See also Scott D. Sagan, *Moving Targets: Nuclear Strategy and National Security* (Princeton, N.J.: Princeton University Press, 1989), 147; Lebow and Stein, *We All Lost the Cold War*, 342.

28. For example, see Richard Ned Lebow, *Between Peace and War: The Nature of International Crisis* (Baltimore, Md.: Johns Hopkins University Press, 1981); Michael Howard, *Studies in War and Peace* (New York: Viking Press, 1971), 99–109; Gerhard Ritter, *The Schlieffen Plan: Critique of a Myth* (London: Oswald Wolff, 1958); D.C.B. Lieven, *Russia and the Origins of the First World War* (New York: St. Martin's Press, 1983).

29. As David Alberts notes, "Information dominance would be of only academic interest, if we could not turn this information dominance into battlefield dominance." See David Alberts, "The Future of Command and Control with DBK," in Johnson and Libicki, *Dominant Battlespace Knowledge*, 80.

30. As Colin S. Gray has noted, "Because deterrence flows from a relationship, it cannot reside in unilateral capabilities, behavior or intentions. Anyone who refers to *the* deterrent policy plainly does not understand the subject." Colin S. Gray, *Explorations in Strategy* (Westport, Conn.: Greenwood Press, 1996), 33.

31. Ashton B. Carter, "Assessing Command System Vulnerability," in *Managing Nuclear Operations*, ed. Ashton B. Carter, John D. Steinbruner, and Charles A. Zraket (Washington, D.C.: Brookings Institution, 1987), 555–610.

32. Richard Ned Lebow, *Nuclear Crisis Management: A Dangerous Illusion* (Ithaca, N.Y.: Cornell University Press, 1987), 25.

33. Ibid., 31–74. See also David Alan Rosenberg, "The Origins of Overkill: Nuclear Weapons and American Strategy, 1945–1960," in *Strategy and Nuclear Deterrence*, ed. Steven E. Miller (Princeton, N.J.: Princeton University Press, 1984), 113–182, especially pp. 135, 143–144.

34. Donald Kagan, *On the Origins of War and the Preservation of Peace* (New York: Doubleday, 1995), 197.

35. L.C.F. Turner, "The Significance of the Schlieffen Plan," in *The War Plans of the Great Powers*, ed. Paul M. Kennedy (London: Allen and Unwin, 1979), 199–221; Holger M. Herwig, "The Dynamics of Necessity: German Military Policy during the First World War," in *Military Effectiveness*, vol. 1, ed. Allan R. Millett and Williamson Murray (London: Unwin Hyman, 1988), 80–115. See also Kennedy's note that German planning was unique and tantamount to war in his introduction to *The War Plans of the Great Powers*, 15–16.

36. See Martin Van Creveld, *Command in War* (Cambridge: Harvard University Press, 1985).

37. Lebow and Stein, *We All Lost the Cold War*, 349–351.

38. Desmond Ball, "The Development of the SIOP, 1960–1983," in *Strategic Nuclear Targeting*, ed. Desmond Ball and Jeffrey Richelson (Ithaca, N.Y.: Cornell University Press, 1986), 57–83.

39. Colin S. Gray, "Targeting Problems for Central War," in Ball and Richelson, *Strategic Nuclear Targeting*, 171–193.

40. Lawrence Freedman, *The Evolution of Nuclear Strategy* (New York: St. Martin's Press, 1981), 245–256.

41. Bruce G. Blair, "Alerting in Crisis and Conventional War," in Carter, Steinbruner, and Zraket, *Managing Nuclear Operations*, 75–120; Sagan, *Moving Targets*, 148–149.

42. David M. Glantz, ed., *The Initial Period of War on the Eastern Front, 22 June–August 1941* (London: Frank Cass, 1993), 28–37, 40–50.

43. Martin Van Creveld, *Technology and War: From 2000 B.C. to the Present* (New York: Free Press, 1989), 247.

44. Lebow and Stein, *We All Lost the Cold War*, 341; Allison, *Essence of Decision*, 138–139.

45. L.C.F. Turner, "The Russian Mobilization in 1914," in Kennedy, *The War Plans of the Great Powers*, 252–268, argues that the distinction between Russian partial and general mobilization was essentially meaningless in terms of Germany's understanding of Russia's actions. See also Marc Trachtenberg, *History and Strategy* (Princeton, N.J.: Princeton University Press, 1991), 80–87, 94–95. Luigi Albertini refers to the plan for partial mobilization as "this bright idea of Sazonov's" and argues that the Russian General Staff had never worked

up a plan for mobilization only against Austria-Hungary. See Luigi Albertini, *The Origins of the War of 1914*, vol. 2, trans. and ed. Isabella M. Massey (London: Oxford University Press, 1953), 292–293.

46. Lebow, *Nuclear Crisis Management*, 150.

47. Sagan, *The Limits of Safety*, 228–231.

48. Bruce W. Nelan, "Nuclear Disarray," *Time*, May 19, 1997, pp. 46–48.

49. Lebow and Stein, *We All Lost the Cold War*, 132. Raymond L. Garthoff, who participated in U.S. Cuban missile crisis decision making as a State Department official, contends that "no U.S. plan for an invasion of Cuba was under way," but acknowledges that previously laid down U.S. contingency plans for military action against Cuba were being refined, updated, and rehearsed. Raymond L. Garthoff, *Reflections on the Cuban Missile Crisis*, rev. ed. (Washington, D.C.: Brookings Institution, 1989), 50–51. See, in particular, his discussion of the memorandum from McNamara on contingencies for military action against Cuba, referred by the Joint Chiefs to CINCLANT (Commander in Chief, Atlantic).

50. Anatoli I. Gribkov and William Y. Smith, *Operation ANADYR: U.S. and Soviet Generals Recount the Cuban Missile Crisis* (Chicago: Edition Q, 1994), 62–63, and Appendix 1, Documents 1–3. See also Mark Kramer, "Tactical Nuclear Weapons, Soviet Command Authority, and the Cuban Missile Crisis," *Cold War International History Project Bulletin* 3 (Fall 1993): 40, 42–46; James G. Blight, Bruce J. Allyn, and David A. Welch, "Kramer vs. Kramer: Or, How Can You Have Revisionism in the Absence of Orthodoxy?" *Cold War International History Project Bulletin* 3 (Fall 1993): 41, 47–50. The best evidence now suggests that prior to October 22 Moscow had given to the commander of Soviet forces in Cuba, General Pliyev, predelegated authority to use nuclear-armed tactical missiles in the event of an American invasion.

51. On Soviet alerts during the Cuban missile crisis, see Richard K. Betts, *Nuclear Blackmail and Nuclear Balance* (Washington, D.C.: Brookings Institution, 1987), 120; Bruce G. Blair, *The Logic of Accidental Nuclear War* (Washington, D.C.: Brookings Institution, 1993), 23–24. On the U.S. DefCon II alert broadcast in the clear contrary to regulations, see Lebow and Stein, *We All Lost the Cold War*, 341.

52. Sagan, *Moving Targets*, 146.

53. In Blight and Welch, *On the Brink*, 52, 195.

54. Allison, *Essence of Decision*, 224.

10

Military Persuasion in War and Policy: Conclusion

REVISITING THEORY

Although all human conflict involves some degree of thinking, not all wars are exercises in military persuasion. Military persuasion is a special kind of psychological strategy. Strategy is the use of the most efficient and effective means to accomplish the goals of an individual or group: Parents, police, governments, robbers, and demonstrators all employ strategies of various kinds. Military persuasion is a psychological strategy with a political object that relates to the use or threat to use military power. Various forms or manifestations of military persuasion appear in politics: coercive diplomacy, psychological warfare, propaganda, negotiating and bargaining strategies, prestige policies, and others. A rich political tapestry in world politics can provide numerous illustrations for each kind of military persuasion.

It would be presumptuous to expect that we could even raise all of the important issues pertinent to military persuasion in a single study. The object was to open a door and walk part of the way through it. Our concept of military persuasion included five elements or attributes:

First, the object of a psychological strategy of military persuasion is to *influence the will* of the opponent, not necessarily to weaken his actual military capability or hardware. The idea is to upset the opponent's assumptions about the course of battle and his optimism about his control over events. This can be done by the use of threats, by actual combat operations, or by both means, but in any case it usually involves careful planning of intelligence and deception. Military persuasion is more about Sun Tzu than about Clausewitz, more about the avoidance of force or the minimum use of it than it is about winning victory in battle (although once in battle the combat-related aspects of military persuasion must be kept in mind).

Second, military persuasion includes the willingness *to adjust initial political and military objectives* without necessarily conceding to the opponent the major stakes or values at issue. This flexibility is especially important when war- or peacemaking aims of one state are interdependent with those of another, as when various states cooperate for specific purposes within a multinational alliance or when two antagonists attempt to settle a crisis without war.

Third, a successful strategy of military persuasion often requires the facility for *perspective taking*; that is, for understanding and taking into account the world as another state or actor sees it, even if this view is antithetical to your own. Getting inside the mind of your opponent is prefatory to understanding his aims and methods, and therefore to defeating him. Some of this is good intelligence work, but all the intelligence gathering or estimation in the world will not pay dividends unless the opponent's sociopolitical culture is comprehended correctly.

Fourth, the *manipulation of symbols and information* is a frequent attribute of military persuasion. One characteristic manifestation of this is the technique of perceptions management. Symbols have two levels: signs that simply denote or refer to other objects or actions and signs that have deeper connotations, often emotional, beyond pointing to a particular object or action.[1] Perceptions management is the ability to influence and manipulate favorably the perceptions that affect the mind-set of your opponent. Skill in perceptions management is also required of commanders who must deal with the "intangibles" of war, including uncertainty, chance, and friction, as well as the inherently paradoxical character of war itself.

Fifth, the importance of *moral influence*, which is something larger than "morale" but not unrelated to feelings of esprit and confidence, is paramount in military persuasion. Moral influence is a combination of a righteous cause, a determined state and society, and a confident military force, among other variables. Moral influence cannot be forced on warriors; although affected by the society, culture, and polity "outside" of the individual, it comes from within.

Before we review and summarize the findings of preceding chapters, let us revisit three examples of military persuasion from very different contexts. The first example, the Battle of Midway, shows how an astute commander can use intelligence to understand and then outwit the mind of the enemy, bringing about a tactical victory with strategic consequences for its effect on the opponent's will as well as his

capabilities. The second example shows how an inadvertent air collision resulted in a diplomatic confrontation in which the weaker side
played a stronger hand than its military power alone might have led
observers to anticipate. The third example shows how a political leader
can exploit a moment of international crisis in order to create a favorable political realignment that at least temporarily enhances his
country's political leverage.

Midway

The Battle of Midway in 1942 was the major turning point in the large
struggle for naval mastery between the United States and Japan in the
Pacific theater of operations. The basic tactical and operational elements
of the battle have been well documented. What is less obvious is how
psychological the Japanese and American strategies were, in terms of setting up the battle, fighting the battle, and the after-battle implications.

Japan had no hope of conquering the continental United States, nor
did her strategy require that she do so. Japan had inflicted a stunning
but temporary defeat on the United States at Pearl Harbor. The assumption made by the military hardliners in the Japanese government
who insisted upon war was that, war being necessary and unavoid-
able in any event (they needed oil and other resources from the British
and Dutch colonial possessions in South Asia), the U.S. Pacific fleet stood
in the way. The United States, if properly demoralized by initial surprise
strikes, would take a long time to regather its nerve and build up its forces
to strike back at Japan. Meanwhile, Japan could cement into place a
maritime defensive perimeter that would delay, if not deny, ultimate
U.S. victory. Japan's own architect of the Pearl Harbor attack, Commander in Chief of the Combined Fleet Admiral Isoroku Yamamoto,
predicted success in the early months of the Pacific War but eventual
defeat if the war became protracted for several years.

Pearl Harbor failed to achieve the knockout blow that Japan had
intended. American carriers had escaped destruction despite the enormous loss of lives and battleships. In addition, and more important,
Japan miscalculated the moral effect of Pearl Harbor on the U.S. population and government. America's reaction was united, white-hot fury.
The American Navy was humiliated, embarrassed, and bent on prompt
revenge. Despite being outnumbered in capital ships in 1941 and for
the first half of 1942, the U.S. Navy determined to strike an offensive
blow at Japan and at the Japanese Navy at its first opportunity. Japan's
military persuasion strategy for the Pacific had already failed in 1941,
years before the United States rebuilt a fleet that could drive the ships
of Japan from the sea.

The United States employed a two-part strategy with important aspects of military persuasion in order to draw the Japanese Navy into a position of possible vulnerability to a U.S. strategic counteroffensive. First, President Roosevelt authorized the "Doolittle raids" in spring 1942 against the Japanese homeland, using Army Air Force B-25 bombers launched from the Navy carrier *Hornet*. These first-ever air attacks on the Japanese homeland were primarily acts of symbolism. They did not inflict any significant loss of military capability on Japan, but the airstrikes sent a powerful message that rattled the cages of the emperor and his military advisors. The message was this: You, personally, are not immune from the costs of war. You cannot hide and your navy cannot protect your imperial person or eminent persons.

This message that bombs might symbolically or actually drop on the emperor's residence stirred the Japanese Imperial Defense Forces. They had been humiliated in the eyes of their emperor and in front of the Japanese people. They were spoiling for revenge. As one of Yamamoto's air commanders later testified, "In Admiral Yamamoto's mind, the idea that Tokyo, the seat of the Emperor, must be kept absolutely safe from an air attack amounted almost to an obsession."[2] The Japanese Navy sought a prompt opportunity to inflict further and more decisive defeat on the American Navy. Midway was the answer for Yamamoto. The Japanese plan had the following as its objectives: (1) attack and occupy Midway Island, (2) extend the Japanese perimeter in the Pacific, and (3) attempt to draw U.S. naval forces into a decisive engagement.[3] In support of the plan the Imperial Navy surged three major task forces toward Midway: a carrier striking force from the northwest, an invasion or landing force from the west, and a main battle force built around heavy battleships and positioned between the other two task forces in order to support both.[4]

An attack on Midway, accompanied by a secondary thrust against the Aleutian Islands, would put the United States on the proverbial horns of a dilemma. The United States would either have to defend Midway or concede it. To defend it, the U.S. Navy would have to surge all of its available carrier strength against a numerically superior attacking Japanese carrier fleet. But defending Midway required a willingness to take an enormous calculated risk. Throwing all of the available and serviceable U.S. carrier strength against the Japanese at Midway exposed the American Pacific coast to direct attack should the United States suffer defeat at Midway. On the other hand, holding back any of the available U.S. carrier strength from the battle at Midway would raise the tactical odds in that battle in favor of Japan. Admiral Chester Nimitz, the U.S. Pacific fleet commander, chose to use all his available carriers against Japan's superior attacking force, with the attendant risks.

In support of Admiral Nimitz's risk strategy, the United States employed military persuasion. First, Navy cryptographers in Hawaii decoded vital parts of Japanese naval communications related to their planning for Midway. When these decrypts were combined with other available intelligence information, they helped Nimitz and his staff to determine with great precision the day and time of the planned Japanese attack. However, Nimitz did not stop with the acquiring of seemingly positive intelligence. He approved a controlled communications deception operation to validate the identity of Midway as the point of attack, sending in the clear fake American messages that he knew would be overheard and translated by Japanese code breakers.

Second, the United States concealed its intentions with regard to the deployment of its carriers from Japanese intelligence. Japanese intelligence was uncertain exactly how many carriers the United States would be sending to meet them at Midway, nor were they sure where those carriers would be deployed at the outset of battle (actually northeast of Midway and just within striking range of the Japanese fleet). A third aspect of American military persuasion at Midway was partly fortuitous and partly a matter of a commander's style. Tactical commander Rear Admiral Raymond Spruance, with characteristic boldness, launched his attacking aircraft at the very first opportunity and at the outer range of their distance envelope from the Japanese carrier task force heading toward Midway. For this and for other reasons, several Japanese carriers were caught in the process of switching between aircraft bomb and torpedo loadings while commanders debated whether to launch additional air attacks on Midway or to strike back at the American carriers.

U.S. victory at Midway was a near thing, but it was a great contest in military persuasion between Admiral Nimitz and Admiral Yamamoto, who held ultimate responsibility for planning and approving the offensive against Midway. The United States at Midway destroyed four Japanese carriers at a cost of one for the Americans: The naval balance in the Pacific war was never again to rest heavily in favor of Japan. Even more important, the results of Midway boosted the morale of fighting Americans as well as those on the home front. The U.S. Navy entered an era of global maritime supremacy that has still not ended. Midway was a large tactical loss to Japan but an even bigger psychological defeat for the Imperial Japanese Navy, for Admiral Yamamoto, and for his government. Midway was to the Pacific war as Stalingrad was to the war on the Eastern front: costly in lives and in ordinance, but even more important as a symbolic turning point in the war.

Midway was made possible by U.S. intelligence successes, especially in timely code breaking, and by some Japanese miscalculation. But the importance of military persuasion at Midway should not be underes-

timated. Admiral Nimitz counted on the boldness of Admiral
Yamamoto and on the self-confidence of the latter and his officers to
help trap themselves. This boldness was manifest, for example, in the
willingness of Yamamoto to assume that the Americans would be surprised at Midway and to make no alternate plan for what to do if they
were not. As Eric Larrabee explains,

An assumption of American ignorance of it [Yamamoto's plan] should not
have been made an essential feature of the Midway operation. To do this was
not only unwarranted but unnecessary. Their preponderance of power so far
exceeded the requirements that the Japanese could have anticipated that every available American warship would be lying in wait for them and still have
enjoyed a comfortable margin of safety.[5]

Nimitz assumed that the Japanese would throw everything they had
into this attack; therefore, he had better do likewise while, at the same
time, outfox them. He resolved to do so: Had he failed, his career and
more would have gone down with his ships. Nimitz steeled the resolve of his component commanders and their air wings, and they, in
turn, responded with performances beyond those previously observed
in battle by American naval air crews. His instructions to his carrier
task force commanders, Admirals Spruance and Fletcher, could not have
been improved upon as an expression of a commander's intent consistent with the requirements of the mission: "In carrying out the task
assigned . . . you will be governed by the principle of calculated risk,
which you shall interpret to mean the avoidance of exposure of your
force to attack by superior enemy forces without good prospect of inflicting, as a result of such exposure, greater damage on the enemy."[6]
Nimitz also steeled the resolve of Washington, D.C., where Navy
headquarters had doubted his strategy and urged a more cautious
approach and intelligence estimate. He was also aware of the doubts
of the local Army commander in Hawaii, who argued that Nimitz's
estimate was based on Japanese intentions, not capabilities: The Japanese could just as easily attack Hawaii again.[7] Midway was, among
other things, the story of a man and his psychology of war as much as
it was a manual of tactics.
Nimitz used some of the most important principles of military persuasion in planning for and carrying out his strategy for Midway. He
took care to understand the perspective of the enemy, to see the Japanese Navy's motivations and expectations as Yamamoto saw them.
Nimitz also used military persuasion to make this clear to U.S. Naval
headquarters: He knew the "enemy" in Washington, D.C. He used
moral influence to obtain the most from his men, officers and enlisted.
He and Raymond Spruance understood the importance of affecting

the enemy's will by making unexpected moves that throw off the other side's sense of control over events. Nimitz was willing to gamble for large stakes because he understood the symbolism and not just the operational–tactical implications of a defeat at Midway. Having nowhere to run and nowhere to hide, he decided on a strategic counteroffensive at a time and place not expected by the enemy. Nimitz used uncertainty and chance to advantage in order to manipulate the perceptions of the Japanese commanders, both before and during the battle.

The EP-3 Incident and Sino–American Diplomacy

The George W. Bush administration had not been long in office when it was handed its first major diplomatic crisis. On April 1, 2001, a U.S. EP-3 Navy surveillance aircraft collided with a Chinese fighter that had been shadowing the American plane. The Chinese fighter crashed into the sea with the pilot presumed drowned. The U.S. spy plane, damaged and needing to make an emergency landing at the nearest available location, radioed a "mayday" call and eventually landed on Hainan Island off the coast of the Chinese mainland, in Chinese territory. Upon landing, the plane and its twenty-four American military crew members were immediately taken into custody by the Chinese military. The crew members spent the next eleven days under confinement in a hotel on Hainan while American and Chinese diplomats negotiated about who caused the incident and the eventual fate of the aircraft and crew.

The essential logic and available facts of the situation were not apparently in China's favor. First, the U.S. aircraft was flying in international airspace, outside of the twelve-mile limit for national claims of sovereignty recognized by most states. Second, the EP-3 surveillance plane was slower and harder to maneuver than the Chinese fighter-interceptor. The Chinese flier should have had the last clear chance to avoid any collision between the two. Third, the United States had film of previous close encounters between its surveillance aircraft and the unfortunate Chinese pilot, who had a reputation among Americans for close buzzing and daring maneuvers. Fourth, regardless of the cause of the incident, international law suggests that crews forced to land after issuing a "mayday" distress call not be held or subject to hostile interrogation by their temporary hosts. Fifth, the United States and other countries had established the precedent during many years of Cold War for flying these kinds of reconnaissance and surveillance flights in airspace contiguous to the Soviet and Chinese borders. It had become routine business, at least in the minds of Americans. Shadowing of flights by Soviet and Chinese fighters was expected and not perceived as especially threatening.

On the other hand, the end of the Cold War and the demise of the Soviet Union had changed the international power system in ways that China found threatening. The United States had emerged in the 1990s as the singular economic and military global superpower, posing for China's Communist Party leadership a perceived threat to interfere with China's own vision and plans for its military development and political influence in Asia. China waxed its military muscle and political influence in the 1990s throughout the Asia–Pacific theater, and the design of the Chinese leadership was to continue in this fashion in the twenty-first century. Unfortunately for China's leadership and game plan, the United States and its singular military capability presented an obstacle. China's ambitions to absorb Taiwan and to extend its effective military reach over the South China Sea collided with U.S. naval power projection forces capable of pulling the dragon's tail in its own littoral waters.

China's situation with regard to the EP-3 collision required it to play a weak hand with an appearance of strength. This called forth the logic of Sun Tzu and the Tao: When weak, feign strength. When strong, offer a facade of weakness. Therefore, China immediately charged the United States with having caused the midair collision, demanded an apology from the Americans, and held onto the U.S. air crew for eleven days. Even after releasing the air crew, China continued to hold the plane for whatever intelligence could be gleaned from its close inspection.

In reaction to Chinese intransigence, the United States first denied that it would issue any apology. Then U.S. Secretary of State Colin Powell issued a statement of "regret" that the Chinese fighter pilot had apparently been killed as a result of the collision (that he, the Chinese pilot, had almost certainly caused, although Powell did not say that). As China kept up the pressure by taking a hard line in public diplomacy that emphasized U.S. responsibility for the mishap, American officials moved closer to an acknowledgment that both shared responsibility for the disaster. Carefully worded U.S. statements stopped short of using the word "apology" but remained consistently conciliatory in their tone and substance. President Bush recognized that the Chinese held a whip hand over American emotions as long as the air crew remained on Chinese territory. Bush did not want to become another Jimmy Carter: denied a second term in the White House on account of a protracted hostage crisis. One can assume that Chinese officials knew this and played this card for its maximum value.

On the other hand, the Chinese, like other states and diplomatic services experienced in dealing with the United States, recognized that the power of American public opinion cut two ways. Initially the public might prefer that the president avoid any obviously precipitate or provocative move that would gratuitously offend the Chinese and thus prolong the crew's captivity. On the other hand, if the United States took a soft line and China held onto the hostages for too long, then the American public could turn quickly against an apparently intransigent Chinese leadership and empower the U.S. president to take drastic action. The card of potential U.S. hostages could be played to advantage by China in the short term, but not indefinitely.

China walked this tightrope with careful timing. After about a week of confinement for the U.S. air crew, attentive Chinese watchers of American television news began to notice subtle shifts in the tone of media reporting and of public sentiment. Media pundits began to refer to the EP-3 crew members as "hostages" with greater frequency, instead of the euphemism "detainees" that marked most early coverage of the crisis. Families of the crew appeared on television expressing increased urgency for the return of their loved ones. A majority of the U.S. public told pollsters that they thought the EP-3 air crew were now effectively hostages. Most important, liberal members of the U.S. Congress added to the usual conservative voices in that body denouncing China's holding of the American military personnel and demanding that the matter be promptly resolved. After eleven days of confinement the crew were released and eventually flown home.

China was criticized in the American media by some expert commentators on military affairs and by others who claimed that Beijing had not handled the diplomacy surrounding the incident very well. We disagree. China actually played a weak hand into a strong position: Its pilot caused the accident and it held innocent American crew members as virtual hostages for eleven days. Despite this, China gained from the Americans (1) several de facto, if not legal or formal, apologies that acknowledged partial U.S. responsibility for the collision; (2) a willingness to hold talks about the status of future American reconnaissance and surveillance flights near Chinese airspace; and (3) a temporary standdown of surveillance flights off the southern coast of China while negotiations continued and the United States reviewed its policy, although similar flights off the northern coast of China continued without dispute or incident. In Sun Tzu's terms, China manipulated the symbols of hurt national pride in order to establish moral influence through the global media against an assumed American aggressor spy plane into or near sovereign Chinese airspace.[8]

The behavior of the Bush administration subsequent to the release of the American air crew suggested that President Bush and his advisors were worried that their crisis-time diplomacy had been too conciliatory. Once the air crew were safely back on American soil, U.S. public diplomacy took a harder line. Secretary of Defense Donald Rumsfeld, whose voice had been muted prior to the return of the air crew, gave briefings explicitly critical of the Chinese role in the collision and showed video of aggressive maneuvers against other U.S. surveillance flights by the same Chinese pilot. President Bush and Secretary Powell reaffirmed U.S. rights to conduct aerial surveillance and stated that the flights would continue. Most emphatically, President Bush, facing an imminent deadline for a decision on arms sales to Taiwan, approved the sale over China's objections.

In addition, Bush went out of his way to volunteer a clarification of U.S. policy toward Taiwan that some felt was an actual change in policy. He stated publicly in April that the United States would definitely defend Taiwan with American military force if Taiwan were attacked by China with the intent of forcible annexation to the PRC. Bush's statement was a notable departure from the previous policy of "deliberate ambiguity" that had characterized American relations with the People's Republic since the early 1970s. In the Shanghai Communique of 1972, the Nixon administration officially acknowledged that there was one China and that Taiwan was juridically part of the PRC. On the other hand, Cold War alliances with the nationalist Chinese regime led the U.S. Congress to legislate that the United States would not permit China to annex Taiwan by force. Of course, these two policies (one China, but with a U.S. veto over the use of force by Beijing to bring it about) were in contradiction, but the contradiction was a concession to the Taiwan lobby in Congress and to other conservatives who argued that the Chinese seizure of Taiwan would be a loss of face for the United States in Asia. The argument was somewhat circular: Because we have held this contradictory and anachronistic commitment for so long, we cannot reconsider that commitment even if conditions have changed without appearing to be weak. There was some element of self-entrapment in U.S. policy here.

Bush's statement on the defense of Taiwan was, given the political realities of the situation and regardless of the supernatural half life of obsolete commitments, purposeful in the signal it sent to China. China was being put on notice that the United States was walking away from the previous policy of tacit commitment but explicit ambiguity. The signal was a strong one, and it was not unrelated to the recent EP-3 episode and the concern on the part of Bush advisors that China may have mistaken careful diplomacy prior to the hostage release to a lack of firmness in dealing with future Sino–American security issues. Bush had, by intent or by inadvertence, also accomplished something else in deterrence as a form of military persuasion. He had "burned his bridges" and left himself and future presidents and Congresses less room to fudge the nature of the U.S. commitment to Taiwanese security. A future president with warmer relations with Beijing would now have a harder time going back on Bush's hard line of an explicit defense guaranty to Taiwan in the face of Chinese military attack. In a sense, Bush had undertaken military persuasion with regard to the American national security establishment and policy-making process: By setting a new benchmark for U.S.–China security relations, Bush had increased the political costs that would have to be paid by any others who wanted to travel back to "deliberate ambiguity" and two Chinas (but one).

President Putin and the "Post–Post–Cold War" World

The terrorist attacks on the World Trade Center and the Pentagon on September 11, 2001, stunned Americans and called forth a global war against terrorism. This incident created a sea change in the priorities of the Bush administration. It also opened the door to a realignment in international politics. Russia's President Vladimir Putin was not slow to seize the opportunity. Putin was the first foreign head of state to call President Bush on September 11 to offer his condolences. He also offered considerably more.

Russia offered to the United States its cooperation in fighting terrorism in Afghanistan. This cooperation included both diplomatic and intelligence support. Russia encouraged states that were former members of the Soviet Union and still closely tied to Russia to permit the United States to establish air bases and other facilities on their national territories. The Russian intelligence services were tasked to provide assistance to their American counterparts and to the U.S. military in its conduct of operations against the Taliban and al-Qaeda in Afghanistan. Russian intelligence was especially valuable on account of the protracted war the Soviets had fought in Afghanistan from 1979 until 1989. In addition, President Putin offered to the United States his support for antiterrorist campaigns beyond Afghanistan.

Putin had several agendas in providing this support to America's new war against terror. The first agenda was that the United States could now be marshaled as an ally against Islamic fundamentalist terrorism in the form of the Taliban and al-Qaeda. Russian intelligence believed that al-Qaeda and Osama bin Laden had provided direct support to rebels in the Russian region of Chechnya during wars from 1994 to 1996 and from 1999 to 2001 (and ongoing). Putin hoped to persuade the United States to see the Chechen rebels as analogous to the al-Qaeda terrorists: An Islamic terrorist in one place is the same as an Islamic terrorist in another location. Putin was not entirely successful in shaping American views on this point, but he hoped that the Bush administration would be less explicitly critical of Russia's war against Chechnya than the Clinton administration had been during the 1990s.

Another and more important objective of Russia's leader in the aftermath of September 11 was to achieve an at least temporary geopolitical realignment. The 1990s had begun with an initial flowering of good will between the United States and Russia's government under President Boris Yeltsin, but as the decade progressed the two states fell out over a variety of issues, including NATO enlargement and NATO's American-led war against Yugoslavia in 1999. By the turn of the century Russian public opinion had turned very sour on U.S.–Russian relations, and Russian political and military leaders and other elites were more openly expressing anti-American sentiment in domestic political debates. Then, too, the George W. Bush administration immediately upon assuming office declared its intention to deploy a missile defense system, very much against the expressed wishes of Russia and requiring an American abrogation of the ABM Treaty of 1972 that Russia regarded as a cornerstone of strategic stability.

Putin seized the moment of September 11 to create an important shift in U.S.–Russian relations, at least temporarily. Whether it would last would depend upon the enduring geopolitical and economic interests of both countries. But Putin had momentarily and dramatically halted the backward drift of American–Russian relations and reversed its momentum into forward progress. Part of this effect resulted from the favorable personal relationship that the two presidents were able to establish after several meetings in 2001. Bush astonished reporters by exclaiming after one meeting with Putin that he had "looked into the man's eyes" and found him trustworthy. For a former KGB operative turned head of state, this declaration from a U.S. president was no small achievement! Nor was it fluff. Personal relations between heads of state are an important part of international diplomacy, as the sour relations between then U.S. President Jimmy Carter and then West German Chancellor Helmut Schmidt demonstrated in the late 1970s, or as the favorably evolving relations between Ronald Reagan and Mikhail Gorbachev showed in the latter 1980s.

However, there was more to Putin than personal diplomacy. He sought to turn Russian foreign and security policy in the direction of the West; in particular, toward increased accommodation with the United States and with NATO. Putin saw Russia's future as one that required Russia to be a participating partner in resolving European security issues. Russia could not stand apart from the United States and NATO and still have a meaningful voice in conflict management and resolution in Western, East Central, and Southern Europe. This need for a Russian security connection to the West was driven home dramatically by NATO's ability and willingness to wage an air war against Serbia in 1999, over Russian objections and at the very time that NATO was admitting three new members that formerly belonged to the Warsaw Pact military alliance of the Cold War. NATO was the military sheriff in charge of European peace and security, and the

United States was the primary military muscle behind NATO. Russia's seat among permanent members of the U.N. Security Council was a Cold War relic that the United States and NATO were free to disregard in the post–Cold War world.

Speaking of Cold War relics, President George W. Bush used that very term to describe the ABM Treaty of 1972. The treaty had been the talisman of arms-control advocates from its signature until the end of the Cold War. The ABM Treaty codified a relationship between the United States and the Soviet Union that helped to limit the arms race and to establish some rules of the road about strategic military competition. One of those rules of the road was that neither side would build a national missile defense of its territory. Each would remain vulnerable to a retaliatory strike by the other in order to preserve mutual deterrence. But in the post-Soviet and post–Cold War worlds, the nature of military threat had changed. The U.S.–Soviet arms competition and political rivalry of the Cold War was replaced by an officially nonhostile U.S.–Russian relationship of the 1990s and beyond. And Russia's debilitated post–Cold War economy could not have competed with U.S. defense spending and military modernization in any event.

Putin recognized that the United States could not be talked out of missile defense. He was equally aware that Russia's economy would not permit the kind of arms race run by the Soviets decades earlier. Putin decided to make the best of an asymmetrical situation. He aligned himself with Bush and NATO against terrorism to obtain diplomatic support for Russian entry into the World Trade Organization, for closer Russian economic integration with the European Union, and for a new Russia–NATO consultative arrangement. The new consultative agreement would provide for improved before-the-fact sharing of information on NATO military interventions inside or outside of Europe and, while stopping short of a Russian veto over NATO decisions, could help to prevent misunderstanding of the kind that characterized Russia's reactions to Operation Allied Force in 1999 (during which an emotive Boris Yeltsin once declared that a world war might result from continued NATO pursuit of its aggression against Yugoslavia).

Putin's use of the terrorism issue to obtain a more favorable relationship with Washington and NATO would not necessarily change other minds in Russia that were suspicious of the West, including disillusioned Communists and other leftovers from the Cold War era still holding seats in the Russian parliament. But Putin had astutely pushed on a swinging door. Bush sought to deploy missile defenses and wanted a Russian reaction that was at least reluctantly acceptant, albeit disappointed. Putin wanted a face-saving exit from Russia's doomed stance against U.S. missile deployments over which Moscow no longer had any leverage. And both Bush and Putin desired to reduce the size of their strategic (i.e., intercontinental-range) nuclear arsenals to levels even below the suggested START III limit of 2,500 deployed warheads for each side. Putin's timing and diplomatic savvy exploited the political moment in order to obtain tacit agreement on arms reductions that would make U.S. deployment of missile defenses more acceptable to discomfited Russians.

In all of this diplomacy in the autumn of 2001, President Putin showed an awareness that the diplomatic–strategic environment had transitioned from the post–Cold War world of the 1990s to the "post–post–Cold War" of the twenty-first century. Russia, to survive in this new world order, had to improve its economic performance, stabilize its military threat assessments, and undertake a realignment of its armed forces that would provide for leaner and smarter troops capable of taking on twenty-first-century missions. In the short run, this meant that Russia had to minimize its conflicts with the United States and NATO. Putin took no small risk in so doing: Future American or NATO decisions might saw off the diplomatic limb on which he was standing, especially NATO enlargement that incorporated the Baltic states of Estonia, Latvia, and Lithuania. But the diplomatic and military fallout in the autumn of 2001 from Putin's "knight's move" across the issue of terrorism to the issue of geopolitical restructuring seemed to be a favorable move for Russia. The Russian president had played a weak military hand into a stronger diplomatic outcome, in the fashion of Bismarck or Richelieu.

REVIEWING OUR FINDINGS

We have just considered three very different examples of military persuasion, in addition to the cases covered in prior chapters, in order to set the stage for our concluding chapter. Some summary of the conclusions from our interior chapters will now be attempted. As we proceed we will propose additional insights or hypotheses related to our findings. Chapters 1 through 3 laid down the concept of military persuasion and outlined its various dimensions. The implications of military persuasion for theory and policy are broadly discussed in these three chapters, with some pertinent references to related concepts in the literature of history and policy studies.

In Chapter 4, we revisited the Cuban missile crisis as an example of military persuasion. The crisis was used as a case study to develop some of the most important theories of coercive diplomacy, which is one very important kind of military persuasion. In addition, the missile crisis also shows the importance of leaders being able to interpret correctly one another's perceptions, expectations, and worldviews. The events preceding the actual outbreak of the missile crisis provide a loud soundtrack for the study of misperception. Each side believed the other would not dare to cross certain lines that, seen in retrospect, the other was quite willing to cross. Soviet Premier Khrushchev saw his missile deployments in Cuba as a defensive measure to deny the United States the opportunity for a successful war against Cuba by conventional means only and to reply to NATO's agreed deployment of medium-range ballistic missiles in Europe capable of striking targets in Russia. President Kennedy saw the Soviet missile deployments in Cuba as provocative for two reasons: The Soviet leadership disregarded what Kennedy felt were strong warnings against just such a course of action, and the Soviet missiles in Cuba would appear to change the balance of strategic nuclear power between the two superpowers.

This last point is of special interest here. Moving Soviet missiles into Cuba did not actually change the balance of power, as U.S. Defense Secretary Robert McNamara pointed out at the time: It adjusted the *perceived* balance of power, and that was what mattered to Kennedy and his advisors. The missile crisis (see Chapter 2) offered a tableau for the practice of deterrence and compellence within the context of larger and more symbolic military persuasion between heads of state and their respective militaries.

The Gulf War of 1991 has been treated for the most part as a triumphal march of American and allied technology over the seemingly decrepit phalanxes of Saddam Hussein's Iraq. In fact, there was much more to the U.S. and allied coalition success in expelling Iraq from Kuwait, as noted in Chapter 5. Technology had to be used within a more inclusive context of strategy, including military persuasion. Some attributes of military persuasion were apparent in, for example, the destruction of Iraqi military command centers; early knockout blows against Iraq's air defense radars, communications links, and control centers; and coalition use of missile-fired chaff against electrical wires in order to disrupt power grids.

All these examples also could be classified as forms of "information warfare" or "cyberwar" in its largest sense, although we prefer a more restrictive usage for those terms. Other military persuasion in the Gulf was less obvious than the objectives explicitly related to targeting and battle tactics. The more subtle military persuasion included the role playing by Bush and Hussein, in which each demonized and underestimated his fictive opponent: the Great Satan and the next Hitler, respectively. Other forms of military persuasion included coalition psychological operations to obtain Iraqi troop surrenders or to demoralize the frontline foot soldiers who were bearing the brunt of the U.S. air war for more than a month before the ground war began.

Intelligence is both a necessary support for military persuasion and a form of military persuasion. The collection of foreign intelligence or domestic counterintelligence involves deciding what information about the "other" is important, gathering the information, analyzing the information, and making it available to consumers or clients. With respect to foreign intelligence the client is usually a government. Intelligence as a form of military persuasion goes on at two levels: between political heads of state or governments, and between rival intelligence services. It cannot be assumed that governments and their intelligence services are always on the same wavelength: A regime and its intelligence organs will sometimes have very different agendas and priorities, especially in democratic systems. Even when intelligence agencies and their political masters are on the same planet, what makes intelligence truly necessary and fascinating is that the enemy or "other" can never be fully understood. Its "otherness" can only be approximated even in general, and a good general understanding of another state or political culture does not necessarily lead to accurate predictions about any single crisis or foreign policy event.[9]

That been said, in Chapter 6 we examine some aspects of the relationship between intelligence and military persuasion during the "war scare" of 1983 between the United States and the Soviet Union. There is little doubt that the early Reagan years saw a worsening of the political climate between Washington and Moscow. Few knew at the time that some Soviet political leaders and intelligence organs were seriously concerned about the possibility of a U.S. or NATO nuclear first strike against the Soviet Union. The Soviet leadership approved an anticipatory, "what if" intelligence and military readiness plan for a nuclear surprise attack based on a series of events that took place between 1979 and 1983. This Soviet mind-set ran into NATO determination to deploy the "572" intermediate-range missiles beginning in 1983. It also overlapped with the president's "Star Wars" missile defense initiative, the shootdown of a Korean airliner over Russia, and other evidence of renewed zest for the Cold War on both sides. The chapter examines some of the historical and anecdotal evidence for the war-scare thesis and complements that with statistical analysis to ascertain whether Soviet perceptions of greater first-strike vulnerability compared to America might have had some relationship to their increased alertness and intelligence pessimism.

In Chapters 4 through 6, we evaluated past cases in which military persuasion played a part in politico–military competition between or among states. In Chapters 7 through 9, we considered present and possible future cases of military persuasion and their significance.

The philosophically complex but very important problem of "friction" in war and its relationship to military persuasion is taken up in Chapter 7. Friction was described by Carl von Clausewitz, the Prussian philosopher of war regarded by many as first among modern military thinkers, as the difference between war on paper and war in practice. Clausewitz took this concept from physics, but he adds depth and breadth to the concept by including the human factor and the potential of each individual to introduce some unpredictable or unexpected twist into planning or military operations. He also enriched the concept by tying it closely to the ideas of chance and uncertainty in warfare. War was the realm of the unpredictable, very much like Machiavelli's idea of *fortuna*. A modern view of Clausewitz's friction would in all likelihood incorporate into the concept his insistence on the maxim that war was the continuation of policy by other means. Therefore, the formulation and execution of policy relevant to military operations is a field of plenty for the appearance of friction.

Chapter 7 considers how friction might impact upon the most studied form of military persuasion in the Cold War years: nuclear deterrence. Whether nuclear deterrence is even relevant any longer between the United States and Russia is in dispute among academics and policy elites. But in the interim the United States and Russia proceeded in the 1990s to engage in cooperative denuclearization of their respective arsenals, on one hand, and in some serious divisions of opinion about geopolitics and security, on the other hand. The most serious of these were about NATO enlargement and NATO's war against Yugoslavia, both in 1999. NATO enlargement and Operation Allied Force against the Milosevic regime in Yugoslavia produced, across the political spectrum in Russia, new demands for military modernization and military persuasion against the Americans. The Putin administration has already shown interesting tendencies toward a more skillful exploitation of military persuasion for deterrence, for arms control, and for the resolution of conflicts on favorable terms (as in Chechnya, 1999) than its predecessor. Given the Russian president's background in the KGB, the conduct of military persuasion was presumably part of his tuition.

In Chapter 8 we discuss the significance of military persuasion in so-called small wars and in peace operations. There is some overlap between the nature of small wars, in which at least one side is fighting with unconventional strategy or tactics and organization, and peace operations. This similarity results from the frequency with which peace operations are called upon to restore civil order that has broken down. The result of a breakdown in civil order is often war between the government and one or more insurgent factions, war among various nongovernmental factions, or both. Another similarity between small wars and peace operations is that traditional military training often neglects to impart the political, social, and cultural cognitions (i.e., the military persuasion skills) that a soldier or commander needs to carry out his or her assigned mission. A third similarity between peace wars and small wars, related to the second, is that the political or military missions given to peace operators and small warriors are often unclear. The environmental conditions often shared by peace warriors or small war fighters are civil anarchy, inappropriate training, and mission malaise.

Military persuasion is especially pertinent to traditional insurgencies as well as to postmodern peace operations. Traditional insurgencies are fought between a government and dissident partisans over the right to rule. Postmodern peace operations are often undertaken to prevent or to limit a humanitarian disaster. In either case the allegiance of political elites and of mass opinion in these failing or contested states may be up for grabs. In multinational peace operations of the 1990s, as in Bosnia or Kosovo, information warfare in various forms became an important factor in the efforts of peace operators and their opponents to sway indigenous and foreign public opinion.

During NATO's Operation Allied Force, for example, my desktop computer hard drive was bombarded by vivid electronic images from Serb and NATO sources testifying to the mendacity of the "other." The Internet, cellular telephones, satellite transmissions, and other accoutrements of the information age have created an infosphere in which it is almost impossible to escape electronic stimuli about public affairs. Many of the messages contained in these stimuli include powerful and seductive condensation symbols: strong emotional tugs and pulls on the receiver' sense of honor, nationalism, religion, conscience, or what have you. A media-centric world in which the media no longer merely report on foreign policy and national security, but in which they also play a role in policy making and execution, is here to stay, to the regret of some and to the amusement of others. He who goes to war without a well-thought-out media strategy will lose the military persuasion, and perhaps the battle as well.

Information warfare, as first noted in Chapter 3, is now a term of art and has taken on so many shades and innuendoes that it is in danger of being all inclusive. Almost anything one does to prepare for war or to fight in war involves information. Accordingly, most U.S. and other professional military planners apply a more restrictive definition: Information warfare is specifically against the command, control, communications, computers, intelligence, surveillance, and reconnaissance systems of the other side. This is no small hors d'oeuvre. There are two concepts of information warfare: transformational and reductionist. Transformational information warfare assumes that information will eventually make a change in kind, not only in degree, in the ways and means of war planning and fighting. Some transformationists even envision entire wars conducted in cyberspace without human casualties. In contrast to this vision of electronic utopia without burns or bruises, reductionists envision that information systems will enhance

the power of militaries to prevail in battle by well-known and historically tested means: increasingly precise and longer-range targeting,
deceiving the opponent as to one's aims and methods, reducing the
cycle time for decisions and actions, and so on.

Of course, in some ways both transformationists and reductionists
are correct: Information warfare is both a new paradigm with as yet
unknown and unrealized potential and an additive support for the faster,
more precise, and less confused conduct of war in the present and near
future. Meanwhile, the military application of either transformational
or reductionist logic to warfare is a sure sign of military persuasion.

We saw in Chapter 3 that deterrence, the preferred form of military
persuasion in the Cold War, has become somewhat more problemati-
cal in the post–Cold War world. Even with respect to the U.S.–Russian
relationship that is now officially nonhostile, nagging questions of
deterrence and arms control linger along with the missiles, warheads,
and other nuclear residues from past global rivalry. It is hard enough
to stabilize or reduce nuclear arsenals in the face of Russian budgetary
squeezes, entrenched Cold War habits of thinking on both sides, and
the potential complication introduced by U.S. missile defenses, if deployed. Further difficulty rises from the uncertain aspect of the Russian nuclear command and control system. This system has been
acknowledged by Russian as well as American experts to be in need of
equipment upgrades. It is also well known that Russia's economic
troubles through 1999 required delayed salary payments and cuts in
living expenses that affected all arms of service, including the Strategic Rocket Forces.

But in addition to these widely acknowledged problems of insufficient resources and discouraged nuclear weapons operators, Chapter 9
adds another possible determinant of a future Russian or U.S. nuclear
malapropism. The additional determinant is the possibility that Russian or U.S. command, control, communications, and other information-
intensive systems are themselves the specific targets of enemy attack.
Official Russian military sources have expressed specific concern about
information warfare as a strategic threat to Russia—strategic, in this
context, means decisive.

The potential overlap of information warfare and nuclear crisis management provides fertile ground for nuclear preemption or for accidental or inadvertent nuclear war. Misleading indicators from faulty
warning or assessment systems could lead operators in the middle
levels of command to raise alert levels unnecessarily. High-level commanders and policy makers, responding to those alerts, could interpret ambiguous information as a clue to hostile intent. In 1995, for
example, a Norwegian scientific test rocket launch, of which the Russian foreign ministry had been prenotified, was temporarily miscon-

strued as a possible U.S. submarine-launched ballistic missile aimed at Russia's Kola Peninsula. President Boris Yeltsin for the very first time opened his *cheget* or special small suitcase containing authenticating codes and option buttons for authorizing nuclear attack (in retaliation, assuming that an attack had already been launched against Russia).

One might say, in relation to the findings of Chapters 7 and 9 especially, but also with some regard to the conclusions of Chapter 3, that nuclear deterrence is among the most fragile types of military persuasion ever devised. That it "worked" for forty-five years of the Cold War is an article of faith among many in the policy community, but this success may be fortuitous. Other conditions between 1946 and 1991 also worked against an outbreak of major war, at least in Europe: bloc consolidation within NATO and the Warsaw Pact, an essential military bipolarity as between the United States and the Soviet Union, the absence of any territory on Soviet or American soil claimed by the other side, and the stabilization of nuclear technology such that offenses were guaranteed to overwhelm any defenses once ballistic missiles with nuclear weapons became plentiful.

In other words, military instability and political uncertainty in the Cold War were limited because allies of the Americans or Soviets had little room to maneuver their senior partners into war; because an essential military equivalence made adventurism and brinkmanship appear too dangerous, especially after 1962; because no "Alsace–Lorraines" or "Kashmirs" existed between America and Russia for nationalist firebrands to draw upon; and because the inferiority of missile defense technology throughout the Cold War enforced a militarily defensive strategy on Washington and Moscow of second-strike retaliation based on survivable offenses. Unfortunately, none of these conditions can be assumed to be as durable for even the next quarter century, and some have already been superseded.

BEYOND THE BOOK

There are many developments related to military persuasion that cannot be covered in a single study. One development is the "revolution in military affairs," about which there is a considerable amount of interest and controversy within the U.S. armed forces and the professional defense community. We are willing to address this here, in a manner that is admittedly speculative, but the reader is warned that our view of this topic is less technology centered than the views of many others.[10] Because innovation in technology is flowing from the civilian into the military world instead of the other way around, the modernization of twenty-first century militaries by means of information technology cannot be separated from the sociopolitical and cultural impact of that technology.[11] Just as commerce once followed the flag, now culture follows technology, except that this culture holds uncertain and perhaps threatening implications for the territorial state and its asserted primacy in world politics.

It may be useful to distinguish among possible schools of thought or contending paradigms with regard to their assumptions about the impact of the revolution in military affairs:

1. *Technology maximalist, strategically minimalist*—in this view, technology related to computers, communications, and electronics will continue to advance rapidly, but its impact on strategy will be selective and discrete. For example, the ability of air forces to conduct long-range precision strikes will continue to improve, as will the speed of data transmission and the ability to see more of the battlefield in real time. On the other hand, these capabilities in seeing, knowing, and reaching the battlefield will not alter strategy in a fundamental way.

2. *Technology minimalist, strategically minimalist*—from this perspective the RMA has been overly hyped. Having the world's best long-range air force and a large number of computer geeks, as the United States does, does not equate to a true military revolution, nor is it apparent that in the twenty-first century as opposed to the 1990s the United States will maintain its lead in civilian-invented but military-related technology. Others will copy or steal what we design, and may eventually surpass the United States in selected technologies. Since current RMA-related technology is overrated by its enthusiasts, it will alter military strategy only at the margin.

3. *Technology maximalist, strategically maximalist*—in this view both technology and strategy will move into new dimensions as a result of the RMA. The early decades of the next century will see knowledge wars and knowledge warriors who achieve military and political objectives without bloodshed and in virtual reality. Those wars that do involve actual combat will be remote from the technologically advanced civilizations and handled by proxies, mercenaries, or by ignoring them. A "system of systems" of interconnectedness information, communications, command and control, and decision-support systems will give the United States or other dominant power an all-seeing, all-knowing, and all-pulverizing (if necessary) command over battlespace.

   Some would cite the successful U.S. military campaign in Afghanistan from October 7, 2001, through December as a case of applying a new technology-driven template for victory: highly integrated intelligence, surveillance, and reconnaissance systems; long-range precision strike by air-delivered munitions and missiles; flexible and adaptable command, control, communications, and computers; and allied ground forces from the Northern Alliance (an anti-Talilban intertribal coalition) working with U.S. special-operations forces and CIA intelligence personnel.

4. *Technology minimalist, strategically maximalist*—although this category would seen oxymoronic, it is at least theoretically possible that one or a few key

technologies would by themselves revolutionize military strategy while most of the other new technologies were a side show. An example of this might be the discovery of nuclear fission by scientists, eventually leading to the development of nuclear weapons that inverted much of the basis of traditional military strategy for total war. Other possibilities would be simultaneous breakthroughs in biological and microelectronic technologies: for example, combination of cloning or genetic therapeutic techniques with nanotechnology for building smart machines of miniature size.

As the 1980s ended, desktop computers were only beginning to be used widely by ordinary citizens as tools for work and play, as opposed to their use by computer professionals and "hackers." The extraordinary growth and development of electronics and communications technology in the 1990s, combined with the fall in price per unit of computing power, brought the computer into the realm of mass culture. Desktop and even laptop computers are now as accepted as household items as were the television sets of the 1950s. Then came the Internet. The key jump here was the movement of the Internet out of the domain of a few networked professionals and government officials. As ordinary citizens plugged into the Internet they realized what had once been only a dream of Marshall McLuhan: a global village. Now persons who lived in the most remote hinterland of the planet could be connected almost instantly, by text and by graphics, with a connected someone who lived anywhere else. This meant that geographical isolation was broken apart by cyberconnection, or that we were all now residents of "cyberia." The implications of this global connectedness, including the political, social, and cultural ones, are both reassuring and troubling.

The tribal or ethnic warriors of the future will have the additional advantage of networked cybersmart tools with which to communicate, navigate, and expedite their military operations. Smarter is as smarter does, as Forrest Gump might say. As information technology spreads among the warrior societies of the developing world, as it must, revolutionaries and terrorists will have available the user-friendly tools of political disruption. Palestinians in the fall of 2000 attacked Israeli Web sites and altered their messages: Israelis responded in kind. What used to be called "hacking" has moved from being a pastime for precocious adolescents to a predictable tool of information strategy as part of war or armed diplomacy. U.S. and allied peacekeepers in Bosnia and Kosovo were quick to appreciate the significance of getting the upper hand over media previously used for Serb propaganda: It was a war of images and words as well as a military operation to calm down the previously engaged combatants.

It bears repetition that, as my colleague Paul Bracken has noted, armies do not travel down the information highway, and airplanes do not fly through cyberspace.[12] War still involves physical movement, destruction, and killing. The globalization of information does not change the essence of armed conflict from that of a killing ground into that of a video game. But it is true as well that the way in which the killing is explained, justified, and put into context may have as much or more to do with determining its outcome than the results of aimed firepower. It goes too far to argue that all strategy is fundamentally about psychology or mindwar: It certainly is not. But to paraphrase Trotsky, you may not be interested in military persuasion, but military persuasion is interested in you.

NOTES

1. Murray Edelman has developed this point with regard to political symbolization in his application of the distinction between referential and condensation symbols to political objects. See Murray Edelman, *The Symbolic Uses of Politics* (Urbana: University of Illinois Press, 1985), 6.

2. Eric Larrabee, *Commander in Chief: Franklin Delano Roosevelt, His Lieutenants, and Their War* (New York: Harper and Row, 1987), 366.

3. Samuel Eliot Morison, *History of United States Naval Operations in World War II*, vol. 4, *Coral Sea, Midway and Submarine Actions, May 1942–August 1942* (Boston: Little, Brown, 1949), 70–75, cited in Carl H. Builder, Steven C. Bankes, and Richard Nordin, *Command Concepts: A Theory Derived from the Practice of Command and Control* (Santa Monica, Calif.: RAND, 1999), 25.

4. Morison, *History of United States Naval Operations in World War II*, 88–89; Builder, Bankes, and Nordin, *Command Concepts*, 25–26.

5. Larrabee, *Commander in Chief*, 382.

6. Morison, *History of United States Naval Operations in World War II*, 84; Walter Lord, *Incredible Victory* (New York: Harper and Row, 1967), 36, in Builder, Bankes, and Nordin, *Command Concepts*, 32.

7. Builder, Bankes, and Nordin, *Command Concepts*, 28.

8. As Richard Ned Lebow has explained, credible threats are usually based on strengths relative to the opponent's weaknesses, or on "favorable asymmetries" for the threatener. On the other hand, sometimes unfavorable asymmetries or weaknesses can be manipulated for success in bargaining. In order to do this, the weaker side must convince the stronger that, although the weaker side would suffer more relative deprivation or loss than the stronger if the stronger side refuses the demands of the weaker, the weaker side can impose unacceptable losses for the stronger of an absolute kind. For example, Khrushchev's bargaining power during the Cuban missile crisis of 1962 was not diminished by U.S. relative superiority in survivable warheads and launchers: The Soviet Union could have "lost" a nuclear exchange in relative terms but still inflicted unacceptable losses on several U.S. cities with its undestroyed forces. See Richard Ned Lebow, *The Art of Bargaining* (Baltimore, Md.: Johns Hopkins University Press, 1996), 122–125.

9. The significance of Robert D. Steele's movement for "Open Source Solutions" applies here. See Robert D. Steele, *On Intelligence: Spies and Secrecy in*

an Open World (Washington, D.C.: AFCEA International Press, 2000) and robert. d.steele@postoffice.worldnet.att.net. Cultures are not best understood by the accumulation of classified and compartmentalized bric-a-brac. The U.S. intelligence culture of secrecy and compartmentalization is also antithetical to a faster-moving Internet world. See Bruce D. Berkowitz and Allan E. Goodman, *Best Truth: Intelligence in the Information Age* (New Haven, Conn.: Yale University Press, 2000), 30–57.

10. For a critique of the technological assumptions underlying disparate views of RMA, see Michael O'Hanlon, *Technological Change and the Future of Warfare* (Washington, D.C.: Brookings Institution, 2000), 7–31. For an assessment of RMA from the standpoint of military strategy, see Colin S. Gray, *Modern Strategy* (Oxford: Oxford University Press, 1999), 243–254.

11. In support of this assumption, see Thomas L. Friedman, *The Lexus and the Olive Tree* (New York: Farrar, Straus, Giroux, 1999), 25–37, 59–82, 267–284.

12. Paul Bracken, *Fire in the East: The Rise of Asian Military Power and the Second Nuclear Age* (New York: HarperCollins, 1999), 10.

Suggestions for Further Reading

Adams, James. *The Next World War: Computers Are the Weapons and the Front Line Is Everywhere*. New York: Simon and Schuster, 1998.

Bellamy, Christopher. *Knights in White Armour: The New Art of War and Peace*. London: Hutchinson, 1996.

Berkowitz, Bruce D., and Allan E. Goodman. *Best Truth: Intelligence in the Information Age*. New Haven, Conn.: Yale University Press, 2000.

Chandler, David G. *The Art of Warfare on Land*. London: Penguin Books, 2000.

Cimbala, Stephen J. *Clausewitz and Chaos: Friction in War and Military Policy*. Westport, Conn.: Praeger, 2001.

Creveld, Martin van. *The Transformation of War*. New York: Free Press, 1991.

Daalder, Ivo H., and Michael O'Hanlon. *Winning Ugly: NATO's War to Save Kosovo*. Washington, D.C.: Brookings Institution, 2000.

Denning, Dorothy E. *Information Warfare and Security*. Reading, Mass.: Addison-Wesley, 1999.

Fitzgerald, Frances. *Way Out There in the Blue: Reagan, Star Wars and the End of the Cold War*. New York: Simon and Schuster, 2000.

Friedman, Thomas L. *The Lexus and the Olive Tree*. New York: Farrar, Straus, Giroux, 1999.

Gates, Robert M. *From the Shadows: The Ultimate Insider's Story of Five Presidents and How They Won the Cold War*. New York: Simon and Schuster, 1996.

Gray, Colin S. *Modern Strategy*. Oxford: Oxford University Press, 1999.

Halberstam, David. *War in a Time of Peace: Bush, Clinton and the Generals*. New York: Scribner, 2001.

Ignatieff, Michael. *Virtual War: Kosovo and Beyond*. New York: Henry Holt, 2000.

Kaplan, Robert D. *Soldiers of God: With the Mujahidin in Afghanistan*. Boston: Houghton Mifflin, 1990.

Keaney, Thomas A., and Eliot A. Cohen. *Revolution in Warfare? Air Power in the*

Persian Gulf. Annapolis, Md.: Naval Institute Press, 1995.

Keegan, John. *A History of Warfare.* New York: Alfred A. Knopf, 1993.

Laqueur, Walter. *The New Terrorism: Fanaticism and the Arms of Mass Destruction.* New York: Oxford University Press, 1999.

O'Hanlon, Michael. *Technological Change and the Future of Warfare.* Washington, D.C.: Brookings Institution, 2000.

Toffler, Alvin, and Heidi Toffler. *War and Anti-War: Survival at the Dawn of the 21st Century.* Boston: Little, Brown, 1993.

Treverton, Gregory F. *Reshaping National Intelligence in an Age of Information.* Cambridge: Cambridge University Press, 2001.

Index

Media, 19–20, 250
Metastability index, 138–139
Metz, Steven, 29, 35, 36
Michels, Robert, 64
Middle East, U.S. objectives for, 123 n.51
Midway, Battle of, 11, 200, 235–239
Military action, 26, 27
Military deployments (buildup), Persian Gulf , 101–102, 103. *See also* Troops
Military persuasion, idea and examples, 5–6, 9–11; dimensions of, 40–41; how it works, 29–41; images, 16–20; information warfare, 20–23; Iranian hostage crisis, 11–14; nuclear deterrence, 14–16; from passive to active, 102–106; theory, 233–235; three examples of, 234–246
Military-technical innovation and ideas, 63–65
Milosevic, Slobodan, 16, 17–18, 27, 187, 188, 189, 191, 192, 249
Mirror imaging, 99, 121 n.14
Missile defenses, 245–246; friction in, 167–168, 171. *See also* Ballistic missile-defense systems; National missile defense
"Missile gap", 76
Mobilization, Russia, July 1914, 214, 217–218, 230–231 n.45
Moltke, Helmuth von, General, 55, 217
Moral influence, 37–41, 182, 234
Morgan, Patrick M., 173 n.22, 207
Moscow Center, 126–127, 132, 133
Murphy, Audie, 20
Muskie, Edmund, 13–14

Napoleon, 186
Nasser, Gamal Abdel, 97
National missile defense (NMD), 59, 165–166, 167, 168. *See also* Ballistic missile-defense systems; Missile defenses
National information infrastructure (NII), U.S., 205

Native American cultures, 34–35
NATO, 53, 84, 85, 86, 97, 170; in Bosnia, 189–191; Operation Allied Force, 16–19, 27, 186, 187–189, 192, 250; and Russia, 244–245, 246; war scares, 127, 127–128, 132–133, 134
Nazism, 17–19
Net-centric warfare, 54
Netwar, 20–23, 29, 54, 204
New Triad, 160
Nicaragua, 4
Nikolai II, Tzar of Russia, 214, 217
Nimitz, Chester, Admiral, 236–237, 238–239
1983 "war scare", 248. *See also* Intelligence and military persuasion
Nitze, Paul, 86, 88
Non-Western cultures and United States, 95
Noriega, Manuel, 119
Normandy invasion, 37, 203
North, Oliver, Colonel, 4
North American Aerospace Defense Command (NORAD), 218
North Korea (North Korean), 96–97, 100–101, 120 n.4
North Vietnam, 112
Norway, 37, 201
Norwegian scientific rocket incident (scare), 140, 201–202, 251–252
Nuclear age, 46
Nuclear balance of power, 78
Nuclear command and control system, 141, 142, 143
Nuclear crises, 15; management of, 136, 137, 211–213, 251–252
Nuclear deterrence, 14–16, 60, 80–81, 86–87, 203, 249, 252; and cyberwar (information warfare), 204–206, 222–223; U.S. school of thought, 214–215. *See also* Friction and nuclear deterrence
Nuclear deterrent: Soviet, 135, 137–139; U.S., 137–139
Nuclear first strike, 126, 130, 133, 138–139. *See also* First strike
Nuclear Posture Review (NPR), 160–161

ABOUT THE AUTHOR

Stephen J. Cimbala is distinguished professor of political science at Penn State University (Delaware County). His most recent work is *Through a Glass Darkly* (Praeger, 2001).